History of France

Of the author

Le Mont Saint-Michel, monastère et citadelle, Rennes, Ouest-France, 1978, préface de Jean Favier, de l'Institut, nouvelle édition, 1984.

Espions et ambassadeurs au temps de Louis XIV, Fayard, collection « Nouvelles études historiques », Paris, 1990 (Prix d'Histoire Eugène Colas de l'Académie française, 1991).

Les Relations internationales en Europe XVIIe-XVIIIe siècles, collection Thémis Histoire, PUF, 1992, nouvelle édition, 2007.

La France moderne 1498-1789, P.U.F., Paris, 1994, édition « Quadrige », 2013.

Dictionnaire de l'Ancien Régime (direction de l'ouvrage), Paris, P.U.F., 1996, nouvelle édition, Quadrige, 2002.

Histoire de France, Paris, Gisserot, 1997, nouvelle édition, 2009.

L'Invention de la diplomatie (direction, avec Isabelle Richefort), Paris, P.U.F., 1998.

La Société des princes, Paris, Fayard, 1999 (Prix Joseph du Teil 2000 de l'Académie des Sciences morales et politiques).

L'Europe des traités de Westphalie. Esprit de la diplomatie et diplomatie de l'esprit (direction, avec Isabelle Richefort), P.U.F., Paris, 2000.

L'Information à l'époque moderne (coordination de l'ouvrage), P.U.P.S., Paris, 2001.

La diplomatie et les compromis dans l'Europe centrale et orientale, Sette Città, Viterbo, 2002, (avec un texte de G. Platania).

La Présence des Bourbons en Europe (direction), P.U.F. Paris, 2003.

« *Les Temps modernes* », dans *Histoire de la diplomatie française*, Paris, 2005, p. 157-404.

« *1589-1789* », *Dictionnaire des ministres des Affaires étrangères* (co-direction de l'ouvrage, avec le concours de Bernard Barbiche), Paris, 2005, p. 1-203.

Louis XIV. Le plus grand roi du monde, Paris, 2005.

L'Art de la paix en Europe. Naissance de la diplomatie moderne, XVIe-XVIIIe siècle, PUF, Paris, 2007 (Prix Albert Thibaudet du Centre Thucydide et prix Thiers de l'Académie française, 2008).

La France au XVIIe siècle. Puissance de l'État, contrôle de la société, Paris, PUF, 2009 (Prix Laurain-Portemer de l'Académie des sciences morales et politiques).

L'Incident diplomatique, XVIe-XVIIIe siècle (direction, avec Géraud Poumarède), Pedone, Paris, 2010.

Les secrets de Louis XIV. Mystères d'État et pouvoir absolu, Paris, Tallandier, 2013, nouvelle édition, 2015.

La Paix des Pyrénées (1659) ou le triomphe de la raison politique (direction, avec Bertrand Haan et Stéphane Jettot), Paris, Classiques Garnier, 2015, 571 p.

Dictionnaire Louis XIV (direction d'ouvrage), Paris, Robert Laffont, Collection Bouquins, 2015.

Lucien Bély

Professeur des Universités (Paris IV - Sorbonne)

History of France

Translated by Angela Caldwell

Éditions Jean-Paul Gisserot
www.editions-gisserot.eu

© 2019 Editions Jean-Paul Gisserot
Imprimerie Pollina, Luçon 85400

N° 87121
Printed in France

France was created by its history, a combination of natural elements and the age-old work of Man.

The French Isthmus

Located at the westernmost tip of the continent of Europe, the territory lies at the crossroads of overland routes. It is an isthmus between north-western Europe and the Mediterranean. It took advantage of influences, populations and languages which, having come from every direction, gave the country its cultural diversity and richness. Roman domination enabled Gaul to take advantage of the skills and experiences of oriental and southern European civilisations. When it became France, it occupied a central position within the Christian world and, therefore, in Europe while gradually, but not without dramatic events, establishing its borders until the country acquired the approximate shape of a hexagon. When major international trade and, later, the Industrial Revolution transformed the economies of northern lands, France followed their example.

The Bounties of Nature

The country had a number of natural advantages which facilitated human settlement and ensured its success. Man was already living in this land and suffering terrifying periods of cold when a temperate climate gradually took over. With mild, damp weather in the west and dry, hot weather in the south, such a climate provided marked winter and summer seasons and was ideal for human activity.

Water was not rare, even if it remained to be conquered and tamed. Villages grew up in locations where water was to be found and, for many years, the local spring and fountain constituted the heart of rural communities while the church gave them their soul. There are also landscapes in which water reigns supreme thanks to the determination and work of Man. The Dombes area is dotted with lakes and was laid out by monks – migratory birds now use it as one of their stopping-places. The springs gushing out of the ground also have medicinal properties that have been recognised since the days of the Ancient Romans, giving rise to « spa towns ».

The country had rivers along whose banks most of its settlements and communities were built. Men, ideas and merchandise travelled along the courses of these rivers because the roads were badly maintained from the end of the Roman Empire to the 18th century. Towns grew up on the banks of smaller rivers, especially beside bridges. For centuries, it was difficult to build bridges across the widest waterways.

Since the sea struck fear into the hearts of the population, country folk preferred to turn their backs on it and France was not always a maritime nation despite the fact that it has three «windows» onto the open sea in the Channel, Atlantic Ocean and Mediterranean. The sea is also a link with other countries and French harbours made a profound contribution to the development of trade, especially major international trade. Since the 19th century and the introduction of «sea bathing», the coasts have become holiday venues.

France has high mountain ranges. The Pyrenees form a barrier to contact with the Iberian Peninsula but the Alps include wide valleys opening onto Italy. For many years, the mountains constituted a hostile environment but the 20th century and winter sports have succeeded in domesticating a number of inaccessible peaks.

The History of the Landscapes

Land that was, in many cases, particularly fertile and set in an area of plains, hills or plateaux has allowed for an active agricultural sector which, in its turn, has provided the food for large populations – for many years, France had the largest population in Europe. Today the population density of under 100 means that it is much less densely populated than its neighbours.

Our scenery has a history; it is our history, carved out by rural populations. France or, to give it another name, Gaul, cleared its forests. The monarchs retained a few, very fine forests for hunting purposes and these areas of woodland became the «lungs» of the major cities. Good food is the most evident and delicious symbol of this «auld alliance» between man and Nature. It reflects the diversity of agricultural production made possible by the climate and soil. Wine is part of this history. France has turned vine-growing into a science and an art form.

The changes that have beset modern farming, the developments in industry, the increasing size of towns and cities, the development of methods of transport and, finally, the spread of leisure activities have sometimes changed the appearance of landscapes with apparent impunity. This, in turn, has led to anxiety about environmental conservancy and to initiatives designed to retain the countryside intact.

The Nation

The people of France have had a common Latin-based language since the Middle Ages; they also shared a position as subjects of the King of

France. It was the monarch who forged the country's unity and identity since France was the territory over which he exercised his sovereignty i.e. first and foremost his justice. Following in the wake of the monarch came a State and, therefore, an administration. With time, the legal connections between the monarch and his people were accompanied by a feeling of belonging to a group of men and women with the same past and the same destiny, in short of belonging to a «nation». For many years, the king was one with the nation, which he wished to embody on his own. When a split occurred between the sovereign and his people, leading to the death of the king and the disappearance of the monarchy, the nation survived. Sovereignty was handed over to the people of France. As to the State, which was already centralised and powerful, it gained even more strength. The State-Nation then had to confirm its position and defend itself in the face of the other nations that it had played a part in bringing to life.

The French People

People and nations are abstract, general concepts. Yet the words reflect the enormous efforts made by successive generations who worked and suffered, hoped and innovated. This collective, anonymous effort should not be forgotten for it is this which carries, supports and encourages action on the part of the men and women who have made the history of France and whose names have come down to us. They would not have been able to invent, build or create without the obscure strength given to them by the French people.

French Uniqueness

France has never been isolated; it has lived in contact with other peoples, other civilisations and other nations. Now, as in days gone by, it is part of a Europe that is under construction. It is open to influences from other countries in the world. However, in Europe and in the world as a whole, it has perhaps enjoyed a unique place that was, and is, totally unrelated to the size of its population or the scope of its natural resources, giving humanity at large a number of ideas which exalt or console, a few inventions which strengthen or help, and a few masterpieces that solicit amazement and wonder. This uniqueness also merits description.

THE BEGINNING

Tautavel

Even if it was, apparently, in Africa that primates gradually evolved into the Hominidae that were the precursors of Man, humans settled very early on in history in the territory that was to become Gaul and, later, France. The sheer number of archaeological artefacts discovered to date is a characteristic of a country in which many sites have served to describe prehistoric eras.

In the Early Palaeolithic Era, prehistoric man had no fire. He hunted animals such as elephants or hippopotami, in a period when the fauna corresponded to a very hot climate (approx. 1.9 million years ago). It was in Chilhac, in the Massif Central area, that the oldest human habitations in France were discovered. The hunters liked to seek refuge in caves such as Le Vallonet in Roquebrune-Cap-Martin. Tools and weapons were made from split flint hence the name Palaeolithic, or Stone Age, to describe the earliest days of Man. The oldest of the skulls found in Tautavel in the Corbières area near Perpignan dates from 450,000 years ago and is thought to correspond to Homo erectus, the Hominidae which finally succeeded in standing up.

Ice and Fire

The climate cooled down and everything changed, beginning with the flora and fauna. Mammoths and reindeer first appeared. Periods of glaciation named after tributaries of the Danube (Gunz, Mindel, Riss and Würm) forced man to adapt to a new environment. He invented fire i.e. he learned how to control it. One theory states that his body structure then changed since cooked meat did not require jaws as strong as those required to masticate raw meat. The lighter jaw then enabled man to hold himself more erect and this facilitated the development of the brain. In Terra Amata, near Nice, a seasonal open-air habitation has been discovered. Large, oval huts were built on a beach using branches pushed into the soil and, in some places, consolidated with stones. The presence of hearths proves that fire existed here c. 380,000 B.C. Fire also had to be maintained and carried and that required social organisation. This was also a vital factor in the hunting of large animals. Fire was useful there, too, to frighten them off or track them, or to harden the spears used to kill them. Implements became more sophisticated thanks to the art of cutting stone, especially flint. When this rock, which is harder than steel, was split, it produced sharp edges for weaponry or tools. Bifaces were the finest masterpieces of this craft used by Neanderthal Man. When the flints were no longer seen as mere stones but were considered as a symbol and a product of human skill, scientists realised that there had been human life before History began – and the study of prehistory was born.

Cro Magnon

Hunting forced man to move – he was therefore nomadic. He was aware of the spatial dimension; he also understood time and death. By burying the dead and giving them graves, prehistoric man became aware of life. The oldest trace, in France, of this preoccupation with eternity (a grave containing gifts of food) is in La Chapelle-aux-Saints (Corrèze).

By c. 35,000 years B.C. Cro Magnon Man who was to be found in Les Eyzies-de-Tayac in Dordogne was tall, with the same cranial capacity as modern day man to whom he is closely related. This was Homo sapiens sapiens. Remains of other men have also been found e.g. Chancelade Man in Dordogne or Grimaldi Man near Menton. Reindeer hunters used to pass through Pincevent near Montereau. In Solutré, it is possible that herds of wild horses were driven towards the rock from where they galloped over the edge. The weapons used were particularly flat bifaces known as laurel leaves or willow leaves.

Lascaux

Prehistoric man was also an artist who did his utmost to represent the world around him. The «Aurignacian Venuses» are strangely-shaped statuettes of women symbolising sexuality and fecundity; they undoubtedly had a religious purpose. The Lady with the Hood, also known as the Lady of Brassempouy (in Landes), shows the same determination to produce an image of a beautiful face. In rock shelters and caves, animal art predominates. It is a feature specific to Western Europe, with one undoubted centre – the Périgord area. Linear skills developed only gradually. The earliest works were clumsy representations of animals. Later, they became more schematic but they were easier to recognise. During a third stage, the animals became stylised, with large bodies and short legs, and human figures were introduced into the works. Finally, the proportions of the animals became accurate, just as this period of artistic creation came to an end.

The cave in Lascaux (c. 15,500 years BC) is the finest example of this art. The colours were carefully prepared and chosen, and the lines showed great skill in the celebration of deer, mountain goats, horses and bulls. Although it is difficult to interpret this work, which places the huntsman centre stage and sublimates him through the game he is tracking, it is easy to see that the artist paid careful attention to nature, wanted to control it, and had a taste for shape and colour. These decorated caves may have been sanctuaries and the representations of animals may have had a magical meaning. Man also used «stencilling» to reproduce the outline of his hands. In Gargas, some of the finger joints are missing. These pictures are not thought to represent mutilated hands but rather hunting signs, obtained by bending the fingers.

The First Villages

When the climate became milder, the forests reappeared, with their populations of stags and wild boar. It was in the Middle East that the main changes occurred. Man learned to cultivate the land and domesticate animals. Agriculture and animal farming enabled him to control Nature instead of submitting to it and to produce food instead of having to hunt or fish – although hunting and fishing were both still practised. Man was no longer a nomad following game; he became sedentary. Tasks were shared and people came together in villages then, later, in towns. The new lifestyles spread along the Danube and the shores of the Mediterranean. The oldest known village in France is Courthézon in the Rhône Valley, dating from 4,650 B.C. The people lived in small huts and grew cereal crops. In order to preserve food, man shaped clay which he then dried; later he learned to fire it and pottery was born. Sheep's wool was spun and weaving appeared, with what were still very rudimentary looms. Although cut stone was still used, polished stone enabled the production of the axes required by woodcutters. This era is known as the Neolithic, or Late Stone Age. Timber became very common in tools and weaponry. Bows became the main weapon.

By allowing for the collection of cereal crops and food, the Neolithic Age stimulated the concentration of wealth. It established long-term differences between people and this social organisation is thought to have encouraged the emergence of political and religious authority, through kings and priests.

Standing Stones

Neolithic Man took great care in building impressive graves. Dolmens were funereal chambers covered with earth (rain has since washed away the earth, to reveal the stone tables below). The manmade grottoes were sometimes grouped in a dry stone construction known as a «cairn». The one in Barnenez (Finistère) included chambers accessed by a narrow passageway and, from the outside, the cairn was a tiered construction. Such building projects presupposed that numerous men could be mobilised to transport stones that were, in some cases, very heavy. Although the graves were used for several generations, they were also reserved for the richest and most powerful members of the community. As to the standing stones, or menhirs, they remain more mysterious, especially as they were, in some cases, combined in alignments e.g. in Carnac (Morbihan). When they were erected, did people want to represent idols or constitute markers that would help them with astrology? For it was doubtless the movement of the stars and the return of the seasons that, along with farming, were of the greatest interest to man, rather than the mysteries of large animals.

Lake Dwellings

One strange form of habitation is worth a special mention – the houses built on piles belonging to the «lake dwelling» civilisation that was to be found all along the Alps. For many years, people saw these houses as poetic examples of «lake villages». It would, however, seem that the houses were actually built on the shores of lakes, in such a way as to withstand floods. In time, the rise in water level covered over many items from everyday life, preserving them for posterity. This was the case in Charavines on the Lac de Paladru near Lyon where the stakes date from 2,700 B.C. On the site, fabrics, ropes and even amber have been found.

The population, which expanded and became more organised, experienced rivalry as a result of attempts to control lands or corn stores. Warfare became more commonplace and many of the skeletons found bear traces of arrow wounds.

The Bronze Age

The great technical changes, however, again took place in the Orient where metals came into use, alongside flint. Bronze, a copper and tin alloy, appeared in the West c. 4,000 B.C. The Bronze Age brought prosperity to countries where there was tin e.g. Cornwall and Brittany, and trade in these precious metals now involved long distances. The fusion of the minerals required high temperatures, kilns, and understanding of a technology that was already very advanced. A wide range of artefacts was forged for every conceivable trade, as were fearsome weapons. All the techniques were improved. The plough already existed. The ploughshare was made of wood and the implement was used to dig furrows. Wheels were used on carts drawn by oxen and horses. New tools were used to build stronger houses. Warring princes took advantage of impressive weaponry. They were buried, with their weapons and jewellery, beneath mounds of earth known as «tumuli». Other peoples used cremation and the ashes of the deceased were put into urns that were then placed in vast underground necropolises or «fields of urns». This civilisation preceded the Celtic world.

Elsewhere, in the Mediterranean area, man invented writing and, at the same time, history. He could then keep track of the past by recounting it. Prehistory had reached its end.

The Celts

Gaul existed before France but it was the Romans who gave the name of Gaul to the territory that they were on the point of conquering. They gave the name of «Gauls» to the people that they had initially feared but then wanted to subject to Roman rule. According to Julius Caesar, the people described themselves as Celts. Gaul as defined by the Romans was, therefore, part of a much larger Celtic world extending to the north of the brilliant Mediterranean civilisations.

This is a world of legends, tales of fantasy and hypotheses for it is known to us only indirectly, through the writings of the Greeks and, more particularly, the Romans i.e. through the documents written by enemies who considered Celts and Gauls as barbarians. For centuries, the French learned the early history of their country through the tale that recounted the end of Gallic independence, Caesar's Gallic Wars. Archaeology then completed the view of the Celtic and Gallic worlds supplied by historians and certain features of the Celtic civilisation have also been retained in the ancient epic tales that are part of Irish literature.

The Iron Age

The Celtic presence might coincide with what has, by convention, become known as the Iron Age, beginning in 800 B.C. Archaeologists have observed the existence of the so-called Hallstatt civilisation (named after a site in Austria) dating from 800 to 450 B.C. Its main characteristics were the chieftains' graves, containing four-wheeled chariots and iron weapons. The Celts, who were already present in Europe, are thought to have been involved in this civilisation, in the west of the continent.

Marseille

The main trade routes along the Mediterranean then turned westwards for the tin mined in the British Isles had become an essential commodity. The Phoenicians had dominated trade for many years and it is they who are said to have invented writing, with an alphabet that the Greeks, Etruscans and Romans then merely adapted. The Greeks sought to establish themselves for the long-term, setting up trading posts along the coasts of the Western Mediterranean. Phocaea, a town in Asia Minor, created the colony of Massalia or Massilia (Marseille) in 620 B.C. Around it, other towns grew up, including Nice, Antibes, Arles and Agde. From then on, the Greeks influenced neighbouring peoples for Marseille was a staging-post between the world of the Greeks and that of the Celts.

The Vix Vase

One of the main trade routes ran to Brittany where traders came to obtain the precious tin. In 1952, on Mont Lassois in Vix, near Châtillon-sur-Seine, the tomb of a princess aged 33 or 35 years was found. Near her was a Greek crater 1.65 metres (5 ft. 6 ins.) tall and weighing 209 kg (approx. 4 cwt). This huge, priceless recipient dating from 525 B.C. showed the importance of the geographical location and those who controlled it. It lies at the junction of the Seine Basin (at the point where the river ceases to be navigable) and the Rhône Corridor. The Greeks sold their wine to the elite, leaving to others the drink made from barley, the ancestor of beer. All the digs have revealed the presence of countless amphorae. Many have also been found in the wrecks discovered on the seabed along the coastlines.

Celtic Invasions

The Second Iron Age began towards the middle of the first millennium B.C; it is also known as the La Tène civilisation (450 to 50 B.C.). The graves of the so-called «warrior chieftains» contained chariots with two wheels rather than the earlier four; they are battle chariots. Iron weaponry became more commonplace throughout the population and there were larger numbers of warriors. This was a world at war. Numerous Celts or Gauls served as mercenaries in the Mediterranean and troops of «Gauls» sold their services to the highest bidder. There were also, however, entire peoples who launched attacks on the Mediterranean countries.

Brennus in Rome

The Romans spoke fearfully of the Gauls, as did the Greeks when referring to the Celts or «Galatians». The Romans remembered the capture of Rome by Brennus and his warriors c. 390 – 383 B.C. and his Vae victis was fairly descriptive of the humiliation suffered by the defeated. The Greeks remembered the expeditions in Macedonia, in Delphi in 279 and in Asia Minor where the Galatians settled and created Galatia. Their fear was akin to terror for the warriors considered themselves to be invincible, thanks to their weaponry, and they fought naked, wearing the heads of their enemies on their belts or hanging them round the necks of their horses. The Celtic world then covered much of Europe. All these peoples had the same lifestyle and, no doubt, the same beliefs. What remains a mystery is the reason for these expeditions against the civilisations established along the Mediterranean. Were the Celts pushed by other peoples from the East, or by internal unrest?

Gold

Mercenaries and conquerors brought gold back from their expeditions because the metal was highly sought after by the Gauls who believed it had religious value. It was the property of the gods and jewellery items were talismans. Torques, the twisted necklets worn by warriors during battles, protected them from death. However, the gold had to be returned to the gods and the Gauls made offerings of gold in the form of artefacts. When Julius Caesar conquered Gaul, he carried off the treasures found in Gallic temples. This facilitated his future career but it also decreased the price of gold in Italy. The Greek influence continued to be felt in the Celtic world which, for example, used the Greek alphabet. Writing was used for public and private affairs. On the other hand, according to Caesar, the Druids refused to write down all that they knew.

The Narbonnaise area

Gauls had settled in Northern Italy. The Romans, having observed that they were allied to Hannibal the Carthaginian during the Punic Wars, sought to gain control over them. They succeeded c. 225 B.C. and Cisalpine Gaul was placed under Roman authority. The Romans also ruled Spain. Between Italy and Spain lay the Greek colonies. The Gauls, however, made their presence felt in this region, mixing with the indigenous population, the Ligurians, to form a people known as Celto-Ligurians. The Greek colonies felt under threat and sought assistance from the Romans who were only too pleased to intervene and who, in order to counterbalance Entremont, a Celto-Ligurian town destroyed in 124, founded Aix-en-Provence (Aquae Sextiae). They then settled in this area of Cisalpine Gaul and turned it into a Roman province. Provence, of course, owes its name to this province which also included the Alps and Languedoc areas. It was known as the Narbonnaise (118 AD) and had Narbonne as its main town. The Via Domitia which crossed it linked Italy to Spain. This Roman province closed off the Celts' access to the Mediterranean.

The Belgae

The situation was further complicated by the fact that peoples from the east, the Celtic-speaking Belgae, crossed the Rhine in the 3rd century. They included the Atrebates who gave their name to Arras and the Artois area, the Ambiani who settled in Amiens, the Bellovaci in Beauvais and the Remi in Champagne and Reims. They crossed the Rhine again in the 2nd century (Nervians and Eburoni in what is now known as Belgium), forcing Gallic peoples to seek refuge in England. It was the presence of these Belgiae in one part of Gaul that Caesar noted in his Gallic Wars. The birth of «Belgium» also meant the establishment of a border area to withstand pressure from the Germans.

The Gauls

In Gaul there were some sixty different peoples. The population of Gaul as a whole has been subject to fluctuating assessments; they were said to number from 3 or 5 million up to 20 or 25 million but the figure of 10 million may be nearer to the truth. In the 2nd century BC, some of the people had immense influence e.g. the Arverni in the centre of Gaul. They, however, were defeated by the Romans in 121 BC. The Edueni (in what we now know as Burgundy) established political links with Rome. Until the end of the 2nd century BC, monarchies existed among the largest peoples but they were later replaced by oligarchies. The peoples were divided into tribes led by a few warrior families seen, by the Romans, as «knights» because they fought on horseback as well as dominating trade and mining. Warriors would meet in assemblies which designated a chieftain, the «vergobret». The Romans had no difficulty setting up similar assemblies in later years. The peoples continued their nomadic existence and did not settle anywhere on a permanent basis. It was Rome which took upon itself to give them stability.

The Slave Trade

These peoples were only too pleased to wage war on each other and, according to Caesar, before his arrival not a single year passed without conflict. These wars provided prisoners who were then sold on in the remainder of the Mediterranean area, in particular to the Romans. The slave trade led, in turn, to further warfare. During the revolt led by Spartacus (72 BC), mention was made of several thousand Gallic slaves. With the wine trade, the market for slaves was one of the main features of trade with the Mediterranean, and one of the factors that led to tension in the Gallic world. There was conflict between the various peoples but, according to C. Goudineau, there was also conflict within single populations, between supporters of the monarchy, of independence, of a return to traditional values who were doubtless «anti-Roman», and supporters of leading families who had an open-minded approach to other peoples and to major trade and who were, therefore, «pro-Roman».

Oppida

The Gauls earned their living from working the land and breeding animals, in particular pigs which provided them with ham, and horses. Hunting and fishing occupied only a limited place in their life. They felled trees to produce huge clearings in the forests and villages were established there, with houses made of timber and clay and roofed with thatch. They were skilled artisans, inventing numerous tools that remained in use for many years, sometimes for many centuries, from scythes to the tools used by cobblers or lumberjacks. They produced fine swords and lances, as well as iron ploughshares for the two-wheeled ploughs that were far superior to the swing-ploughs used in the Mediterranean area. If danger threatened, the people would seek refuge in oppida, vast areas protected by fortifications. Each of the peoples had an oppidum which it considered as a capital. These fortified places became marketplaces and trading centres. Bibracte was the capital of the Edueni and, although the town was said to have lain on the site of Autun, archaeological digs proved that the Gallic settlement was actually built on Mont Beuvray, some 20 kilometres (12 miles) away.

The Druids

Priests formed the hub of Gallic society. They were feared and respected, yet they remain a mystery for us. They created a comprehensive vision of the world, doubtless by studying the stars and their movements. They worked to discover the secrets of nature but were also involved in laws and ethics. According to Caesar, they taught people that souls do not die but that, after death, they pass from one body to another.

They retained all this knowledge, never writing it down but passing it on by word of mouth and insisting on the art of memorisation. Because of this, we know little about the beliefs and ideas of the Gauls. Again according to Caesar, young people flocked to the Druids to acquire their knowledge. They also had to learn a considerable number of lines of poetry containing age-old wisdom and for the initiated, in particular those destined to become Druids themselves, studies could take twenty years.

The Forest of the Carnutes

The priests trained the young aristocrats and formed close ties, based on this teaching, with the world of princes and warriors to whom the Druids provided guidance through their moral authority. According to Caesar, they settled nearly all the conflicts between States or private individuals. They were also a federating element for the Gauls since they met, every year, in the Carnutes Forest between Orléans and Chartres. The forest was considered as the centre of Gaul. For all these reasons, they formed the basis of the resistance to the Roman Occupation.

The Gods

The Gauls had a large number of gods. Lug was the god of craftsmen. Gods were often associated with springs, trees, rocks or natural phenomena. The god of the skies or the «god with the wheel» was Taranis. Cernunnos was the god with antlers. Esus was the god of war while the god of war and peoples was Teutates. Oak trees were venerated and the Druids were known as the «men with the oak trees». According to Pliny, priests dressed in white robes would climb into the tree and cut off mistletoe which was collected in a piece of white cloth. Mistletoe is said to have been used as a remedy against all types of poison. The Druids were intermediaries between men and the gods and they were responsible for sacrificial offerings for, in Gaul, worship included the sacrifice of human victims who were smothered, hung or burnt in order to ensure the goodwill of the god concerned. War also led to ritual sacrifices. Prisoners-of-war were cut to pieces and decapitated then their bodies were placed on public view for some considerable time. Their weapons were destroyed and the sacrifices were followed by general banqueting. In addition to the Druids, there were soothsayers who foretold the future and bards or lyric poets who sang hymns or satires to their own musical accompaniment.

The Greek and Roman influence had already percolated through to this world of religion but it was the Roman Conquest which totally transformed it, firstly by putting an end to the Druids' ministry while retaining the Gallic gods.

ROMAN GAUL

Julius Caesar

This ambitious young man was the nephew of Marius who had successfully put an end to invasions by the Germans (the Cimbri and Teutoni) and he acted jointly with two other men of ambition, Pompeus and Crassus. The Senate appointed him Proconsul of Transalpine Gaul and Cisalpine Gaul and ordered him to support the Edueni, who were friends of Rome. However, the Helvetii in Switzerland, encouraged by the Germans, wanted to reach the Santones area (now known as «Saintonge»). The Edueni, worried by this move, called upon Rome and Caesar pushed the Helvetii back towards Switzerland. This marked the beginning of the stabilisation of the Gallic peoples who then put down roots and formed the pagi of Gaul (areas now known to the French as «pays») to which they gave their names.

The Rhine as a Frontier

Again at the request of the Edueni, Caesar attacked the Suevi, a German people under the command of Ariovistus, and defeated the invaders. The Roman general considered that the Rhine, which he had reached, would then serve as a border between what he called «Gaul» on one side and Germany on the other. «Caesar therefore created the «Gallic nation». He imposed the name of «Gaul» which dated back to the very end of the Pre-Roman period and used the Rhine as its border» (Karl-Ferdinand Werner). On the other bank of the Rhine, there were still Celts. However, the priority, for the Romans, was to fortify this frontier along the Rhine and Danube, turning it into a limes.

And in Gaul, which was sometimes described as «hairy» (comata) or «wearing breeches» (braccata), Caesar distinguished, in addition to the Belgiae, between the Aquitanians to the south of the River Garonne (they were not a Celtic people) and the Gauls or Celts themselves.

The Conquest

Once the Roman army had entered Gaul, it remained there and, in just a few years, conquered the entire country. In 57 BC, the Belgiae were defeated and Caesar could announce the conquest of another province to the Senate in Rome. However, in 56 BC, the Veneti rebelled and were severely punished. In 55 BC, Caesar risked an incursion beyond the Rhine and crossed the Channel, repeating the expedition in 54 BC.

These campaigns amazed his contemporaries. In the following year, he put down a revolt on the part of the Eburoni and Treviri in the north.

Vercingetorix

In 52 BC, Gallic insurrection became, if not general, at least widespread. The Arverni led the movement because they had succeeded in reinstating a monarchy and had acquired a chieftain, Vercingetorix, an Arverni nobleman who was not only brave but who also had a feeling for organisation and command. Faced with Caesar and his legions, he adopted a fearsome tactic – he refused to fight a pitched battle. Instead, he kept the Romans under pressure by launching attacks by the Gallic cavalry and he instituted a scorched earth policy in the area in which his enemies sought supplies. By his strategy, he drew the Roman legions towards a town and could then attack them during the siege. He succeeded in defeating Caesar who had thought he could capture Gergovia by surprise. Vercingetorix enjoyed the trust of the Druids in the Carnutes Forest and he had command of all the Gallic rebels. Many Gallic peoples, including the Edueni, then revolted against the occupying forces of Rome.

Alesia

Caesar, however, succeeded in defeating the Gallic cavalry and Vercingetorix retreated to Alesia. The Roman army laid siege to the town but was itself attacked by Gallic coalition forces. It took all the skill of the Romans in building fortifications to enable Caesar to maintain his position. The Romans erected a double set of walls, one facing the beleaguered town and the other opposing the rebel reinforcements. Finally, the Romans routed the Gallic army and forced Alesia to capitulate. Vercingetorix offered to surrender personally to Caesar and this he did, throwing his weapons down at the General's feet. The defenders of Uxellodunum in the Quercy area were also forced to surrender and they all had their hands cut off (51 BC). Caesar showed great mercy towards the rebels but he included Vercingetorix in the triumphant procession that marked his entry into Rome, before having him executed. This triumph marked the end of the Roman Republic and the imminent birth of the Empire in which a single man, the Emperor, would exercise almost total control over the huge territory conquered on the shores of the Mediterranean.

Roman Control

Gaul was part of this mighty empire and, as such, belonged to an admirable civilisation. Latin, used by admirable writers, was a universal language – and it remained so long after the ancient civilisation had died out. Roman law took root in much of Gaul. The achievements of Rome inspired admiration for centuries to come and were tirelessly imitated. However, the arrival of the Romans also meant the arrival of an invader. The legions had proved their efficiency in the face of Gallic bravery.

Roman culture crushed much of the culture that had preceded it, in particular the knowledge of the Druids who were considered with awe, mistrust and, perhaps, disdain by the new arrivals. The history of Gaul reflected the vicissitudes of the history of Rome.

Romanisation

The noblemen of Gaul retained their rights and aspired to Roman citizenship. The spread of Roman culture was encouraged by the presence of the Narbonnaise area in the south. Roman towns were established and populated with army veterans. Gallic towns, which became Roman towns, also enjoyed exemplary development. Gradually, the administrative map of «hairy Gaul» was drawn with three Gauls (Aquitania, Celtica and Belgica) coming together in Lyon, a town founded in 43 BC. It was there that, in 12 BC, the federal sanctuary of the Three Gauls was inaugurated near the confluence of the Rhône and the Saône. Rome left Gaul to its own devices, being more concerned to defend the Rhine through the setting up of two Germanies (Argentoratum (Strasbourg) was one of the main fortresses). Roman culture spread more quickly during the reign of Emperor Claudius (41-54 AD) who was born in Lyon and who, in a speech preserved in the town through the Claudian Tables, was careful to recall that Gaul was enjoying a period of security and peace and had been totally loyal to Rome. There were to be Gallic senators in Rome and this great aristocracy was to last longer than the Roman Empire itself. A single cohort garrisoned in Lyon was sufficient to maintain law and order in a Gaul that had been pacified.

Towns

Rome had developed an urban civilisation. Each of the Gallic peoples lived around a town (civitas) which took on the Roman way of life. A forum at the junction of the two main streets was the centre of public life. Aqueducts carried water to the baths where the population could relax. The baths were also centres of art and leisure. The Pont du Gard, one such aqueduct, serves as a reminder that this type of construction remained unrivalled until the 18th century. The circus, or Roman arena, was used for gladiatorial combat or horse racing, indeed for all the games which the Romans considered to be as essential as bread. The amphitheatres and theatres could hold thousands of spectators and they provided the stage for more serious entertainment. In Lyon an indoor odeum was used for singing. Monuments decorated the towns and triumphal arches recalled the victories of Rome, like a discreet reminder that law and order had to be upheld. Finally, the town withstood the passage of time by building in freestone. Many Roman buildings have survived every form of destruction.

The Gallo-Romans

These towns were settled by civil servants working for the Roman administrative departments and, in some cases, by army veterans. They also attracted craftsmen and shopkeepers. Through marriage, links between Romans and Gauls who had espoused the Roman way of life were strengthened, giving rise to a Gallo-Roman society. This symbiosis was also evident in religion. Although the Romans venerated their own gods, for example in the Maison Carrée in Nîmes, they also respected the Gallic gods and a veritable merger was achieved through Gallo-Roman gods. Oriental churches gained a following in Gaul and Christianity also spread through the country. It was in Lyon that Christians were martyred in 177 AD, among them St. Blandine.

Villae in the country

The Roman influence also left its mark on rural districts where leading Gallic families or rich Romans built up huge estates. They produced pork meat products, corn and wine, for vineyards were becoming increasingly commonplace. In their country houses, these wealthy Gallo-Romans led the same lifestyle as they did in their mansions in town. To work the land, the owners could have slaves but most of them tended to divide their land into small areas and lease them out to colonists. In 322 AD, Constantine forbade the colonists to leave their land and the sons were obliged to take over their fathers' farms. This hereditary dependence of tenants on landlords was also to survive the collapse of the Roman Empire. All that Rome required was that taxes be paid into its coffers and that, therefore, the land be carefully tended. The taxes became increasingly heavy. Small areas (pagi) were organised around a local centre (vicus), a small town. The towns and vici constituted the network which was to structure French geography to a large measure until the present time.

The First Stirrings of Discontent

This period of balance and peace lasted only until the end of the 2nd century. The Roman Empire, whose political, economic and social weaknesses became apparent over time, suffered attack from every direction at the end of the 2nd century. It was also racked by internal strife. Disputes between men seeking to occupy the highest echelons of power led to civil wars. Lyon, which had not been swift enough in selecting the party of Septimus Severus, was pillaged when he became Emperor. Bandits and deserters also reflected the exasperation of the people at large. Maternus, a soldier known for his bravery, decided to desert in 186 AD and it took an entire army to put down the rebellion that he fomented.

Franks and Alemanni in the 3rd Century

The Roman Empire had to defend its far-off provinces, especially in the East, and to do so it used the legions that had been guarding the limes in the west. The Germanic peoples were then tempted to take advantage of the situation by raiding Gaul. The Franks, installed on the right bank of the Rhine, consisted of a league of minor people such as the Bructeri or Salians. The word «frank» is thought to have meant «free» i.e. free of Roman domination. The Franks, like the Alemannic league further south, launched expeditions into Gaul.

The legions on the Rhine reacted by choosing their own emperor in 260 AD. By acknowledging this «Gallic» emperor and his successors until Tetricus was deposed in 275, the people and soldiers of Gaul, Spain and Great Britain showed their determination to defend themselves, having felt abandoned by Rome. It was in 275-276 that pillaging forces overran the country and destroyed, it is said, sixty towns. Buried treasures show that a wave of attack swept across the country.

Constantine

Resistance to invasion and subsequent recovery were enabled by the construction of superb walls around towns which could then serve as refuges in case of attack. The Roman emperors, beginning with Probus, succeeded in defeating the barbarians and negotiating with them, using them in the Roman army where they soon occupied positions of command or installing them on territories that guarded the frontier. The Empire was reorganised by emperors named Augustus or with the title of Caesar and, gradually, two distinct areas came into being. On one side was the Latin world; on the other side, the Greek civilisation. The rebirth of the Empire coincided with a religious quest. Diocletian authorised persecution of the Christians; another emperor, Constantine, supported them. In order to take power, he had been obliged to get rid of his rivals and he then succeeded in containing the Franks and Alemanni. Through the Edict of Milan (313 AD), the emperor granted Christians freedom of worship. He made gifts of magnificent basilicas before being baptised prior to his death. Constantine bound the Empire to Christ and this choice led to the conversion of the entire Roman world.

Christianity

In Gaul, after being the belief of a few minority groups from the Orient, Christianity became an official State religion and, finally, the only authorised religion. Instead of a multitude of gods, it imposed a single God like the God of the Jews but it also proposed the teachings of the Son of God, Christ. The emperors convened oecumenical councils at which the main tenets of the faith were discussed. The Nicene Council in 325 defined the Creed and condemned arianism, a form of heresy. A Church, i.e. an assembly, was created with bishops at its head. The Bishop of Rome, the Pope, who was considered as St. Peter's successor, was to occupy a special place in Christianity. St. Martin of Tours (317-397), a former soldier, was loved for his kindness (he cut his cloak in half in order to share it with a pauper) and he founded the first monastery in Gaul, Ligugé near Poitiers. Later, having been elected Bishop of Tours, he founded another, Marmoutier. This was how monasticism, an oriental practice, became established in the western world.

The Final Roman Reforms

Society changed but the senators, the clarissimi, retained their power because the emperor nominated to the Senate leading figures from right across the Empire and even, in some cases, barbarians who had entered his service. Their villae were veritable rural palaces in the 4th and 5th centuries. One example is the Montmaurin villa. These palaces combined enormous luxury with a strong system of defence and small private armies were recruited. The senatorial order survived and was renewed through the mediaeval nobility. Something else that survived for many years was the land tax which was reorganised, affecting mainly people in country districts. An administrative reform resulted in a new map of Gaul, showing divisions that were taken over by the Church. The bishop sat in a town and, within a former province, there was a «metropolitan». Around the emperor were counts (from comes meaning «companion») who held the highest positions in the army and the State.

Julian the Apostate

The confrontations between pretenders to the imperial throne weakened the Empire and, in 355 AD, Franks and Alemanni were again able to invade it. Gaul was then the key element in resistance to invasions. Julian saved it by leading a number of victorious campaigns. In 358 AD, he authorised the entire Salian people, which had been defeated, to settle on the left bank of the Rhine. These Salian Franks were under an obligation to serve in the Roman army and they were well integrated into the Empire by the time of the fall of Rome. Julian had re-established the defence of the Rhine. He considered that the new capital of the western world, Trier, was too exposed and he preferred to stay in the Parisii's town, Paris. It was there that he was proclaimed emperor by his troops and lifted aloft on the shield, like the barbarian kings. Julian was nicknamed «the Apostate» because he broke away from the Christian faith in which he had been brought up and his reign corresponded to a new rise of paganism. He went to war in the Orient and died there (363 AD).

The Goths

The Franks occupied an increasingly large place in the army and in affairs of State, especially those Franks who were part of the emperor's entourage. However, they were confronted by other peoples. The Goths, Vandals and Burgundians came from Scandinavia c. 100 and settled in Central and Eastern Europe where they posed a threat mainly the east of the Empire. Among them were the Visigoths who served the Emperor of the Orient. In 406, another wave of invaders, Vandals, crossed the

Rhine with the Suebi and Alani. Standing in their path were the Franks who appeared to be defending Gaul itself. In 410, considering that he had been insufficiently rewarded by the Emperor of the Orient, Alaric the Visigoth pillaged Rome. However, still in the service of the Empire, the Visigoths settled in Aquitaine with Toulouse as their main town, and in Spain. These Goths had been converted to Christianity but they were Aryans i.e. they did not believe in the divinity of Christ. They were therefore regarded as heretics by the Roman Catholic bishops.

Aetius and the Huns

Aetius had lived with the Huns and, having become the chief commander of the armies of the western world, he used their troops to defeat the Burgundians whom he then settled near Lake Geneva. He also defeated the Salian Franks and the Visigoths. He appeared to be Gaul's new saviour. However, the Huns then posed a threat. Their king, Attila, was the master of a vast empire centring on the plains of what is now known as Hungary. The Huns were a nomadic people, living off the tribute-money paid to them by terrified princes such as the Emperor of the Orient. Attila decided to obtain the same submission from the western world by attacking Gaul. His targets were the Visigoths in Aquitaine and he succeeded in advancing as far as Orléans. Theodoric's Visigoths then allied themselves with Aetius despite the fact that he was a friend of the Huns. The invaders fought the allies at the Battle of the Catalaunian Fields, a location possibly situated near Châlons-sur-Marne (20th June 451). Attila was defeated and left Gaul. Paris had been saved. The ambitious Aetius, on the other hand, was personally assassinated by Emperor Valentinian III in 453 AD. He was the last man to maintain unity in a Gaul that was both Roman and barbarian.

CLOVIS AND THE MEROVINGIANS

In 476 AD, Romulus Augustulus, the «Little Emperor», was overthrown by Odoacre who had been elected king and who sent the imperial insignia to the Emperor of Orient in Constantinople. This was a means of acknowledging his authority and the Byzantine Empire was to continue to keep alive memories of the Empire – albeit a Greek Empire, far removed from the Roman Catholic religion. The date (476 AD) has been retained as the date marking the end of the Roman Empire which was already in decline in the western world. In Gaul, Syagrius upheld the Roman tradition. He commanded the Roman army between Somme and Loire, is said to have used the title «Rex Romanorum» («King of the Romans») and settled in Soissons.

The Defeat of Syagrius

In 486 AD, Syagrius was defeated by King Clovis of the Franks. This easy victory was perhaps not the break-point that has long been described. The King of the Franks took over the army which dominated part of Gaul, as other barbarian chieftains had done before him with the approval of Rome and the Romans when they were seeking to uphold public law and order. However, there was no longer any need for approval from Rome; its authority had disappeared and the Emperor of Orient was too far away to intervene. The Franks were entering a political vacuum. It was after this battle against Syagrius that the famous episode involving the Soissons vase occurred.

The Soissons Vase

Clovis accepted a complaint from a bishop who was demanding the return of a liturgical vase, thereby showing that he respected prelates. He was shortly to be converted to Christianity. The king demanded the vase for himself, as if it was his share of the booty but in fact to return it to the Church. Resistance on the part of one of his warriors, who struck the vase, also showed that Frankish traditions were maintained and that the sharing of booty remained the rule for pillaging troops. It indicated that the pagan Franks had no regard for Catholic bishops and that the chief did not have the right to act entirely as he wished. In the following year, while reviewing troops, Clovis punished the rebel on the grounds that his weaponry was badly maintained then, reflecting the insult inflicted upon him by the same rebel. Clovis declared «This is what you did to the Soissons vase» and, by his violent act, indicated that he would brook no discussion of his authority. This also marked the birth of a kingdom.

Tolbiac

For the bishops of Gaul, the goodwill shown by the Franks was a sign of hope for, above all, they feared the Visigoths who were Christians but who had chosen Aryanism, a doctrine which denied the divinity of Christ and which the bishops were fighting fiercely. The pagan Franks, who could be converted, seemed less fearsome than heretics who continued to ignore the error of their ways. Gradually, Clovis and the Church authorities moved closer together. Tradition has it that Clothilda, a Burgundian princess and supporter of the Christian religion, played a major role in the conversion of Clovis who had taken her as his second wife. Clovis' biographer, Gregory of Tours, tells how, during a battle against the Alemanni in Tolbiac near Cologne, possibly in 496 AD, the king promised to be converted to Christianity if he was victorious – and God gave him a victory. This was a way of taking up the thread of Constantine's conversion and historically situating Clovis in the wake of the emperor who had linked the destiny of the Roman Empire to Christianity. In fact, Clovis followed his father's policy and found, in the bishops, men capable of supporting his power while seeking to obtain his military protection.

The Baptism of Clovis

Baptism became an essential act, a sign of the alliance between the Roman Catholic Church, which led and controlled the people, and the King of the Franks who commanded the army and was determined to expand and stabilise his influence. There is still some doubt as to the date of the baptism – it took place between 496 and 508! But it did take place. At Christmas, in Reims. Bishop Remigius is said to have encouraged and supported this movement towards the Christian faith. He presided at the ceremony during which Clovis was no doubt immersed three times in a pool then anointed with consecrated oil. The bishop's admonition, which was translated, for many years, as «Bend thy head, proud Sicambrian» is thought to have really meant «Leave off thy amulets» since the magic amulets symbolised paganism. There is equal uncertainty as to the number of people who embraced Christianity at the same time as Clovis. They no doubt included his companions, if not all the Franks. From then on, a precedent had nevertheless been set and the Franks would eventually be converted.

The Kingdom of the Franks

Did this act mark the country's foundation? Whether it was or not, Gaul was gradually to become the kingdom of the Franks and, later, the kingdom of France before finally becoming France. From then on, there was also a vital dialogue between the king of the Francs or, later, the king of France and the Roman Catholic Church, especially the Pope, successor to St. Peter. On some occasions, the dialogue turned into a terrible conflict or a silent struggle. Clovis was the only Christian prince in the western world and he was supported by bishops who, in the towns, inherited the Roman traditions. The king of the Franks launched military operations – he failed against the Burgundians but defeated the Visigoths at the Battle of Vouillé in 507 AD and took over Aquitaine. He then had himself acknowledged as the king of all the Franks at the end of his reign, by murdering the other chiefs. Not only had he gathered under his authority almost the entire area of Ancient Gaul; he attempted to give it coherence by convening a national council of all the bishops, from north and south alike. In the long term, Catholicism was to defeat Aryanism. Clovis annexed Gaul to the lands of the Franks and this changed the centre of gravity of the country as a whole. The sign of this change was the choice of Paris as his capital city. Finally, by drawing up the Salic Law based on the traditions of the so-called Salian Franks, he set his mark on a society which, first and foremost, aligned itself with the Roman law that remained very much alive in the south.

Fredegund and Brunhild

Clovis' successors described themselves as «Kings of the Franks», which showed that a monarchic idea had begun to take root. This did not mean stability, however, for the warrior nobility retained its right to elect a chieftain by «carrying him aloft on the shield», but Clovis' successors were selected from among his descendents. Distribution of wealth between the sons remained a rule inherited from Frankish tradition. This led to an eventful history, full of twists and turns during the days of the «Merovingian» Kings, so-called after Clovis' mythical ancestor, Merovech. The monarchs were long referred to as the «lazy kings» and little is known about them, although a number of terrifying tales have been handed down on the subject of palace intrigues. Division of property gradually led to the creation of three areas – Austrasia in the east, Burgundia, and Neustria in the west, the latter being the forerunner of Francia. Together, the three separate territorial entities constituted the regnum Francorum. Two women were locked in a power struggle at the end of the 6th century – Fredegund, wife of the King of Neustria, and Brunhild, Queen in Austrasia. After a struggle lasting several years, Fredegund's son captured the aging Queen Brunhild and sentenced her to be dragged along the ground, with her hair tied to the tail of a spirited horse.

King Dagobert

Clothar II (548-629) succeeded in bringing a semblance of order to the Frankish civilisation but it was more particularly his son, Dagobert I, who stands out as the best of all the Merovingian kings. His reign lasted from 629 to 639 AD. His life was extolled by the monks in Saint-Denis Abbey to which he afforded his protection and where he chose to be buried, as did all the kings of France after him. The legend of King Dagobert was born. A close companion of Dagobert, St. Ely, who was a skilful goldsmith, serves as a reminder of the importance of treasure for princes who descended from pillagers. They adored objects decorated with precious stones and took care to decorate their churches with gold. Beside these kings were the «mayors of the palace». The major domus was appointed to manage one of the three sections of the kingdom of the Franks but, over the years, he became the representative of the nobility of Neustria, Burgundy and Austrasia in their dealings with the sovereign. The mayors of the palace were in conflict with each other and they attempted to impose their own candidates among Clovis' descendents. A dynasty of mayors was finally established. Dagobert I had succeeded in controlling the mayor of the palace of Austrasia, Pepin, in whose care he had been placed during his youth. However, after the death of Dagobert, the kingdom suffered no little upheaval and the grandson of this Pepin, Pepin of Herstal, succeeded in rebuilding the unity of the Frankish kingdom while retaining a Merovingian king with very limited powers.

St. Columban and St. Owen

Historians now have a tendency to gild the Merovingian period by emphasising the religious fervour that was one of its main aspects. Monasticism received a decisive push thanks to the influence of St. Columban and his companions who came from Ireland. Columban founded the monastery in Luxeuil in the Vosges. In Normandy, St. Owen, a close companion of Dagobert, played a decisive role.

Monasticism

Monks eager to find God sought out marshes in the depths of valleys, rocks lashed by the waves and inaccessible mountains. They carried with them a model of an austere life dedicated to prayer, and they chose to live in solitude. Yet they were not hermits; they lived in communities. From the 7th century onwards, numerous monks found a law that suited them in the Rule of St. Benedict. A community was set up with a «father» at its head, the abbot chosen by the brothers who then obeyed his commands. Daily life was organised with great precision, in accordance with a rigorous, unchanging order. Often, the monks' solitude was only temporary, for fervour begets fervour and their communities attracted other strong believers or simple people in search of guidance. Monasteries formed the heart of villages, or even towns, and monastic communities became major agricultural enterprises or collective landowners. The monks did not remain immobile. They travelled throughout the Christian world, converting people and circulating ideas and knowledge by copying and transporting manuscripts. The presence of these monks, in addition to the power of the bishops, led the Franks to embrace Christianity. The Frankish people took over the inheritance of the Romans and this led to linguistic romanisation at a time when the Gallo-Romans were taking on the Frankish way of life.

Charles Martel

The kingdom of the Franks was to withstand many a threat, from the Saxons in the east, the Frisians in the north, and the Basques and Arabs in the south. Charles, Pepin of Herstal's son, succeeded initially in retaining his position as Mayor of the Palace. He then stood up to these threats and proved himself to be a fearsome warlord. After crushing the Frisians, Charles turned his attention southwards. The Moslems had taken over Spain and were threatening to launch invasions on the other side of the Pyrenees. Aquitaine, which had acquired a form of independence, was threatened and Eudes of Aquitaine had to call on Charles who stopped the Saracen advance on 25th October 732 near Poitiers. It was a limited victory; he did not pursue the defeated forces and left them to ransack Aquitaine. However, the event was soon considered to have dealt a death blow to the expansionist policies of the Saracen and was seen as a success for the Christians, even though the Moslems had never intended to settle in the territory into which they had pushed rather too far. Charles acquired huge prestige and this was confirmed by his never-ending expeditions. They enabled him to take over Provence, giving the Frankish kingdom access to the Mediterranean. The Frank imposed rough justice and this earned him the nickname «Martel» i.e. «the Hammer». Rome sought to obtain protection from the victorious chief. With Charles Martel, it was the eastern influence that won the day, through a rebirth of germanisation. Although he was not a king, Charles was able to govern for some time without a monarch. His son, known as Pepin the Short, decided, in 751 AD, to depose Childeric III, with the approval of the Pope and the support of the bishops who, for the first time, anointed him with consecrated oil, giving a new, sacred character to the function of sovereign.

CHARLEMAGNE AND THE CAROLINGIANS

Pepin's sons, Charles and Carloman, divided the kingdom between them. When Carloman died, his brother Charles, who had already gained distinction in battles against the Gascons and Aquitanians, took over his lands and became sole monarch. He has come down through history as Charlemagne, Carolus Magnus, Charles the Great.

The Mountain Pass at Roncesvalles

He proved to be an outstanding warrior and his kingdom eventually covered most of Europe. He had no hesitation in using terror to force people into submission. He went on an expedition to Italy and captured the kingdom of the Lombards, imprisoning their king, Didier, in a monastery. He did the same thing with Carloman's sons who had sought refuge with the Lombards. He led victorious expeditions against the Saxons and, after many mishaps, forced the chief, Widukind, to accept conversion. The Saxons then acknowledged the power of the Frankish king. He next turned his attention to Saracen Spain where, initially, he failed. While coming back after this expedition across the Pyrenees, his rearguard led by his nephew, Roland, was attacked and slaughtered by Basques in Roncesvalles (15th August 778). This tragic episode, in which Roland showed his heroism, was to inspire the poets who dedicated the first known chanson de geste, the Chanson de Roland, to his memory. Later, Charlemagne placed his son, Louis, on the throne of Aquitaine and he succeeded in setting up the «Spanish Marches» to the north of the Iberian Peninsula. Charlemagne's presence could be felt in every corner of the vast area controlled by him and his successes silenced any revolt and resistance.

Aachen

The king was also an administrator, capable of providing a strong base for his authority. He sought support from the bishops and counts whose loyal soldiers ensured law and order. He controlled the overall structure by sending out his personal representatives, known as missi dominici. Charlemagne had a palace built in Aachen, linked to a chapel. It was a perfect octagon with a dome in which there was a representation of

Christ. Charlemagne's throne stood above a gallery, making it look as if it was midway between earth and heaven. The monarch stayed frequently in Aachen. Indeed, it became his permanent residence and capital from 807 AD onwards. This marked the birth of a second Rome, or a second Byzantium. Charlemagne aimed to create his own court and he sought to attract literate people from every corner of his land. A palace academy came into being, centring particularly on Alcuin. Its policy, which was laid down in 789, was to open schools «to teach children to read». There was a need, it was said, for «each monastery and each bishopric to teach the psalms, notes of music, song, calculation and grammar and carefully to correct books of piety for often, while there are those who wish to pray to God, they are unable to do so because of the faults filling the books». The court was also to be a school. Young noblemen received board there and it was from among their number that Charlemagne chose the counts placed by him at the head of the pagi. Charlemagne's lands enjoyed a cultural renaissance symbolised by a more careful, clear, regular style of writing known as «Carolingian minuscule». The period was also marked by the construction of chapels and abbeys. The church in Gremigny built by the Bishop of Orléans is a fine example of this.

An Emperor in the Western World

Military and administrative success led to political change. Since Pope Leo III had been attacked in person, he sought refuge with the powerful King of the Franks who then appeared to loyal followers as the sole guide for Christian peoples. He enabled the Pope to return to Rome and soon travelled to Italy himself. The Pope granted him the title of Emperor and placed himself under the Emperor's protections, especially since, in Byzantium, it was a woman, Irene, who had declared herself to be empress. This usurpation seemed to indicate that the imperial throne was vacant. On Christmas Day in the year 800 AD in St. Peter's in Rome, the Pope crowned Charlemagne who was then acclaimed by those in attendance. This marked a «renovation» of the Empire – renovatio imperii. The Emperor found himself in a position to control the Church of Rome which, in exchange, had found a means of regaining the initiative as regards Byzantium. After the fall of Irene, the Emperor of the Orient acknowledged the accession of the new Emperor in the Western world.

The Failure of Louis the Pious

The imperial structure, which had brought organisation and administration to much of Western Europe, was linked to the strong personality and the activity of Charlemagne. The Emperor had planned the division of his kingdom after his death but fate stepped in and, by 814, only one of his sons was still alive – Louis who acquired the title of Emperor along with most of the Carolingian empire. Known as «Louis the Pious», he was unable to act as arbitrator in the quarrels between the members of his family and he soon became the target of his own sons – Lothar, Pepin I of Aquitaine and his son Pepin II, Duke Louis of Bavaria, and Charles the Bald, his son by a second marriage.

The Treaty of Verdun

When Louis the Pious died, Lothar became emperor but his brothers refused to submit to his authority. Charles the Bald, who controlled the small area of Neustria around Le Mans, allied himself to Louis «the German». The two princes met in Strasbourg on 14th February 842 and swore not to separate until they had achieved a common victory. Charles took an oath in the German language in order to ensure that his brother's soldiers understood him and Louis swore the oath in the Romance language. This is the oldest known text drawn up in the language that was a forerunner of French. The Frankish aristocracy eventually imposed a division rendered easier through the efforts made to find out more about the Carolingian empire. It was known as the Treaty of Verdun (August 843 AD). The division left Lothar with Italy, Louis with Bavaria and Charles with Neustria. Between Louis the German and Lothar, the border was the Rhine; between Lothar and Charles the Bald it was the Scheldt, the Meuse, the Saône and the Rhône, although there were numerous enclaves along the way. Lotharingia corresponded to a central line cutting across Europe from Italy to the Aachen area. As to Charles, he obtained the legacy of Clovis and Dagobert.

The Robertians

Some of the aristocracy refused to accept the division. Robert the Strong, for example, left the Rhineland and sought the protection of Charles the Bald. He was given a leading command in the struggle against the Bretons who, led by Nominoë, had created a large, independent duchy that included Rennes and Nantes. He was also involved in the struggle against the Normans, formidable seafarers who came from the north and whose presence added yet another difficulty to the many political crises. Robert the Strong was the first in the line of Robertians who were, in later years, to be known as Capetians.

The Viking Siege of Paris

Charles the Bald succeeded in overcoming every intrigue and, after Lothar's death, he took Italy where he was crowned Emperor by the Pope on Christmas Day 875. However, he left his own lands to fend for themselves and they were attacked by the Vikings. After the death of Charles the Bald, Carolingian monarchs continued to reign but with increasing numbers of princes at their sides. Hugh the Abbot, lay abbot of Saint-Germain d'Auxerre, held any weak or sick monarchs in his sway. Gozlin, who had charge of Saint-Denis Abbey, also played a vital role. It was he who had Robert the Strong's son, Odo, named Count of Paris and it was his friend, Thierry de Vermandois, who asked the

Emperor, Charles the Fat, to bring all the Franks together under his authority, for the last time. Odo then became the Emperor's confidant in the west and he led the heroic defence of Paris when it was attacked by the Vikings. Gozlin, who had become Bishop of Paris, died during the siege in 885-886. Odo received the entire estates of both Hugh the Abbot and Gozlin. In particular, he became lay abbot of Saint-Martin in Tours, Saint-Germain des Prés, Saint-Denis and Saint-Amand. On 29th February 888, Odo had himself crowned. His first intention was to defend the western kingdom against the Vikings and he was recognised by the Carolingian Emperor, Arnoul. He was succeeded, however, by a Carolingian king, Charles the Simple, grandson of Charles the Bald.

The Duchy of Normandy

It was at this point that «princes» gradually took the title of duke after establishing huge principalities such as Aquitaine, Burgundy, Gascony, Toulouse, Septimania-Gothia and, more particularly, Neustria which became the property of Robert, brother of King Odo. This was the model used as the basis of the agreement that put an end to the Norman question in 911. The Frankish aristocracy and the princes had begun by reacting and adapting to the forms of combat imposed by the pillaging hoards from the north. One of them, Rollo, settled at the mouth of the River Seine. He was the signatory of the agreement known as the Treaty of Saint-Clair-sur-Epte. Rollo became Count of Rouen, the only authority recognised by the monarch, Charles the Simple. Rollo was required to gain mastery over the other Vikings, in particular those who held the Loire. In order to ensure that there was peace with the Normans and the Bretons, Normandy gradually expanded. Rollo became Robert and was converted to Christianity. His religion became the religion of his companions and conversion was achieved rapidly. He began using Latin and the Normans then took as their own the Carolingian form of administration.

Duke of the Franks

Charles the Simple implemented an ambitious policy and captured Lotharingia, the heart of the Carolingian world. In fact, he was the primarily in control of the Laon area and, for the remainder, he was happy to acknowledge the power of the dukes, counts or marquises and the hereditary nature of this power. This enabled him to reign for a long period. However, he eventually annoyed his kingdom's aristocracy and he was deposed by its leaders. They then chose as their monarch Robert of Neustria, Robert I. He lost his life in a battle against Charles the Simple but the latter was nevertheless defeated and forced to flee (923 AD). Robert I's son-in-law, Ralph of Burgundy, was then designated as king (923-936). Ralph's reign, however, was difficult and, on his death, Robert of Neustria's son, Hugh the Great, did everything in his power to ensure that a Carolingian mounted the throne. The choice fell on Charles the Simple's son, Louis IV from Overseas, so-called because his mother had taken him to England. Hugh, who then became Duke of the Franks (dux Francorum), travelled with the new king all across the lands belonging to the Robertians. The young Louis IV attempted to shake off this stifling protection and his life was a succession of wars and alliances against Hugh. It was during these struggles that the word «France» first appeared, describing the western kingdom of the Franks. The powerful Duke of the Franks retained his power and again imposed it on Louis IV's successor, a child named Lothar.

The Robertian State

The Robertians controlled the major counties in Neustria, around Paris but also in the Loire Valley and they received backing from «Viscounts». They also owned leading abbeys, in particular St. Martin's in Tours, to which they were lay abbots. These were the count-abbots or abbacombes. The cloak which St. Martin had split in two, the «cappa», had already been a relic in the days of the Merovingians and Carolingians and it gave its name to the palace «chapel». Hugh the Great's son, Hugh Capet, also takes his name from the relic as did the dynasty that came after him, the Capetians. The assets from these abbeys enabled the prince to maintain his living standards and to reward those loyal to him. Such administrative and ecclesiastical power led to the birth of a veritable Robertian State in which there was a total lack of civil strife. It seemed to be an exemplary model in troubled times.

The Days of the Abbeys

The Robertians skilfully took advantage of the monastic revival centring on Cluny Abbey which was founded in 910 AD. The Benedictines obeyed the Rule of St. Benedict, which was revised during the days of Emperor Louis the Pious by Benedict of Aniane. The abbeys were structured around the abbot, the father of the monks over whom he had full authority. The Robertians also took advantage of the increasing role of the bishops. Six of them became counts (Reims, Laon, Châlons, Beauvais, Noyon and Langres). Later, they were to be the six ecclesiastical peerages of the realm.

The Rebirth of the Empire

The Empire revived in the east where King Otto of Germany had become emperor in 962 AD. It was perhaps thanks to his backing that the Carolingian King Lothar regained some of his power and initiative, therefore delaying the investiture of Hugh Capet after the death of his father, Hugh the Great. Hugh Capet also had to face the ambitious viscounts who had obtained the title of counts and were building new principalities, around Blois for example. Events were to reverse this development. War broke out between Lothar and Emperor Otto II for reasons relating to flouted honour. Lothar won Aachen and ransacked the imperial palace (978). The emperor launched a counter-attack and the Carolingian monarch had to seek refuge on lands belonging to Hugh Capet, who implemented skilful defence. Since Lothar continued with his intrigues, Hugh Capet gradually moved closer to the powerful Otto and won support from Archbishop Aldaberon of Reims whom the Carolingian king wanted to accuse of high treason.

Hugh Capet's Accession

When Lothar died in 986 AD, followed shortly afterwards by his son (987), the situation was favourable to Hugh Capet. Adalberon invited the leading noblemen to choose Hugh Capet as sovereign (his family had already given France two kings) and he was crowned on 3rd July 987. Hugh Capet also had his son crowned a short time later and he succeeded in ridding himself of Lothar's brother, Charles of Lorraine, who could have been a dangerous rival.

France grew up around this western kingdom based on the Carolingian empire then took root in the lands held by the Robertians around Paris. Even though his power and territory were limited, the Carolingian king had maintained his power for some considerable time for he was cloaked in the earlier prestige of Charlemagne and acknowledged as a sovereign by princes in distant places. Gradually, the Duke of the Franks became an integral part of the political landscape. It was a slow, gradual move towards the new, Capetian dynasty which was to fill a vacuum. At the same time, the western kingdom had shaken off the hold of the Ottonian empire.

THE FRANCE OF THE FIRST CAPETIANS

The first kings (Hugh Capet, Robert II the Pious, Henri I and Philippe I) had very little authority. The ordinary people were led, controlled and guided by noblemen and monks.

The Power of the Capetian Monarch

The king's power depended on his relationships with princes (dukes and counts) and his only room for manoeuvre was to take advantage of their rivalries. His authority was exercised over a very small territory around Paris, the royal estate. The Capetians were especially anxious to hand the royal function down through their lineage and in this they succeeded. To this end, they had no hesitation in marrying several times, which scandalised the Church, in order to ensure male descendants. They had their eldest son crowned during their own lifetime so that his accession to the throne would be undisputed. By ensuring this continuity, the Capetian dynasty took root and eventually took control of the other authorities in France.

The Miraculous Coronation

The alliance with the Church was highlighted by the coronation. Like the kings of Israel, the monarch was anointed with the consecrated oil and, through this anointing, he became like a king-priest. The men of the Church were tempted to claim that it was the anointing ceremony which produced a royal sense of dignity because such dignity was then dependent on them. During the days of the Capetians, the idea gradually spread that the king was capable of working miracles and had thaumaturgical powers enabling him to cure scrofula, a disease that affected the glands in the neck. Originally such healing took place in the church in Corbeny which was dedicated to St. Marcoul and located within the royal estates. Robert the Pious (996-1031) already had a reputation of being able to cure the sick by the laying-on of hands but it was Philippe I (1060-1108) who worked the miracle mainly for scrofula. Piously collected legends had doubtless created this belief which became one of the characteristic attributes of the Capetian dynasty.

Feudal Hierarchy

During the Carolingian period, it had been necessary to grant the counts a certain amount of public power by honouring them with a public charge, a position of command enabling them to mete out justice. They clung to these positions and, in their turn, bequeathed their power to their descendents. When external threats increased with new invasions, the people turned to them for greater help than they received from the king far away. This led the counts to create veritable «principalities» linking together several pagi. Once a count had been «promoted» to prince, viscounts then rose to the rank of counts in their turn. This change was to be a characteristic feature of the western world in the Middle Ages and it was to affect every layer of society, in a form of fragmentation and legal privatisation of public authority. At the same time, through marriages, numerous links were built up between these princes and counts who, in turn, contracted alliances or opposed each other. Thanks to this situation, the King of France was able to take advantage of the rivalry between the Duke of Normandy and the Count of Flanders or draw benefit from the permanent dispute opposing the Count of Anjou and the Count of Blois.

Personal Ties

Another preoccupation of authority, whether in Roman or Merovingian times, had been to ensure military assistance by means of strong commitment in the form of a contract for the Romans or a form of military «guild» for the Franks. It was during the Carolingian era that the first report of an oath taken on relics was mentioned. A vassal would swear allegiance to his lord («seigneur» in French, from «senior» meaning «older»). This created a personal bond between the two men. It was to develop from top to bottom of the social scale through the nobility, especially when the noblemen were warriors. An entire, new social hierarchy came into being with the king at the apex of the pyramid in his capacity as lord of all lords. Gestures accompanied this social ritual in addition to the oath itself, among them the kiss (osculum). The gestures symbolised peace and instigated a personal bond, in appearance at least, between the lord and his vassal.

Estates

In addition to this spiritual exchange, there was a material guarantee in the form of a gift of a benefit, an estate (feodum); it is this word which has been used by historians to describe the entire system of feudalism. The estate also became hereditary, like the power over the local people, an inheritance from royal authority. Soon, the lords in turn sought to attract followers by granting benefits. This being so, the feudal system was more than a network of personal commitments; it was also an intricate structure of material interests and complex rights. Vassals owed assistance to their liege lord in at least three situations – in order to pay a ransom if the lord was taken prisoner, to raise the eldest son to the knighthood and to pay the dowry of the eldest daughter.

Castles

The Capetian monarch could only exercise his authority through these princes who, themselves, had to take account of a fragmentation of the country into several hundred castellanies. For many years, the building of a castle was the monarch's prerogative or, at the very least, a count's prerogative – until the early 11th century that is. Invasions by Vikings or Hungarians encouraged people to think in terms of defence. Gradually, outer walls were strengthened around towns and abbeys; towers were added along their length. Then, after the year 1000, lords (or «sires» i.e. viscounts, the younger sons of leading families or supporters of the princes) built castles or captured those already in existence that, in some cases, they were guarding on a count's behalf. France was a country dominated by castellans who were recognisable for their lifestyle and strange residences.

Feudal Mottes

Over time, the feudal motte, the strongpoint in any fortress, also became a symbol of power since royal authority was in decline. On one hand, the weakening of central authority led the strongest or the most enterprising to seize power by seeking to establish it through a castle, i.e. the motte and the bailey, or tower, that topped it. On the other hand, the absence of strong authority led to a decline in public law and order, a climate of violence and private warfare. This in turn led to the building of fortified shelters. Not until late in the day did the feudal mottes abandon their timber fortifications in favour of stone walls and towers and the warriors preferred to choose impregnable sites. The fortresses are stone lookouts dotted across our countryside. Nature came to the assistance of men who revealed and, in their turn, heightened the beauties of nature. Such an enterprise also reflected the pride of dynastic families. The eagle's nests encouraged the reproduction of great rapacious species. A feudal citadel was both a natural refuge to which people could turn in case of danger and a symbol of obedience, even servitude, towards the knight.

Nobles, Men-at-Arms and Knights

And so a group of noblemen (nobiles) came into being, a group which it is difficult to define. Indeed, definitions of this nobility compared to, or confused with, the knights has engendered major controversy between historians. Originally, a nobleman was undoubtedly a free man who possessed freehold land in the form of ancestral estates. Realities changed, however, and the concept of nobility became confused with the ability to carry arms and own a horse – the military function took precedence over any other. It was also of importance in the traditional distinctions made by Adalberon of Laon between those who pray, those who fight and those who work. The concept of «nobility» was therefore extended to include all those who carried weapons and served the lords. They were the milites and they were to form the group of barons and knights. In their turn, they owned fortified houses with towers. The solemn dubbing of a knight was the ceremony which marked the entrance of a young man into this world of combat.

Lordships

The Carolingian period also led to increasing numbers of inventories of assets known as polyptychs. The inventory carried out in Saint-Germain des Prés, the large abbey on the outskirts of Paris, shows the division between the reserve and the small manor houses entrusted to free peasants. Historians are unsure as to the origin of these huge estates which may, in many cases, be an extension of the Gallo-Roman villae and which might have inherited the earlier operating methods, albeit with slaves (servi) being replaced by bonded peasants known as serfs. Slavery had gradually died out. The important thing was to tie the peasant to the land in order to enable the owner to earn good income from the land and live on his income. The logic behind the system was that the person working the land could not easily run away but that he should earn enough in the way of resources to avoid his wishing to leave and to ensure that he enjoyed good enough health to work his field properly. However, all over the country but especially in the south, there were free peasants who owned free land or «allodia».

The Peasant Community

With the strengthening of the lords' position, the burden placed on free and bonded peasants alike became much heavier. They were subjected to the same pressure to provide work. New demands were placed on them and were quickly integrated into the system under the name of «customs». The peasants showed great solidarity in the face of the taxes and tithes, many of which were paid in kind but sometimes in silver, and in the face of the services demanded by the lord. Monasteries, which were also collective estates, followed this example and veritable competition grew up between the lay lords and the monastic communities. In the face of this, or perhaps thanks to it, the villages gained greater strength. It was the lords, whether «sires» or monks, who were also the founders of the villages or «castelnaux» in the south of France, designed to bring families more closely together in geographical terms.

The Development of the Monasteries

The monks spent their lives in prayer for the salvation of all Christians. They abandoned their personal wealth. Abbots were originally elected; in later times, they were often appointed by the lords whose ancestors had founded the abbey. The Benedictines, who wore a black robe, were the predominant order, arousing many a vocation. The Rule of St. Benedict was both humane and strict. The blackfriars gave great beauty to religious ceremonies held in grandiose architectural surroundings. The work recommended by the Rule was primarily aimed at finding manuscripts and copying ancient tests in the scriptorium. This was a way of saving the ancient heritage of the western world but it was also an opportunity for intellectual reflection. The abbeys provided schooling for young monks and it was there that many future bishops or prelates were educated. The monks brought an aesthetic dimension to this intellectual work by illuminating the manuscripts and turning them into masterpieces.

The Role of the Monks

The princes who had decided against becoming lay abbots called upon the Benedictines, especially those following the Cluniac Reform, to reform or found religious communities. Duke Richard II of Normandy asked an Italian, William of Volpiano, to take over the monasteries in his duchy. A community of Benedictines was established on Mont Saint-Michel, replacing with some difficulty the chapter of canons already settled there. William the Conqueror found, in the abbeys of Normandy, some of the framework for the Church in England. The princes donated lands and presented gifts to the monks who thus built up huge estates of which the abbot was the lord. The working of these estates was often exemplary. Certain historians have insisted on the close ties between the world of the knights and the monastic world. Although the monks prayed for all, they began with the founder of their abbey and with the generous donor. They themselves came from the nobility and they also remembered their families and relations in their prayers. At the end of their lives, lords would seek refuge in monasteries, or ask to be buried there.

Cluny

Cluny in Burgundy lay at the centre of this monastic revival. Strong characters such as Odilon (994-1049) or Hugh of Semur (1049-1109) set up a whole network of communities (one thousand in all throughout the Christian world) which eventually constituted the «Cluniac Order» and a veritable «monastic empire» since the abbot had authority over all the other monasteries. The monks passed from one abbey to another and there were countless links between the main abbey and its daughter-houses which were independent inasmuch as they were dependent only on Rome and were not under the control of a bishop. The Abbot of Cluny was, in some ways, the second most important person in the Christian world and in Canossa in 1077 he acted as mediator between the Pope and the Emperor.

Cîteaux and Bernard of Clairvaux

Fervent Christians soon considered the blackfriars to be too wealthy and new orders appeared in which purity and austerity were the main tenets. In Cîteaux Abbey founded by Robert of Molesme a new ideal came to the fore – monks were to engage in manual work. The future St. Bernard (1091-1153) left Cîteaux in 1115 and went to Clairvaux from where he founded a large number of monasteries. St. Bernard was actively involved in the controversies of the day and he set himself up as a guide in the Christian world. He condemned heretics, supported the Pope and preached the Second Crusade in Vézelay in 1146. Cistercian austerity led to increasing numbers of architectural successes in which the same layout, endlessly repeated, underlines the same desire for grandeur through simplicity. Sénanque, for example, lies in an enclosed valley, at the end of a field of lavender. Fontfroide stands in Cathar country, its golden stonework apparently forgetting that it was the source of the struggle against the heretics and the mooting of the concept of the much-feared Inquisition.

Romanesque Architecture

Romanesque architecture came into being in the 11th century and it marked this blossoming of Christianity. It was first and foremost a monastic architecture and, for many years, Cluny was the largest building in the Christian world. Europe was then covered with a white cloak of churches, to use the expression coined by Raoul Glaber. The stone barrel vaulting in these sturdy churches required thick walls, piers and columns. In order to increase the number of ceremonies and embellish their contents, numerous chapels were built to house the «relics», or remains, of saints. The doorways and capitals on the columns were carved, often very exuberantly. This style of architecture was initially described as «Norman» by historians and was then renamed «Romanesque». The finest examples of Romanesque abbeys are to be found in Normandy – Jumièges, for example, still has its vast white West Front. In Caen, the West Front of St. Stephen's (Saint-Etienne) with its massive square outline topped by two tall, symmetrical towers, established a norm, a form of architectural harmony which the Normans then took to the British Isles and which cathedrals used endlessly throughout much of the western world.

Gregorian Reform

The monks were also instrumental in the reform implemented by the Popes. For the Church and the clergy, it was known as the «Gregorian» reform, named after Gregory VII, Pope from 1073 to 1085, even though the reform was launched before his accession to the papal throne. The main aim was to impose, as bishops and priests, men whose behaviour more closely complied with the rules of the Church. This would combat the wheeling and dealing in ecclesiastical benefits and religious sacraments («simony») and would prevent the marriage of priests (doctrine of the «Nicolaitans»). It aimed to prevent lay people taking over Church assets and controlling clerics.

The Peace and Truce of God

It was the monks who encouraged a movement launched by the bishops, the «peace of God». The idea was to condemn all those who attacked the assets and men of the Church or who took over property belonging to peasants. Abbot Odilon of Cluny offered the lords of Burgundy an opportunity to take a solemn oath in 1016 in an attempt to combat private violence. The peace of God led to a simple «Truce of God» imposed upon the combatants. Even though warfare remained legitimate, the men of the cloth did their utmost to limit its effects, trying to prohibit fighting during times of major liturgical importance such as Sundays, or even from Fridays to Mondays, as well as during Advent and Lent. The movement was supported by the Cluniac Order and by the bishops; it spread mainly in the south of France. On the other hand, in the north, powerful princes and bishops well settled in their towns were not tempted by these new commitments. The peace and truce of God were mainly ideals but they marked the involvement of spiritual authorities in political life in order to ensure public law and order at a time when it was no longer guaranteed.

The Crusades

It was Pope Urban II, formerly a monk in the Order of Cluny, who brought all these changes together. In Clermont, on 8th November 1095, in order to impose peace between warring noblemen, he offered Christians an opportunity to undertake a new mission which was sure to be pleasing to God, a mission that would take them far afield in order to free Jerusalem from the Moslems. By placing a Cross on their clothing, crusaders made a public statement about their holy commitment. The reason for this crusade was the presence of the Turks who were making it more and more difficult to undertake pilgrimages in the Holy Land. The crusade against Islam was the Pope's business; the princes were pushed aside. The Pope thought of a military expedition to free the holy places but his call created an army of ordinary Christians who had been convinced by Peter the Hermit, a marginal figure within the Church. The crusade of poor people set off first, without preparation and without waiting for military backup. It was a dramatic event. After reaching Byzantium where they were given food but did not receive permission to enter the city for fear of pillaging, the first crusaders were scattered by the Turks in Asia Minor in October 1096.

Christians in the Orient

The noblemen's crusade, which was organised by the papal legate, was led by Godefroy de Bouillon, Duke of Lower Lorraine, and his brother Baldwin, by William the Conqueror's son, and by the Count of Toulouse, Raymond de Saint-Gilles whom the Pope considered as the leader of the crusade. After passing through Byzantium, the crusaders captured Antioch

(1098) and Jerusalem (1099). Godefroy de Bouillon held Jerusalem in the name of the Holy See and his brother, who succeeded him, became its king in 1100. Other crusades were to follow.

The King Confronts Princes and Castellans

Louis VI (1108-1137) sought support from his friend, Abbot Suger of Saint-Denis. He attempted to bring into line the knights who, even on the royal estates, contested the king's authority. The days of the castellanies were over, for such fragmentation hindered the expanding commercial links. The same moves were also keenly felt in all the principalities in which the princes tried to weaken the feudal elements. By doing so, they hoped to satisfy the burghers in the burgeoning towns who were anxious to obtain safe roads. Finally, the king tried to remind the princes (the Duke of Normandy or the Duke of Aquitaine) of his authority and, occasionally, he succeeded. Louis VII (1137-1180) proceeded in the same way. He even succeeded in marrying Eleanor of Aquitaine in 1137 and she brought as her dowry the Duchy of Aquitaine, with its vast estates. Suger was also his adviser and he became Regent when the king set off on a crusade. In 1152, the royal marriage was annulled at the request of the king and this decision has remained something of a mystery ever since. Was Eleanor lacking in prudence or were there differences in character or culture? The break-up of the marriage had far-reaching consequences.

Normandy and England

The Duchy of Normandy had long since seen its destiny change, thanks to William, the illegitimate son of Robert the Magnificent. He succeeded in taking control of the Normans. In England, the succession of King Edward the Confessor hung in the balance. William was the king's cousin; his rival was the leading Anglo-Saxon nobleman, Harold. When King Edward died, Harold declared himself to be king but William decided to land in England. He won the Battle of Hastings on 14th October 1066 and, on Christmas Day, he was crowned. The Norman presence was imposed on England through William the Conqueror, who also brought rigorous organisation based on the administration existing in the Duchy of Normandy. When William died, the duchy was initially separated from the kingdom of England but the two territories were reunited by Henry I Beauclerc. Since he had no male heir, wars of succession broke out after his death with, on one side, Stephen of Blois, grandson of William the Conqueror through his mother, who finally gained the throne of England, and on the other side Geoffrey Plantagenet, Count of Anjou, who had married Henry I Beauclerc's daughter and who conquered Normandy.

Henry Plantagenet

It was Geoffrey's son, Henry Plantagenet, who succeeded in seducing the wife of King Louis VII of France, Eleanor of Aquitaine. Since the Church had agreed to the spouses' separation, Eleanor remarried, with Henry Plantagenet, bringing him Aquitaine as a dowry. Finally, on the death of Stephen of Blois, Henry had himself acknowledged as the King of England. This meant that a considerable territorial power had been created. Within the kingdom, Aquitaine combined with two essential principalities (Normandy and Anjou); on the other side of the Channel lay England. For many years, this state of affairs was to cast a long shadow over the history of France. Henry II proved to be an excellent administrator even if, at the end of his life, his sons rebelled against him.

The Towns Gain Strength

From the 12th century onwards, the towns enjoyed a new vitality. The distinguishing features of a town were the wall it built to protect itself, the existence of many different activities (civil and religious administration, trade, crafts), the size of its population (more than 2,000) and the density of its housing. Paris was the largest town in the kingdom but there were several other large urban communities, especially in Flanders which was then part of France (Ghent, Bruges, Lille, Arras and Douai). There were also large harbours such as Rouen, La Rochelle, Bordeaux and Bayonne. More importantly, there was a whole network of small towns which were to play an important part in the history of France. In Champagne, four large towns (Troyes, Provins, Lagny and Bar-sur-Aube) hosted fairs which attracted merchants. By doing so, they became the largest financial centres in the western world.

Trades (we would now say «corporations») were organised in the 12th century and they drew up their statutes in the following century. Their aim was to monitor the quality of products, train apprentices and prevent unfair trading. Merchants' guilds also came into existence.

The Communal Movement

The burghers in the towns became aware of their own importance and strengthened their identity by taking an oath, the «entreaty». In the north of the country, «communes» (urban communities) were set up and the communal movement came into being in the 1070's. Certain towns such as Soissons or Tournai had obtained total independence. Others obtained charters defining their rights vis-à-vis the local lords. In the south, there were consular towns in which the nobility played a role in municipal government.

Universities

Reflecting the expansion of towns, there were changes in the search for intellectual advancement. Schools set up within monasteries declined while, on the other hand, new schools were established in towns that were bishoprics, in the shadow of the cathedral. Certain teachers had distinguished careers, among them philosopher Pierre Abélard. Knowledge found new bases through the rediscovery of Aristotle as a metaphysician and the rediscovery of ancient science which was known through Arab scientists. Law gained strength thanks to the reading of the Justinian Code. Such intellectual curiosity led to a form of higher education that found a new framework at the end of the 12th century – universities consisting of students and teachers. This type of community, like a «trade guild», defended its rights and customs in the face of the remainder of society.

The Sorbonne

In Paris, the University was recognised by the papal legate in 1215 and it imposed itself on the king, the bishop and the burghers only by using its right to strike i.e. by ceasing to provide courses. The left bank of the Seine became the University district as opposed to the «Cité» and the Town. In 1257, St. Louis' chaplain, Robert de Sorbon, founded a college for some twenty or more theologians. This marked the birth of the Sorbonne and the Faculty of Divinity in Paris was to be one of the leading intellectual centres in the western world. Thomas Aquinas, the famous Italian, came to teach here on two occasions. His work, Summa Theologica, sought to reconcile Christian revelation and Aristotelian rationalism. Other intellectual centres also developed, e.g. Toulouse and Orléans for Law and Montpellier for Medicine.

Dominicans and Franciscans

The towns also attracted new defenders of the faith who were very different to the knowledgeable Benedictines in rural areas. The Dominicans, who first established a strong foothold in order to combat Cathar beliefs, founded their preachings on study and encouraged poverty through their own example. This was also true of Franciscans, the followers of St. Francis of Assisi. Their sermons, which were well adapted to the new social classes in the towns, attracted crowds of people in search of the absolute.

Ogival or Gothic Architecture

It was in towns that ogival, or Gothic, architecture developed. Ribbed vaulting resulted in walls of inordinate size and openings that did not weaken the overall solidity of the construction, while enabling light to flood in through stained glass. Cathedrals were built, demanding several decades of hard work but also attesting to the pride of great towns.

THE DAYS OF GREAT MONARCHS

The Capetian sovereign succeeded in confirming his authority over the castellans on his estates and over the leading vassals present in much of the kingdom who accepted, albeit grudgingly, to pay homage to him. Chief among these vassals were the Duke of Normandy, the Count of Flanders, the Count of Champagne and the Count of Toulouse in the south of the country. The king had successfully manoeuvred his way through European intrigue, in the face of the other princes of the Christian world, and he had taken part in the Crusade.

Philip Augustus

It was Philip Augustus (1180-1223) who gave a whole new dimension to the Capetian monarchy. For many years, he had to stand up to Henry II's elder son, Richard the Lionheart who provided protection for Normandy by building the fortress known as Château-Gaillard. When Richard was killed by an arrow at the Siege of Châlus in the Limousin area in 1199, Philip regained the upper hand over Richard's brother, John Lackland, who had become King John of England. Château-Gaillard fell and, with it, the whole of Normandy followed by the Loire Valley.

Bouvines

John Lackland succeeded in mobilising troops against Philip, gaining as allies Count Ferrand of Flanders and Emperor Otto IV whose rival was supported by the Capetian monarch. While his elder son, the future Louis VIII, was holding John Lackland at bay in Anjou, Philip Augustus decided to engage the imperial and Flemish armies massed in the north of the country. It was Sunday 27th July 1214. He won the day. Ferrand of Flanders was captured and kept prisoner for fifteen years. This victory was celebrated as a sign of God's will and a major stage in the strengthening of the Capetian kingdom which also took advantage of the crusade against the Albigensians.

The Albigensians

Spiritual demands had been a constant feature of the history of the Church and the religious orders had, for example, tried to meet this need for purity and austerity. However, the Church was criticised and, in secret, movements grew up which were deemed by the clerics to be contrary to the official doctrine i.e. heretical. Catharism developed against this background. It was a concept by which two totally separate forces, Good and Evil, confronted each other in the world. Manicheism in the East and Bogomilism in the Balkans had proposed the same ideas. Its arrival in the western world remains shrouded in mystery. Soon, though, the men of the cloth became aware that the doctrine had spread, especially in the south of the country, in Languedoc. The Church was suspicious of this double divinity, Good and Evil, and disliked the moral despair implied by this faith. The Cistercians led the fight against the heresy and the heretics were burnt at the stake.

The «Good Men»

«Cathar» means pure and this description has been chosen by historians to define the mysterious religious movement whose followers were also known as Albigensians, even though the town of Albi was not at the heart of the conflict. The movement grew up from 1167 onwards (Cathar council in Saint-Félix de Caraman). Cathar missionaries called themselves «Perfects». They refused marriage in the name of purity and offered their own lives as examples to follow. According to them, since Man was ensnared in matter, he was condemned to do evil and could not achieve salvation for himself. This doctrine, which was easily stamped out in the north of the country, took root in the south, attracting fervent souls from every layer of society, especially at the courts of noblemen. The Count of Toulouse tolerated, or even supported, the heretics. Warriors in the south of the kingdom showed tolerance for those known as «Good Men» and, in many cases, the warriors' wives, mothers or sisters became «Perfects».

The Murder of Pierre de Castelnau

The Church had already taken action. A Spaniard named Dominic arrived in Languedoc in 1205, adapted his preaching to take account of the aspirations of the Cathars, insisted on the importance of study and, in order to meet the demands for poverty, had no hesitation in begging. At the same time, a papal legate excommunicated Count Raymond VI of Toulouse. It was one of the Count of Toulouse' squires who committed an irreparable act – the murder of Pierre de Castelnau, the papal legate. Pope Innocent III called for a crusade in 1208, offering the Count of Toulouse' lands to anybody who captured them. Raymond VI submitted to papal authority, but in vain.

The Crusade

The noblemen from the north threw themselves into the adventure. A baron with little wealth or influence, Simon de Montfort, and his companions had several successes in battle. After supporting the crusaders, Raymond VI changed sides but he was defeated at Muret

(12th September 1213). Simon de Montfort captured the County of Toulouse. The Perfects were sent to the stake, refusing to deny their faith and abjure.

The French monarchy succeeded in taking enormous advantage of this crisis by gradually integrating new territories into the king's estates. After the death of Simon de Montfort, the king again laid claim to the lands that once belonged to the Count of Toulouse. Philip Augustus' son, Louis VIII, led an expedition in Languedoc. He died on the way home.

Montségur

Peace finally returned in 1229. Raymond VII, Count of Toulouse, gave his daughter, whom he had designated as his heir, to Alphonse of Poitiers, the brother of King Louis IX. In the long term, this paved the way for the inclusion of the lands in the Capetian estates. Carcassonne and Beaucaire became royal seneschalships. For the first time, the royal estates extended as far as the Mediterranean. In 1229, the Inquisition was set up and soon entrusted by the Pope to the Dominicans. They tirelessly sought out heretics by increasing the number of rigorous, systematic interrogations. A few citadels held out for a long time thanks to alliances between leading dynasties and the heretics. Among these fortresses were Montségur and Quéribus. Montségur valiantly resisted between April 1243 and March 1244. In 1255, it was the royal seneschal who besieged Quéribus. This crusade against the Albigensians has sometimes been seen, in the south of France, as marking the end of a southern civilisation that was more tolerant, liberal and enlightened than the civilisation in the north of the kingdom which imposed its law and its control.

Blanche of Castile

When Louis VIII died, his son, Louis IX (1226-1270) was only 12 years old and his mother, Blanche of Castile, became regent of the kingdom. She was a dynamic woman who left her mark on the early days of the reign by bringing order back to a kingdom in which revolts were rife and she continued to wield strong political influence until her death in 1252. Louis IX overcame the many attempts on the part of leading vassals to oppose his authority.

A Pious, Just King

Louis IX also left his mark on his time through his own personality. He was a very pious man who appeared to contemporaries as an exemplary Christian prince implementing policies that complied with his religious convictions. He tried to reform the kingdom by creating a system of royal bailiffs who held military functions in the bailiwicks or in the senelschalships in the south of the country. They mobilised the noblemen, bringing them into the king's service, took receipt of revenue from the estates and, more particularly, meted out justice in the sovereign's name. Through them, royal administration stood strong in the face of lords and princes. The demand for justice was reflected in the picture of the sovereign dispensing justice underneath an oak tree in Vincennes, a form of justice designed to be the same for all, whether nobles or commoners. This determination for equality led the king to prevent quarrels between barons and to impose peace on the country. In 1249, the king's brother, Alphonse of Poitiers, received the legacy of his father-in-law, the Count of Toulouse.

The King's Coinage

Louis IX also wanted political power to impose moral rules that would prevent corruption. He attacked those who handled money, especially the Jews who practised usury which, in theory, Christians were not permitted to do. It was, though, a vital practice if trade was to flourish. Monetary reform was prepared and the king's coinage became mandatory throughout the realm while the right to mint coinage because a royal prerogative, even though lords continued to do so in their own areas. Following the example of Italian towns, the monarch also had a gold coin minted, the ecu.

An Arbitrator in Europe

Finally, Louis IX imposed his will on Europe. Through his own marriage with Margaret of Provence and the marriage of his brother, Charles of Anjou, with the heiress to Provence, the Capetian monarch extended his influence towards the Mediterranean while his brother, Charles of Anjou, launched an Italian campaign. Gradually, Louis IX was seen as the foremost prince in the Christian world and, after the Crusade, as an arbitrator on the European stage. Through the Treaty of Paris in 1259, he granted extensive, some said excessive, concessions in order to re-establish peaceful relations with England. Louis IX was asked to intervene and take decisions in many cases. By choosing the path to peace, he contributed to his image as a saintly king.

A Crusader

In particular Louis IX prepared to take part in a crusade since that was the mission of a Christian king. In 1248, he set off from Aigues-Mortes and led the Crusade against Cairo. He was defeated at al-Mansurah (1250) and captured. Freed in return for the payment of a heavy ransom, he remained in the Orient until 1254 and strengthened the defences of the Latin States. On his return to France, his failure, which he attributed to his sins, dominated his policies. He made a further attempt in 1270, this time attacking Tunis, but he died during the siege of the town. Although Louis IX's personality and action resulted in his being made a saint to whom the Roman Catholic church prayed at the altar, a fact which was proudly proclaimed by the Capetian dynasty and the French monarchy, his image has been slightly tarnished in more recent times because his convictions were accompanied by persecution and intolerance.

The Beautiful 13th Century

The 13th century was a time of growth. In the countryside, clearance had made additional land available. New villages had been created and a robust peasant population could be nourished. The noblemen realised that it was profitable to involve the peasantry in the development process and the movement towards emancipation put an end to serfdom.

Philip the Fair

By developing the presence of the monarchic State throughout the kingdom and ensuring that it was the king's justice which was dispensed, the Capetian sovereigns had weakened the feudal structure, tending to consider lords and peasants alike as subjects. The strengthening of royal power was also based on the weakness of the emperor. The King of France (for so he styled himself from this period onwards) could proclaim himself «emperor in his own kingdom». Such a doctrine reflected the vision of public power held by the ancient Romans. During the reign of Philip IV the Fair (1285-1314), lawyers with in-depth knowledge of Roman law, specified this new legitimacy of the Capetian State and contributed to the definition of royal sovereignty by giving it new resources. Political bodies came into being, centring on the king. The royal household dealt with the monarch's everyday life. He summoned leading noblemen to advise him but also called upon burghers or lesser noblemen, and his lawyers. Major decisions had to be taken «by grand counsel» for the king had to consult his advisers before taking any decision. As a final resort, justice increasingly became the business of the Court, or «Parlement», and it was a court of justice with specialists i.e. judges, which was developed, although the sovereign retained the right to quash rulings handed down by the Court. The Chamber of Accounts was responsible for controlling and monitoring the administration of the royal finances.

The Counterfeiter

It is true that an extended territory had given the sovereign new resources but the Capetians had ambitions, beginning with the Crusade, which had aroused new requirements. The king, who held a monopoly on coinage, gave in to temptation and took full advantage of it. He instigated veritable devaluations and, because of this, the Pope later referred to Philip the Fair as «the counterfeiter». The revenue from the royal estate was no longer sufficient and the principle of a contribution from the king's subjects, a royal tax, was mooted. To this end, and to obtain military aid, with the imposition of extraordinary taxes, the king convened the three states of the kingdom in 1314 – representatives of clerics, noblemen and towns. This marked the birth of the idea that, because the king should normally «live off his own wealth» i.e. the ordinary revenue from his estate, the «extraordinary» finances were to be agreed to by assemblies representing his subjects.

Financial needs were all the more apparent when the king engaged in political ventures. He wanted to attack south-western France, Guyenne, but eventually left it for King Edward I of England, whose son married King Philip's daughter, Isabelle. Philip the Fair wanted to bring under control the Count of Flanders who enjoyed total support from Flemish towns. A crushing defeat was inflicted on the French cavalry in Courtrai in 1302 – the bourgeois militia, especially the craftsmen of Ghent, showed no mercy whatsoever.

The Assassination Attempt in Agnani

Financial questions were also the reason for initial tension between the monarch and the papacy. The Pope could grant the king tithes, taxes levied on ecclesiastical revenue which were to be used to fund the Crusade. Philip the Fair wanted to misappropriate the funds and this led to conflict with Pope Boniface VIII (1294-1297). When a bishop contested the legitimacy of the Capetians, the king decided to have him judged, again defying the sovereign pontiff. Boniface VIII summoned a council and replied to the king by a papal bull entitled Unam sanctam by which he recalled the superiority of papal authority and proclaimed himself competent to sit in judgement on the king of France whom he nevertheless hesitated to excommunicate. The conflict became increasingly bitter. The king and his advisers, acting in the name of the entire realm, asked that the sovereign pontiff appear before a universal council for judgement. One of the king's advisers, Guillaume de Nogaret, travelled to Italy and, on 7th September 1303, he was able to approach the Pope in Agnani and announce the king's riposte. It caused a riot in which the Pope almost died. It was known as the «Assassination Attempt in Agnani» and Boniface VIII died one month later.

The End of the Temple

The struggle between the papacy and the leading State in the Christian world led to an attack on the Order of the Temple. Founded as support for the Crusade, it had lost its primary purpose after the fall of Acre in 1291. However, because of the Order's huge assets, the Knights Templar were leading bankers. They were unpopular because of their wealth and accused of sodomy. In fact, the Knights Templar became an ideal target for Philip the Fair who had them all arrested on 13th October 1307. Subjected to torture, the prisoners confessed to anything and everything. In 1312, Philip obtained from the Pope, who had long shown reticence in this respect, authorisation to wipe out the entire Order. The Grand Master, Jacques de Molay, who protested his innocence, was sentenced to be burnt at the stake. It was long thought that the reason behind this operation was purely financial since the king wanted to obtain the Temple's assets. However, as they were transferred to the Order of the Knights of St. John of Jerusalem, the king's attack was doubtless aimed at the reform, by popular demand, of an Order that had lost its primary purpose.

Succession Through the Male Line

The end of Philip the Fair's reign was marked by a series of scandals that cast doubt on the honour of his daughters-in-law. The reign of Louis X the Stubborn (1314-1316) was short. On his death, he left a daughter who was distanced from the throne but who received Navarre as a legacy from her mother. Louis X's posthumous son, John I, did not live. The child's uncle, Philip V the Long, was preferred to the niece. He died in 1322, leaving only daughters, and was succeeded by his brother, Charles IV. When he in turn died in 1328, there were no more sons descended from the King of France, even though Philip the Fair's daughter had a son, Edward III of England. Attention turned to one of Philip the Fair's nephews, Philippe de Valois, Philip VI. He was easily recognised as king because it seemed impossible to call upon the King of England to reign in France. This also meant that, henceforth, women did not pass on rights to the throne, even to their sons.

THE HUNDRED YEARS' WAR

The accession of Philip VI de Valois was not contested but it enabled the King of England to lay claim to the crown of France. In order to counter his arguments, some fifty years later, lawyers used a tradition dating back to the days of the Salian Franks by which women were disinherited as regards land assets. This was the so-called Salic Law.

Tension

Tension rapidly grew between the King of France and the King of England, initially over Guyenne on which the French monarchy ceaselessly put pressure. Yet, in 1329, Edward III agreed to pay homage to his sovereign. The two monarchs were nevertheless dragged into further quarrels between leading noblemen, especially when difficult questions of inheritance arose. Robert of Artois who had supported the accession of Philip VI, hoped that the Artois area would be his. He was discontented with the king and changed his allegiance to England. The same chain of events applied to Brittany where the Montfort faction which was supported by Edward III confronted the Penthièvres who supported Philip VI. The conflict lasted for many years and included a number of epic events such as the Battle of the Thirty during which the champions of both sides engaged in a murderous fight.

The Battle of Sluis

By 1337, Edward III felt in a stronger position and he threw down a challenge to Philip VI. He began by intervening in the affairs of Flanders where economic crisis had gripped the leading towns. Cloth was selling at a lower price and trade had taken a downturn. Revolt broke out in Ghent, led by Van Artevelde who sought help from England. Pro-English and anti-French feelings had spread since Philip VI had come to the area in 1328 to put down social unrest and had dealt a crushing defeat on the rebels in Cassel. The Count of Flanders turned to his sovereign, the King of France, who had a fleet that had taken forty years to build up. He wanted to blockade the arm of the sea leading to Bruges. This was the Battle of Sluis (24th June 1340). The French military commanders showed themselves incapable of organising a naval battle, the English archers showed that French crossbows were decidedly out of date and many men lost their lives, perhaps as many as 20,000. Thereafter the King of France no longer had the resources necessary to prevent the English landing on the continent. The affair, though, had an unfortunate end for Edward III. Van Artevelde offered him the County of Flanders but the Flemish leader was killed by his own people.

Crécy

In 1346, the King of England landed in the Cherbourg Peninsula. Near Caen, he routed an army which had come to stop his advance, then he avoided Paris and moved northwards. Philip VI finally encountered him at Crécy (26th August 1346). Battle raged but the heavy knights were stopped in their tracks by the arrows of the English archers. Philip was forced to flee. Edward III took time to capture Calais, which resisted for some considerable time. Six burghers were to bring out the keys to the town, dressed in their shirts and wearing a rope round their necks. Tradition has it that King Edward wanted to make them pay for the excessively long resistance but that Queen Philippa of Hainault intervened and saved their lives. More simply, it was a submission ritual. King Philip was discredited and the States which he convened sharply criticised their sovereign.

Black Death

There is no question of repeating the theoretical discussions on the origins of the difficulties, on their date and precise location, or on the evidence of the crisis. Suffice it to say that they were widespread, even if they did not have the same intensity everywhere at the same time. The misfortunes of the day were first and foremost the Black Death and war. The plague had disappeared from Europe and leprosy had become the most feared disease. Suddenly, at the end of 1347, the plague reappeared in harbours along the Mediterranean. It spread through France in 1348 and disappeared again in 1349. Wherever it passed, it ravaged the population, killing one person in three. From then on, it became the most highly-feared scourge of the people, for it returned periodically, approximately every ten years. Fear of the disease and of death was to cause major mental distress, especially as contemporaries were ignorant of the causes of contagion – flea bites. Even though the people regained their optimism after each plague outbreak, in the long term, it accelerated a demographic decline which had been apparent to a lesser extent before its arrival.

War

The «Hundred Years War» was not total warfare; it was interspersed with numerous periods of calm, even periods of happiness. However, the military situation weighed heavily on the life of ordinary people. When armies passed through areas, there was pillaging; mills or ovens were destroyed. Armies on the move facilitated the spread of epidemics.

Mobilisation led to the renewal and increase of royal taxes. It was expensive to arm noblemen and when they were taken prisoner they had to pay a ransom in order to regain their freedom. This was a heavy financial burden for certain families and their peasants. Money was also required to fund the building of defences for towns and the construction of new walls. The crisis was also economic. Climatic difficulties may explain poor harvests and the reappearance of famine. Occasional sharp price rises did not prevent long-term collapse. On the other hand, salaries increased because of the labour shortages. The general depression was favourable to salaried workers but unfavourable to those who lived off their income i.e. the nobility. At the same time, changes in fashion led to the decline of heavy woollen serge and, therefore, to problems for clothmaking towns. International trade routes changed and the fairs in Champagne fell into decline.

The King-Prisoner

Philip VI's son, John the Good, succeeded him in 1350 and did his utmost to restore the concept of chivalry by creating the Order of the Star in answer to the Order of the Garter created by Edward III. The English monarch's son, the Black Prince (so-named because of the colour of his armour), launched operations from Guyenne. Finally, John the Good tried to stop him near Poitiers, in a battle fought on 19th September 1356. It was a disaster. With his cavalry routed, John had to fight on foot. Near him was his son, Philip, now described as «the Brave». John was taken prisoner and, once the sovereign was in the hands of the English enemy, the kingdom was subjected to an awesome test of its courage. Negotiations did not reach a conclusion until 1360 (Brétigny Negotiations, 8th May 1360; Treaty of Calais, 24th October 1360). The territory of Guyenne was extended to include the Poitou area which, like Calais and the Somme Estuary, belonged to the King of England. A heavy ransom had to be paid in order to secure John the Good's release. Commitments were to be made for the future but, in fact, they were not taken. They involved Edward waiving his rights to the crown of France and John's waiving of right to sovereignty over Guyenne.

Summoning the States

John the Good's captivity aroused a wave of unrest that was like a brutal reaction, sometimes organised and sometimes spontaneous, against the servants of a king whose prestige had been whittled away to nothing, against a monarchic State which had been strengthened since the 12th century, and against John the Good's eldest son, Charles. Since 1349 when the Dauphiné area had been purchased, Charles had been known as the «Dauphin», the heir to the throne. He had plotted against his own father and it was he who was now to face the storm. The pressure was initially to be applied through the «States», the States of Languedoïl in Paris for the north of the kingdom and the States of Languedoc in Toulouse for the south (although these were not «States General», they represented every social group, albeit unevenly). The monarchy convened them because it needed their support in order to obtain the payment of new taxes by the people. Such meetings became increasingly frequent from 1355 to the spring of 1358. The representatives of the three social orders (clergy, nobility and the Third Estate through the country's towns) demanded reforms in return. An Order of 3rd March 1357 placed the monarchy under the control of the States. It demanded a shake-up of the civil service, regular sessions and control of income and expenditure.

Charles the Dauphin

The discontented people of Paris found a spokesman in the person of Etienne Marcel, a rich burgher of Paris who became Provost of the Merchants, the equivalent of a mayor today. The Dauphin was also subjected to the political manoeuvring of King Charles of Navarre. Nicknamed «the Bad» because of his many acts of treachery, he was a cousin of the King of France, being the grandson, on his mother's side, of Louis X the Stubborn. He drew support from his possessions in Normandy and Navarre, as well as from his family and friends, and used this to instigate an increasing number of conspiracies. Even though the interests of the various parties were different, they allied themselves against the Dauphin. On 22nd February 1358, crowds in Paris entered the young Charles' bedchamber and killed two of his companions, Maréchal de Champagne and Maréchal de Normandy. Etienne Marcel saved the prince by forcing him to wear a red and blue bonnet – representing the colours of Paris.

Peasant Uprisings

The Dauphin decided to declare himself «Regent» and left the capital. His opponents were then divided, each acting to his own benefit. It was on 28th May 1358 that the peasants' revolt known as the «Jacquerie» broke out. It got its name from the nickname applied to peasants – Jacques Bonhomme, hence the name of «Jacques» given to the rebels. It began in Saint-Leu d'Esserent near Chantilly and spread throughout the north of the kingdom. This was no revolt based on abject poverty. It began in rich, fertile countryside and was a symbol of general anxiety linked to the economic crisis. The rebels marched on Compiègne, attacked a castle and took as their leader a former soldier named Guillaume Carle. The nobility, terrified, reacted swiftly and it was Charles the Bad who commanded the bloody reprisals, dealing the «Jacques» a crushing defeat near Creil on 9th June 1358. Charles of Navarre then decided to look into an alliance with the English.

The Death of Etienne Marcel

Etienne Marcel, on the other hand, had decided to ally himself with the rebel peasantry since he thought he would find support for his struggle against the Dauphin. In the end, he wanted to open the gates of Paris to the army from Navarre and, consequently, to the English. The Parisians saw this as treachery and he was murdered by one of his own cousins on 31st July 1358. Charles the Dauphin re-entered Paris. He was to continue governing until 1360 and he was to negotiate with the English.

Ransom and Hostages

At that time, once the Treaty of Calais had been ratified, John the Good was free, on condition that he paid a huge ransom. To guarantee payment, hostages were to be taken. John the Good had time to create a gold coin, the franc, and to condemn monetary changes. This met the demands of the nobility whose income was fixed and who, therefore faced financial ruin in the case of monetary devaluation. In order to pay the ransom, the States of Languedoïl agreed, in 1363, to the tax becoming permanent. However, one of the hostages, Louis of Anjou, the king's son, did not want to remain in captivity and he fled. His father, a perfect knight, set off again for London where he died in 1364 and France had to continue paying his ransom. Charles the Dauphin became Charles V; he was aged 25. This pious king was not a knight-king; he preferred to work in his study. He was a wise monarch.

Great Companies

The new king took action to restore security in the kingdom by ridding it of the «great companies». In order to go to war, the rules of feudal society entitled a nobleman to convene the regulars and reserves from among his vassals. In order to find soldiers, it had become increasingly necessary to call upon volunteers. A captain was responsible for recruiting the men of arms who bound themselves to him by contract – they were the retainers. This method produced a company of some one hundred men, often of noble extraction. The return of peace put these professional warriors out of a job and they became peripatetic pillagers feared by the general population. Arnaud de Cervole, alias «The Archpriest», formed several companies into one «Great Company» tempted by the wealth of the Popes in Avignon.

Du Guesclin

Du Guesclin, a Breton baron with no great wealth, rose to fame in 1360 by defeating the troops of Charles the Bad in Cocherel. Du Guesclin then succeeded in taking the Great Companies to Spain where there was conflict between the pretenders to the throne. Here, the warriors found work again.

The King of France lent an obliging ear to the complaints that reached him from lords who were vassals of the Prince of Aquitaine (the title given to the Black Prince, son of Edward III) for the Gascons were discontent with the fiscal demands from their lord. And just who was their lord's sovereign? The King of England? Or the King of France who remained the monarch since the waivers included in the Treaty of Calais had not been implemented? War began again in 1369. In 1370, Charles V made Du Guesclin a Constable. The English sent mounted troops across the country but Du Guesclin refused to do battle, shying away and contenting himself with fortifying towns to ensure that they were not captured, exhausting and ruining the enemy. This gradually enabled the Constable to recapture the provinces, after numerous campaigns. Eventually the Plantagenet estates were reduced to Bordeaux and Bayonne.

The Reconstruction of the Realm

Charles V, who had been successful in the military campaign thanks to the appointment of outstanding captains, set his dynasty on a firmer footing by highlighting the «Salic Law» which laid down the rules of succession and excluded women. Another idea which took hold was that a king should hand over power to his successor just before death. Finally, the monarch encouraged study of the State and himself worked to improve the wheels of government. The King gathered a collection of manuscripts in the «library in the Louvre». He embellished the Louvre Palace, which was his private residence. The administrative departments were still housed in the Palais de la Cité and a new wall was built round the capital, with a fortress called the Bastille. In order to fund these projects, Charles V imposed heavy taxes on his subjects. Yet the king, who had accumulated a veritable treasure trove, decided on his deathbed to abolish the direct tax known as the «fouages». This was a way of showing the love that bound him to his people; it also weakened his successor.

Charles VI and his Uncles

In 1380, Charles VI was only twelve years old and had not yet reached the age of majority, fixed by his father at 14. It was his uncles who governed the country, and they soon began to quarrel. They were the deceased king's three brothers. They had already received generous appanages i.e. a group of provinces in which they represented the king and enjoyed most of his prerogatives. Charles of Anjou pillaged the treasure but, having been chosen as heir by Queen Joan of Naples, he set off to conquer this throne and died in Italy in 1384. John of Berry had control of almost one-third of the realm and he was responsible for guarding Languedoc. Finally, Philip the Bold had Burgundy and, thanks to his marriage with the heiress to Flanders, he had built up a vast estate including Flanders, Artois and Franche-Comté. He was soon at the head of the royal government but was principally concerned with his Burgundian and Flemish interests. All the princes around Charles

VI were involved in countless intrigues and projects but, in the end, achieved nothing more than a general ceasefire between France and England in 1388. These were difficult times marked by riots between 1380 and 1385 – a phenomenon that affected much of Europe. The revolts were led by craftsmen from towns or by wealthy peasants who no longer accepted the burden of taxation. Soon, the revolts mobilised the humbler sections of society which were weighed down by poverty. The revolts were aimed at the rich and, in many cases, at Jews and foreigners who became the scapegoats. Violence became increasingly rife. The king's uncles took reprisals. The rebels had to be engaged in pitched battles or towns had to be recaptured – and there were executions designed to imprint themselves in the minds of onlookers.

Charles VI's Insanity

In 1388, when the young king was twenty years old, he succeeded in removing his uncles from power and he placed his trust in the men who had been his father's advisers and whose career and fortune depended solely on him. Encouraged by this confidence, they attempted to reform the State and pacify the kingdom. The improvement was short-lived for, on 5th August 1392, the king had his first attack of insanity. He was in the forest at Le Mans when he thought he was being attacked. He threw himself at his brother, killing four people as he did so. One year later, during the «Ardents' Ball», his costume caught fire and the king's life was only just saved. The fright he suffered worsened his mental state.

Burgundians and Armagnacs

The king's insanity stoked up rivalries and intrigues among those closest to him. The King's brother, Louis of Orléans, was in conflict with the Duke of Burgundy, John the Fearless, who had him assassinated on 23rd November 1407. Soon, there was a veritable civil war between the «Burgundians» and those who defended the memory of Louis of Orléans. First and foremost among the defenders was Bernard of Armagnac, hence the name «Armagnacs» given to his followers. John the Fearless encouraged the King to hold the States of Languedoïl in Paris. This encouraged those present to voice their discontent. Caboche, the leader of the corporation of butchers and flayers, led the movement demanding reforms. A government programme known as the «Cabochian Order» was drafted but never applied because leading figures took fright and turned to the Armagnacs for support. This confrontation between French people from two factions doubtless reflected the conflict between two princely dynasties but it also reflected very different interests. The Duke of Burgundy sought support from Burgundy and Dijon on the one hand, and on Flanders and Lille on the other. His aim was to take control of Paris, a takeover which was resisted by the Armagnacs. The conflict also revealed two views of the world and two methods of government.

Azincourt

In England, the Lancastrian dynasty had taken control and Henry V wanted to wage war to strengthen his hold on power. He demanded the crown of France. Having landed near the Seine Estuary in 1415, he tried to reach Calais. The French attacked at Azincourt. The French nobility was trapped in the mud by the bad weather and was decimated. Many of the combatants were killed; the richest were taken prisoner. Among the captives was Charles of Orléans who devoted himself writing poetry.

The Montereau Bridge

This defeat aggravated still further the splits in the kingdom and they, in turn, helped the English sovereign to victory, after which he gained a strong hold on the country. After the death of several heirs to the throne, the surviving heir, Charles, the future Charles VII, was aged only 13. The Burgundians seized power in Paris and instigated a reign of terror. The Dauphin succeeded in escaping and, with his followers who were Armagnacs, sought refuge in Bourges where he took the title of «King's Lieutenant». Another murder, committed in his name, created an irretrievable breakdown of relations. In order to allow for a reconciliation between Armagnacs and Burgundians, a meeting was arranged between the Dauphin and John the Fearless on the bridge in Montereau on 10th September 1419. The Dauphin's men assassinated the Duke of Burgundy in revenge for the murder of Louis of Orléans. This led to the revival of the civil war for the new Duke, Philip the Good, wanted revenge. He decided to ally himself with the King of England.

The Treaty of Troyes

Henry V offered the unfortunate Charles VI and the Queen, Isabel of Bavaria, an agreement under the terms of which he would marry their daughter, Catherine. The Treaty of Troyes, signed on 21st May 1420, named the king's son-in-law as his heir and entrusted him with the government of the kingdom. Neither Charles VI nor his new son-in-law nor Philip of Burgundy would agree to negotiate with Charles «the so-called Dauphin». Henry V and Charles VI both died in 1422. Their successor, named in place of the Dauphin, was a child, Henry VI. His uncle, John of Bedford, governed in his name over a territory stretching across the north and west of the realm, especially around Normandy and the Paris Basin. King Charles VII was recognised only in the south of France. He was known as the «King of Bourges». Philip the Good had acquired slightly more independence and control over his vast estates.

Joan of Arc

The kingdom was falling apart and two kings of France were locked in conflict. Signs of resistance were apparent, however. Mont Saint-Michel, which was besieged by the English in 1424, was not captured and St. Michael, the archangel was gradually seen as the protector of a

France doing its utmost to survive. Salvation could only come from God and His saints. It was they who spoke to a young girl born in 1412 in Domrémy near the border with Lorraine, in an area in the grip of war. Other women described as prophetesses had also had visions. Joan of Arc succeeded in persuading the Lord of Baudricourt, Lord of Vaucouleurs, to assist her and, on 6th March 1429, she was in Chinon where Charles VII's Court had settled. Her virginity was checked because a witch could not be a «maiden» and Joan of Arc described herself thereafter as «the Maid». She succeeded in convincing the fragile king by a sign and, more especially, by her determination. She also proved to be a leader in battle, galvanising energies and succeeding, on 29th April, in entering Orléans which had been besieged by the English. She led operations and forced the enemy to lift the siege on 8th May. On 18th June, the Maid inflicted a crushing defeat on the English army in Patay. She then had to continue with the mission she had set for herself. She led Charles VII through areas held by the Burgundians to Reims where he was crowned on 17th July 1429, making him the «true king» in the face of Henry VI. The towns then submitted to the authority of the French monarch. Paris resisted.

The Stake in Rouen

Joan of Arc was relegated to minor operations, taken prisoner near Compiègne on 23rd May 1430 and sold to the English. The trial was presided over, early in 1431, by Bishop Cauchon of Beauvais, a theologian who had chosen the Burgundian faction and who did not want to be disavowed by Joan's message if it was inspired by God. The English saw her as nothing more than a witch who could only be deprived of her malevolent powers by death. There were lengthy discussions about the men's clothing worn by the Maid; this seemed to be a sign of disobedience towards the Church. On 23rd May, after consultation with the University of Paris, she was declared a heretic and, frightened by the inevitable death sentence, she confessed, on 24th May, to everything suggested to her by her judges. Capital punishment would have to be reduced to a life sentence. On the following day, she took decisive action - she no longer denied hearing voices. This admission made her an apostate i.e. she had again become a sinner. She was sentenced to be burnt alive at the stake on Place du Vieux-Marché on 30th May 1431.

The epic adventure had given Charles VII back his self-confidence. He realised that his enemies were more fragile than he had thought and that it was possible to win back the lands he had lost. The terrible death of a young girl of the people, abandoned by the king she had supported and condemned by the ecclesiastical authorities, haunted the memory of France and Joan of Arc came to embody the love of country, a «national» sentiment further strengthened by religious inspiration.

The Treaty of Arras

A major meeting of prelates and lawyers in Arras in 1435 enabled the reconciliation of Charles VII and the Duke of Burgundy after Charles had made honourable amends and disavowed, on his knees, the murder of John Lackland. The situation changed suddenly. In 1436, Paris surrendered without a fight. In the following year, the king made a triumphant entry into the town but he soon returned to live in the Loire Valley, as did subsequent Kings of France. Charles VII had to stand up to the mercenaries known as «Flayers» commanded by former companions-in-arms of Joan of Arc, men such as La Hire and Xaintrailles. He stood firm in the face of a revolt of princes including his own son, Louis, then aged 16. This conflict was known as the Praguerie (1440), an allusion to similar events occurring in the same period in Bohemia. He obtained a ceasefire from King Henry VI of England.

Permanent Taxes and a Regular Army

The States were convened every year from 1422 to 1440 so that the king could obtain money. The need to levy a tax to fund the war became more evident but clerics and nobles were to be exempted from payment. A permanent tax came into being, was linked to the establishment of a regular army known as the companies of the «Grand Ordonnance» (15th May 1445), in all 12,000 horsemen with their archers and companions-in-arms. The permanent tax and regular army presupposed a strengthening of the State.

Again in an effort at clarification, Charles VII asked that customs should be drafted in writing (Order of Montils-lès-Tours, 1454). The king succeeded in finding talented servants such as his Chancellor of the Exchequer, Jacques Coeur, who was engaged in major trade in the Mediterranean area then under Venetian and Genoese domination. However, the rise of this new man eventually aroused criticism and Charles VII left him to his fate in 1451. He narrowly escaped a death sentence. The failure showed that royal authority had been restored and that the monarch had again become the supreme arbitrator and master of the finances and destiny of his subjects.

The Church had been shaken by the Great Schism opposing the Pope in Rome and the Pope in Avignon. In 1409, there were actually three Popes and it took a council in Constance (1414-1417) to heal the breach. The French monarchy hesitated between the idea of a concordat which would give the king the right to appoint the highest-ranking clergy such as bishops or abbots, and the re-establishment of elections for these positions. In 1438, the French clergy imposed the Pragmatic Sanction of Bourges and, consequently, the second solution. However, papal authority had been weakened and the King increased his hold on the Church in France.

Formigny and Castillon

Thanks to a strong army, Charles VII decided, in 1449, to begin reconquering territories. The recapture of Normandy was swift - an English army sent in as reinforcements was defeated in Formigny in 1450. The Battle of Castillon, on 17th July 1453, enabled him to recover Guyenne. While England, which retained Calais, was slipping into the War of the Roses, a de facto peace was installed in France.

Louis XI and Charles the Bold

In 1461, Louis XI mounted the throne after the death of his father. He who had been an intractable crown prince then found himself confronted by a rebellion of intractable princes grouped together under the name of the «League of the Public Weal», in 1465. He overcame the revolt, with some difficulty. In particular, the King of France was faced with Charles the Bold, Duke of Burgundy, the son of Philip the Good. The «Grand Duke of the Western World» enjoyed a large measure of independence from the crown of France and he was thinking about being elected to the head of the Holy Roman Empire and building himself a kingdom. He sought support from prosperous, well-developed estates to which he wanted to give greater cohesion and organisation. However, he also worried his neighbours. Louis XI met his cousin in Péronne in 1468 but, at the same time, the monarch had encouraged a revolt in Liège. Charles held him prisoner for three days and forced him to watch as the revolt was crushed. In 1470, the Burgundian army failed to capture Beauvais, an event at which Jeanne Laisné alias Jeanne Hachette won fame. The King of France could then sit back and wait. Charles the Bold succumbed to those who were worried by his hegemony, in particular the Swiss and the Duke of Lorraine, and he died at the Siege of Nancy (5th January 1477). The King of France, however, was unable to take advantage of this providential death. Marie, the daughter of Charles the Bold, married the Emperor's son, Maximilian and took Burgundy with her as her dowry. When she died in 1482, however, Louis XI obtained the Duchy of Burgundy and Picardy while the Hapsburgs took the Netherlands.

A New Era for France

During the reigns of Charles VII and Louis XI, the kingdom of France rebuilt itself after several decades of war. The «good towns» were the most dynamic element in this reconstruction since they allowed for the development of trade and industry, encouraged in this by the monarch. The peasants also took advantage of the demographic crisis – landlords were forced to rent out lands at conditions that were favourable for the tenants. All that remained was the need for the monarchy to give greater coherence to the territory, thereby marking the end of the large independent principalities. The lineage of the Dukes of Anjou died out and the King of France inherited Anjou, followed by Maine and Provence in 1481. In order to take over Brittany, Louis XI's son, Charles VIII, forced the young Duchess Anne of Brittany to marry him. The new queen made a commitment to marry Charles' successor if he predeceased her and this was exactly what happened. She soon married King Louis XII. Their daughter married François I and Brittany became a French province.

NEW HORIZONS

The 15th century had been a time of major changes. To the east of Europe, Constantinople, the last bastion of Greek Christianity, had collapsed under the attack of the Moslem Turks who then constituted a huge threat for Christian countries. Europe had opened new windows onto the world. Portugal had sent seafarers further and further afield, along the coasts of Africa. In the west, Christopher Columbus, who was in the service of Castile, had discovered lands that were to prove to be an entire continent. The Christian kingdoms adapted to this never-ending geographical expansion which led to a change in trade routes, economic links and everyday life.

The upheaval was also cultural and spiritual. The invention of printing accelerated the circulation of knowledge and ideas, aroused new curiosity and permitted audacious intellectual thought. Humanism meant rediscovering the texts and civilisation of the Ancients, often through manuscripts from Constantinople. In France, Guillaume Budé was a fine example of these early 16th-century scholars. The lessons learnt from Antiquity also enabled free thinkers to go beyond received ideas, contest ancient traditions, and propose new concepts and methods.

The Italian Campaign

From the reign of Charles VIII onwards, the kings of France had regular income and a sound army. They had reconquered their land and had established a long-lasting peace. They had forced the great lords and nobility into submission – and they offered them new battlefields in Italy where the sovereign and his knights could find military glory and make their fortunes. Charles VIII laid claim to the Kingdom of Naples in the name of the House of Anjou which had reigned there and which he had inherited. He was initially welcomed as a liberator in Italy but he failed to establish French influence in any sustainable fashion. Louis XII, his successor, was the son of the poet Charles of Orléans. He laid claims to the Milan area and also did his utmost to retake Naples. After a series of vicissitudes, the French occupation failed.

Marignano

On the death of Louis XII, it was his young cousin and son-in-law, François of Angoulême, who mounted the throne as François I. He, too, dreamed of conquests in Italy and, in 1515, he won a fine victory in Marignano against the Swiss who were defending Milan. On the battlefield, a young gentleman from Dauphiné, Bayard, knighted his own sovereign who paid homage, in this way, to his nobility and to chivalrous ideals. The campaign in Italy enabled the king to clarify the situation of the Church in France through the signature of the Concordat in Bologna in 1516 which laid down the relationship between France and Rome for the following three hundred years. The Pope recognised the king's right to make appointments to major benefits (bishoprics and abbeys) and then granted him canon appointment. This meant that the sovereign could choose the bishops who, in turn, controlled parish priests. In fact, he could allocate ecclesiastical revenue as he saw fit. There was resistance from the parlement in Paris and the University, both of which feared this alliance of pontifical and royal authority.

After these undoubted successes, the political situation changed in Europe. Opposite the King of France was the grandson of Emperor Maximilian, Charles, who had inherited the estates in Burgundy (1506), then Castile, Aragon and Naples (1516). In 1519, despite manoeuvring on the part of François I, he succeeded in having himself electing Emperor under the title Charles V. His possessions also included Austria and he reigned over all the American territories conquered by the Spaniards. This global empire encircled and smothered the small kingdom of France and its entire history after this period was aimed at releasing this stranglehold. Friction concerned Burgundy which Charles V, the descendent of Charles the Bold, could not bring himself to abandon. More friction concerned the Milan area which the King of France wanted to obtain at all cost.

Pavia

War broke out frequently between François I and Charles V and it was to the Emperor that the Constable of Bourbon, cousin of the king of France, turned when he deemed that his interests were being damaged par his sovereign. In 1523, this treachery gave François I an excuse to confiscate a large part of the constable's vast estates and advance the unification of the kingdom. However when he set off again for Italy, François was defeated and taken prisoner in Pavia (24th February 1525). His mother, Louise of Savoy, acted as regent, putting a great deal of energy into the task, but the difficult period left its mark on the kingdom even though the concessions made by the king in Madrid during his captivity were then contested after his liberation in 1526. The «Ladies Peace» (Treaty of Cambrai) in 1529, which was negotiated by Louise of Savoy and Margaret of Austria, Charles V's aunt, laid down the huge ransom that France was required to pay. War with the Emperor broke out again several times and François I had no hesitation in establishing diplomatic relations in 1535 with the Great Lord, the Sultan of Constantinople, much to the disgust of the Christian world. This reverse alliance became a natural source of assistance for French diplomacy.

François I's reign strengthened the State even more. The Order of Villers-Cotterêts (1539) obliged parish priests to maintain parish registers indicating the dates of baptism, marriage and burial of their parishioners. French was also instituted as the official language of legal documents.

The Peace of Cateau-Cambrésis

François I's son, Henri II, mounted the throne in 1547; he, too, was a knight-king. He confronted Charles V and instigated a policy which became a permanent temptation for France – alliance with the Protestant princes of Germany against the Roman Catholic Emperor. This was a paradoxical choice because, at the same time, the King of France was regarding his own Protestant subjects with increasing suspicion. During the «journey to Germany» as the 1522 expedition was described, he occupied three bishoprics (Metz, Toul and Verdun), all of them situated within the Empire. France was never to give them back again. Since Charles V had divided his lands in two, leaving the Empire for his brother and Spain for his son, Philip II, the latter became the King of France's main enemy. His armies won a resounding victory at the Battle of Saint-Quentin (10th August 1577). Although Calais was recaptured in 1558 from the English who had occupied it since 1347, the military situation rendered negotiation necessary. This was the Peace of Cateau-Cambrésis (2nd/3rd April 1559). French concessions were deemed to be excessive by contemporaries for all the lands conquered in the Alps and Italy (Savoy and Piedmont) were abandoned and, with them, all the hope that had led to the Italian campaign. Henri II, however, wanted peace in an effort to resolve the religious problem in his kingdom and eradicate Protestantism.

The Renaissance

The Italian campaign had given French soldiers a view of the splendours of the Italian Renaissance and they were dazzled by what they saw. From the 15th century onwards, in particular, Italy had enjoyed intense artistic creativity. The urban oligarchies and princes encouraged and funded creators who outshone each other through their originality in every field, especially painting. A new way of life was developed in which aesthetics and refined pleasure were more important than physical prowess and this was expressed in the architecture and design of mansions. The French did not forget the lessons they had learned in Italy. They sought to embellish their fortresses and make them more comfortable. On the banks of the Loire and its tributaries, rich servants of the monarchy, especially financiers, commissioned admirable châteaux. François I had Chambord built. Although the layout was still mediaeval, it allowed for a number of audacious features such as the double spiral staircase. In Fontainebleau, there was a veritable school and the François I gallery summarises the importance of allegories and the symbolism that was the trade mark of this erudite art form. The Renaissance took care to gather and combine all forms of knowledge, even the most obscure, even the strangest.

The Reformation in France

While the Roman Catholic Church was subject to internal questioning and the clerics were willing to consider the idea of reform, Luther enjoyed a following throughout much of Europe and this brought about a break with Rome. Such a break did not tempt the French monarchy because, through the Concordat of Bologna, François I had obtained close control over the Church in France. The new ideas nevertheless spread throughout the kingdom. The Christian faith, however, formed the basis of the sacred character of royalty and established the might of the ecclesiastics, social organisation and the rhythms of personal, family or collective life. It founded and directed every view of the world and every hope. When the Reformation was introduced into France, it proposed another view and another type of hope. The choice was crucial for each individual. In 1528, spurred on by Chancellor Duprat, the main tenets of the Roman Catholic doctrine were reaffirmed. Tradition (and not only the Scriptures) was one of the sources of faith. Man could make his own decisions. Divine Grace was not everything. The Roman Catholic Church was infallible. The seven sacraments were valid. Salvation could only be obtained through good works. The worship of saints was useful and Purgatory existed.

For a long time, François I regarded the new religious ideas with benevolence but provocation on the part of the Protestants, for example during the Cupboard Affair in 1534, led the monarchy to instigate repression. This was also the path followed by Henri II but he eventually noted that Protestantism had taken root in the country. Because the monarchic State had been built up and strengthened since the beginning of the century, Henri II wanted to place this new strength at the service of the true faith in order to re-establish the kingdom's religious unity. To this end, he had no hesitation in abandoning his dreams of glory and making peace with the Spanish enemy in Cateau-Cambrésis in 1559. A few weeks later, the king died as a result of a fatal wound incurred during a tournament.

THE WARS OF RELIGION

Paradoxically, the death of Henri II was the first stage in civil war. It gave the Protestants respite which they used to build up their own defence.

Calvinism

Conversions increased in number in the 1560's, among the royal princes such as Antoine de Bourbon and Louis de Condé, among the main dynasties e.g. among the nephews of the Constable de Montmorency and, more particularly, Admiral de Coligny, but also more widely throughout the nobility, through the bonds of loyalty and clienteles. Protestantism also affected the educated members of urban society such as craftsmen. Generally speaking, the peasantry was less receptive. The spread of the Reformation was assisted by the influence of Calvin. This time, a Frenchman living in Geneva at the gateway to France, proposed a vigorous doctrine and rigorous organisation, both of them adding greater stimulus to the Reformation in France. Calvinism allowed for a changeover from the hesitant empiricism of the first few decades to a systematic construction of new religions.

The Guise family

The death of Henri II also weakened royal authority because of the young age of the king's sons, François II then Charles IX. The short reign of François II enabled the Guises, the king's uncles, to take over the royal favour and material benefits that it brought with it, to the benefit of their loyal supporters. The monarchy could no longer silence the rivalries between leading figures, between powerful dynasties and rival factions. Nor could it impose its arbitration and sustainable political choices.

Finally, the king's death provided an opportunity for a political reaction after marked reinforcement of royal power during the reigns of François I and Henri II. Legal experts and theorists demanded a return to a mixed monarchy in which power would be shared with the States General or the Council of Princes; this was supposed to be a system from days gone by. The nobility in particular was tempted to take advantage of the troubles to regain its independence in the face of monarchic authority, especially as the royal coffers could no longer dispense favours and peace no longer allowed anybody to make a living from warfare against foreign powers.

Catherine de Medici

After François II's brief reign, Catherine de Medici, widow of Henri II, became regent for Charles IX in 1560. Until her death in 1589, she was to direct royal action using her vast intelligence but she was unable to re-establish peace and unity in the kingdom. With the chancellor, Michel de l'Hospital, she eventually decided on dialogue with the Protestants but this policy of concord resulted in civil war for the Roman Catholics could not accept the fact that the foundations of their view of the world and of life itself might be called into question. The edict of January 1562 had authorised Protestant worship in the suburbs of towns. On 1st March, the Duke de Guise and his escort massacred Protestants in Vassy because the sermon was given in a barn, apparently within the town walls. This marked the beginning of the cycle of civil wars in France. Very soon, there was a desire to gain control of the monarch. The Guise family succeeded in 1562 with the assistance of Constable de Montmorency; the Protestants, on the other hand, failed during the «Surprise of Meaux» in 1567. The belligerents also looked to foreign countries for political support, mercenaries and financial aid. Queen Elizabeth lent a favourable ear to her fellow Protestants under threat, just as the King of Spain encouraged the French Catholics as part of his vision of a new religious conquest. The hesitant situation of France became an essential element in the map of Europe.

Jarnac and Moncontour

In military terms the Protestants grouped behind princes who had been converted to the new religion or behind noblemen. They captured fortresses which formed a robust network within the kingdom. It was a means of withstanding all attacks and keeping control of low-lying country round about. Then came the days of veritable military campaigns once the Protestants, sometimes with the help of mercenaries, lansquenets or ruffianly soldiers, had built up veritable armies. In 1569, during the third War of Religion, the Duke of Anjou, the king's brother who was in command of the royal army, won fame during the Battles of Jarnac and Moncontour. However Admiral de Coligny still succeeded in leading troops across the entire country before threatening the Paris area.

Inhuman Violence

Eventually, violence broke out everywhere between Catholics and Protestants. The idea of a crusade began to spread among Catholics. Denis Crouzet sees the wars of religion as holy wars «because it is even more difficult to kill a brother than the Infidel and because, for man, it is an even greater mark of divine election to succeed in casting off one's humanity in order to kill somebody who is none other than one's other self». It led to family murders, anthropophagic gestures and words, and «inhuman» cruelty. Political assassination also appeared to be a means of ending the war. At the beginning of 1563, a Protestant gentleman murdered the Duke de Guise but his death strengthened the prestige of the Guise family among fervent Catholics. After the Battle of Jarnac, the Prince de Condé was shot dead, an action which contravened all the laws of warfare, and his body was carried on a donkey to the town square.

Charles IX's Tour of France

Throughout these years of warfare, the King and Queen Mother tried to re-establish peace. Catherine tried, when she could, to recover the initiative. She decided to show King Charles IX off to his subjects, through a long trip lasting for more than two years that took them through the entire kingdom (1564-1566). She was suspected of being a follower of her compatriot, Machiavelli, because her attempts at reconciliation went against the tide of religious tension. Yet in her subtle negotiations and complex intrigues, she always kept sight of the need to uphold the State by seeking a policy based on the «unity of hearts», a fact which her dark, legendary figure has tended to conceal.

St. Bartholomew's Day

Catherine and her son, Charles IX, were undoubtedly behind the St. Bartholomew's Day massacre. On 18th August 1572, the marriage of Jeanne d'Albret's son, King Henri of Navarre, with Margaret de Valois, the King's sister, was to symbolise the reconciliation between Catholics and Protestants, as well as constitute recognition for the religious divide in France. It could even be seen as marking the victory of the Protestants. The mysterious attack on Coligny on 22nd August 1572 increased pressure. On the evening of 23rd August, Charles IX, encouraged by his mother, agreed to the idea of having the main Protestant leaders assassinated, with the exception of Henri of Navarre and Condé who were the King's cousins. On 24th August 1572, on St. Bartholomew's Day, the massacre spread throughout the population. Certain historians saw the St. Bartholomew's Day massacre as a trial of strength on the part of Catholic extremists, supporters of the Guise family. There is, however, another possible explanation – the royal determination to massacre Protestant gentlemen appeared to be a means of weakening their faction and re-establishing a balance while satisfying popular hatred of the Huguenots in Paris. The royal decision was amplified by this hatred and the massacre was repeated countless times in the kingdom's largest towns.

The St. Bartholomew's Day massacre had ambiguous consequences. The trial of strength solved no problems whatsoever. It is true that it deprived the Protestant faction of many of its leaders, the murdered noblemen, especially as two princes of the royal household were being held prisoner. However, the event reinforced the Huguenots' convictions. They fell back on the provinces in the south and centre west of the country and strengthened their organisation. During the Millau Assembly in 1573, they set up what Jean Delumeau has called the «United Provinces of Southern France», an allusion to the United Provinces (now the Netherlands) that were created to oppose Spain. This independent organisation was a thorn in the flesh of royal authority and the kingdom seemed to be on the edge of break-up when Charles IX died.

«Monarchomaques», Malcontents and Politicians

The King had taken responsibility for, and admitted to, the violence against the Protestant noblemen, claiming that there had been a conspiracy. Gradually, the royal personage, like the monarchy itself, became a target for attack. Legal experts and polemics eventually contested the traditional order of the monarchy. Such protesters, among them François Hotman, Théodore de Bèze and Duplessis-Mornay, were known as «Monarchomaques». According to the Vindiciae contra tyrannos, there was a contract between the sovereign and his people at the very beginning of the monarchy. If the sovereign committed a breach of contract, the people could legitimately rebel, led by representative institutions or a providential prince. A tyrant could be killed. This was the basis of the tyrannicide theory.

Protestant thinkers found allies among the Catholics who were discontented with royal government, the Malcontents. Support also came from those who were tempted by religious indifference – the Politicians who no longer understood this violence. This alliance has been well described by Arlette Jouanna. All were careful to instigate civil concord. Monarchomaques and Malcontents were obsessed with tyranny but the former wanted to see authority controlled while the Malcontents, like the Politicians shortly afterwards, wanted to avoid lessening royal dignity. As to the Politicians, they claimed that sovereignty belonged to the king alone, that he should not share it with anybody and that preservation of the State was separate from religious unity. Among the Malcontents, the most representative figure was Maréchal Henri de Montmorency-Damville: «he felt threatened in his honour, his assets and his life» (Arlette Jouanna). He was a leader of men who saw the persecution of his family, the Montmorencys, as part of a systematic attack on the nobility. As Governor of Languedoc, he was like a viceroy, having no hesitation in criticising royal policy and moving closer to the Protestants. Such alliances prevented the new king, Henri III, from reigning over more than two-thirds of his kingdom.

Political Crisis in the Days of Henri III

Religious strife led to a general crisis. Conflicts around the King became awesome. The royal family divided for political reasons with the king's brother, François, or on religious grounds with Henri of Navarre. The main families in the kingdom were engaged in conflict which set the Guise dynasty against the de Montmorency. The lords contested their sovereign and his favourites whose climb up the social ladder was considered to have been too swift and, therefore, scandalous. Henri III's political ideas weakened royal power still further. He wanted to give the Court of France an etiquette whose strict rules seemed to show disdain for courtiers. The benefits heaped by the monarch upon a few gentlemen known as the «royal favourites» were deemed to be immoral although his real aim was to build up a group of gentlemen in whom he could have confidence and who would give him personal loyalty to counterbalance the weight of old, established dynasties and their own system of loyalty. According to Arlette Jouanna, Henri III was especially concerned to «attempt to promote a new model of aristocratic behaviour and to introduce to the court refined ethics and a spirited mind... In doing so, he took sides in a debate that was dividing opinion, especially among the nobility who were so fond of warlike values. Was it possible to be valiant yet clean, brave and refined? Many answered in the negative».

Tyrannicide

This unpopularity led to a veritable hatred which soon developed, paradoxically, among the Catholics. They took as their own the criticisms levied by the Protestants; they even took over the theory of tyrannicide. Henri III tried to govern and negotiate with the Protestants, to resist the break-up of the kingdom and, eventually, he set himself up as arbitrator in the religious struggle. However, it was the question of the succession that reopened the floodgates of war. In June 1584, the king's younger brother died. The leader of the Protestants, Henri of Navarre, would mount the throne if, as everybody believed, Henri III could not have children. The Catholics refused to accept a Huguenot as heir. Hatred for the present king combined with fear of the future monarch. The hostility to royal power blended with the fear of a final victory on the part of Protestantism.

The Catholic League

The League was set up in 1584-1585, a «Prophetic and Mystical Union» to use the expression coined by Denis Crouzet. It began life as a Parisian secret society but the movement was taken over by the Guise family who were themselves at the head of an aristocratic association that received financial backing from Spain. With his brothers, cousins and loyal followers, Henri de Guise, alias «Scarface», who was immensely popular, controlled a large area of Northern France. The unity of the kingdom had been lost and the king was personally under threat. The League sought to attract the nobility (outraged by the benefits granted by the king to his «royal favourites»), Catholics (worried about the inroads being made by Protestantism) and taxpayers (hostile to the proliferation of taxes since the reign of Charles IX). Events gathered pace. The war of the three Henri's did not enable the king to defeat his cousin from Béarn and this made Henri III suspect in the eyes of zealous Catholics. Thereafter, Parisian militants openly criticised royal policy which seemed to be particularly hesitant.

The Murder of the King

Paris rebelled on 12th May 1588 and barricades filled the streets, preventing royal troops from gaining control of the town. The king fled on horseback with a few companions, on 13th May. There was a total breakdown of relations between the king and zealous Catholics. Henri III tried, as Charles IX had done in earlier times with the Protestants, to re-establish his authority. On 23rd December 1588, his «Forty-Fives» executed Henri de Guise. Again the «stroke of majesty» achieved nothing. A veritable revolution was beginning, a «revolution of parish priests» to use Arlette Lebigre's fine expression. Henri III's murder by a monk on 2nd August 1589 was only one of the stages in the revolution. On his deathbed, Henri III acknowledged Henri of Navarre as his heir but Henri IV found himself confronted by a divided kingdom and this time it was Northern France that had seceded.

The League had princely connections (through the Guises) as well as links with the nobility and town dwellers. The Guises sought support from their governments in order to prepare veritable independent principalities where they had at their disposal money and royal offices. Soon, as Michel Pernot puts it, there was «territorial decomposition» in France.

Clienteles

The civil war had overturned social conventions among the nobility. Traditional links between sovereign and vassal were nothing more than a carryover from mediaeval times. Obedience to the king as the supreme authority was no longer mandatory when his authority was contested, or even cursed. In the nobility, clientele bonds were strengthened; they did not necessarily correspond to the breaks running through political life – Protestants against Catholics, Catholics against Catholics or royalists against Leaguers. A gentleman «gave himself» to a leading aristocrat or war chief and followed him through the vicissitudes of life, possibly even when he changed allegiance from one side to another. Historians have revealed these changes; Roland Mousnier has shown these bonds in a master/servant relationship and Arlette Jouanna has insisted on the ties of friendship between these men of action. Social fragmentation had been pushed to its utmost limits.

The urban component of the League recruited its leaders among the «bourgeoisie», the wealthy middle class which, as Robert Descimon has shown, wanted a return to the old order in town. It also wanted to shake the foundations of the new oligarchies. The Leaguers were hostile to officers, especially the magistrates in sovereign courts who sought to take over municipal office and direct urban life. They would have had difficulty accepting the closure of this system of obtaining office, as a result of excessively high prices and by the practice of inheritance which made them an asset like any other in a personal estate. The cleansing of the parlement in Paris in mid-January 1589 was one example of this confrontation and social violence was evident in the execution of Barnabé Brisson, President of the parlement, on 15th November 1591.

New Forms of Popular Piety

New forces were brought into play through the action of parish priests and monks involved in warfare through their preaching but who also took up arms. Popular religion was marked by a «huge wave fed by fear, calamities and the passions of struggle» (Marc Venard). Piety took spectacular forms. Old churches and chapels attracted crowds of pilgrims from the 1580's onwards. «White processions» came into being, processions of men and women dressed in white who travelled from one sanctuary to the next, not without worrying the authorities. New brotherhoods gave structure to these spiritual aspirations. They were controlled by the clergy and undertook charitable actions. They also encouraged better practices as regards the sacraments. After their establishment in the south of the country, they were introduced into Paris. With the League, their role became essential and processions in towns often aroused passion while channelling warring energy.

Henri IV and the Reconquest of a Kingdom

What was Henri IV to do? The monarchy had lost much of its strength even though the king's officers had rallied to support the man from Béarn. He could count on the Huguenots who had, of course, become royalists. He could count on the strong organisation of the Reformed churches led by the ministers and on the mobilisation of Protestant provinces. More and more, Henri sought support from the Politicians who defended legitimate royal authority, accepted the concessions made to the Calvinists, wanted to change the Roman Catholic church from the inside and also wanted to reform the State.

Recantation

Henri IV had simultaneously to convert to a different faith, reconquer the kingdom and restore the monarchy. He eventually took control thanks to his courage, skill and charisma. He took, somewhat reluctantly, the giant step of abjuring his faith on 25th July 1593. Although Rome had not given its approval, it was a reconciliation with the Church in France and it also opened the way to Paris. National territory had yet to be regained from Spanish hands. The victory at Fontaine-Française satisfied national sentiment and flattered the pride of the aristocracy by making Henri IV a glorious monarch. The Treaty of Vervins was signed in 1598. Henri IV had to rebuild the kingdom by negotiating with leading noblemen and obtaining their allegiance, at very high cost, in order to put an end to the many secessions. By granting these strange rewards, the monarch again became the source of all benefits. Finally, the keystone of his policy was the implementation, with some difficulty, of a religious peace that guaranteed the interests of the Calvinists since freedom of worship was recognised in places where it was already being openly undertaken. The act did not cause a long-lasting grudge among the Catholics since Protestantism was not openly permitted; it was merely tolerated. However, the Huguenots were treated as privileged subjects, with their political assemblies and numerous places of safety.

Reconciliation with the Church of France, a return to the capital, the defence of national territory, the allegiance of leading aristocrats and religious equilibrium – Henri IV had rebuilt the State on the basis of absolute power. By doing so, he met the immense need for peace felt at every level of French society.

The First Bourbon King

The first Bourbon monarch could then think of founding a dynasty. He separated from Queen Margot and, in 1600, married Marie de Medicis. France gained a Dauphin, Louis, the future Louis XIII, on 27th September 1601. His birth was followed by that of his brothers, Nicolas (who died in 1611) and Gaston. It provided complete reassurance as to the future of the new royal House of Bourbon and put an end to the political and religious crisis of the late 16th century.

The king re-established the finances that had been ruined by successive wars, thanks to the action of his minister, Sully. He confirmed the hereditary nature of royal offices through an annual tax called a «paulette», which enabled an office-bearer to transfer his charge to an heir. An office, which had been financial in nature for many years, then became hereditary, part of public power whether in the field of justice or finance. A modern State was formed also thanks to this convenient system which was inexpensive for the monarch. Henri IV, who had his main residence in Paris, encouraged the improvement of the town and the economic reconstruction of the kingdom.

The Tridentine Spirit

He had promised to ensure that France accepted the decisions on the reform of the Catholic Church taken by the Council of Trent which had ended in 1563. In fact, the King was careful to do no such thing for, like many Frenchmen, he feared an increased role for the Pope and this was rejected on the basis of Gallican liberties and the independence of France from Rome. Despite this, the Tridentine spirit spread in France.

The Church had organised itself financially through regular assemblies of clergy who decided on a «gratuitous gift» for the King. Parish priests were given better training and secondary teaching was strengthened through the opening of schools, many of which were run by the Jesuits.

Ravaillac

Henri IV, having freed himself from conflict with Spain, turned his attention to European affairs. He imposed the Treaty of Lyon (1601) on the Duke of Savoy, thereby obtaining the Bresse and Bugey areas for France. He lent an attentive ear to the complaints of the Protestant princes in Germany who feared that the Catholics would regain the upper hand in the Empire. He had even decided to wage war when he was murdered. Although the «Gay Old Spark» (his nickname was an allusion to his many love affairs) had blunted much of the opposition, he also had to withstand, throughout his life, plots fomented by leading dignitaries. There were also attempts on his life for, in some cases, the hatred he had aroused remained inexpugnable. On 14th May 1610, Henri IV was assassinated by Ravaillac, an exalted visionary, probably working on his own. Although Henri IV had been hated during his lifetime, he was very popular after his death. His simple clothes, sincere bonhomie and care for his people were emphasised; his intelligence, policy of tolerance and sense of statesmanship were also praised. He embodied a generous, humane, open-minded royalty and a return to unity for France.

FRANCE IN A EUROPEAN WAR DURING THE DAYS OF
LOUIS XIII AND RICHELIEU

When Henri IV was murdered on 14thh May 1610, the young Louis immediately became King. He was only eight years of age. Marie de Medicis was declared Regent by the parlement of Paris and Louis XIII was crowned in Reims on 17th October 1610.

Marie de Medicis' Regency

When Henri IV died, he had been on the point of waging a major war against the Hapsburgs because of the Juliers succession. The military campaign took place but was limited to a number of restricted, albeit successful, operations. The Regent, a vain woman with a love of luxury, who sometimes treated her son somewhat brusquely, held him at arm's length while she governed the country. She placed her trust in one of her compatriots from Florence, Concini, who accumulated high rank and became Marquis d'Ancre. Henri IV's ministers, Sully being the first among them, were removed from power. This change enabled Marie de Medicis to break away from the policies implemented by her deceased husband.

Spanish Marriages

She encouraged a rapprochement with Spain in the name of solidarity between Catholic princes and the struggle against Protestantism. To achieve this, a number of marriages were contracted. Louis XIII was to marry an Infanta of Spain, Anne of Austria (i.e. of the House of Hapsburg) and Philip of Spain, the future Philip IV, was to marry Louis XIII's sister. These «Spanish marriages», which were negotiated in 1612, aroused opposition, for example among members of the Reformed Religion who were worried by these pro-Catholic politics. As to the influence exercised by Concini who had become a Maréchal of France in 1613, it angered leading aristocrats who were only too willing to support the Prince de Condé, the King's cousin, when he led a revolt early in 1614.

Marie de Medicis was forced to negotiate. She agreed to convene the States General of the realm to consult them and, as Catherine de Medicis had done before her with Charles IX, she undertook a long trip in France with her son. She succeeded in keeping control of the government of the country when the regency came to an end once the King reached his majority, declared on 2nd October 1614.

The States General of 1614

Although the States General met in 1614, this was to be their last meeting until 1789. The three orders could not agree and, eventually, they turned to the government in an effort to settle their differences. The monarchy appeared to be the best of all possible arbitrators. A prelate had drawn attention to himself during these discussions – Richelieu, Bishop of Luçon. He became adviser to Marie de Medicis. The queen mother did not abandon the idea of Louis XIII's marriage and it was celebrated in Bordeaux in 1615. However, the opposition maintained the pressure and, in 1616, Marie had Condé arrested. He was to remain in prison until 1619.

Monarchic Success

The young king found it increasingly difficult and humiliating to bear the control exercised by his mother and her favourite, Concini. He prepared to take action to overcome this authority with a few of his closest courtiers, headed by Luynes who looked after his birds of prey. On 24th April 1617, on the King's orders and without a Court ruling, Maréchal d'Ancre was shot dead as he was arriving at the Louvre. The capital was overjoyed. This majestic blow for freedom indicated that Louis XIII was thenceforth to take power and make the decisions. He removed his mother from court, recalled his father's former ministers, the prudent «greybeards», and obtained the support of his friend, Luynes, who became a Constable of France but who apparently did not have the talent needed to play a major political role. Louis XIII had to withstand the intrigues fomented by Marie de Medici who did not accept her defeat and, in 1620, there was even a minor battle between royal troops and supporters of the queen mother. More importantly, Louis XIII was wary of the Protestants whom his father had protected and his policy led to a revolt on the part of the members of the Reformed Religion. Military campaigns had to be mounted against them in 1620 but they failed. As Luynes then died, Marie de Medicis regained influence, became a member of the council, and obtained prominence for her protégé, Richelieu. In 1622, the King obtained his nomination as cardinal.

The Thirty Years' War

Internal opposition did not conceal international tension. The situation had suddenly worsened in Bohemia in 1618 and in the Empire. The conflict between Roman Catholics and Protestants degenerated into a European war. Louis XIII followed the advice given to him by the «greybeards» and remained prudent. As a Catholic prince, he did not support the Protestant princes and proposed mediation. This facilitated the Catholic victory at La Montagne Blanche in 1620. However, the battle did not solve any of the problems and the conflict became widespread.

Richelieu in the Council

On the advice of Marie de Medicis and not without some hesitation, Louis XIII drafted Richelieu into his council in 1624. He was to ask him to draw up French foreign policy in the midst of all the dangers. Louis XIII had found a man capable of imagining an ambitious policy for the French monarchy as a leading power throughout Europe. He was also sufficiently talented to find the human and financial resources required to achieve this aim.

Richelieu as Principal Minister

Cardinal de Richelieu first had to gain influence over the King and, by removing his rivals, he became Principal Minister in 1629. He once stated that it was more difficult for him to conquer the four square feet that constituted the King's study than to win victories on the battlefields of Europe. Richelieu always passed major affairs to the King and he never took decisions without seeking the King's opinion, in order to let the monarch have the final word. In exchange, Louis XIII usually agreed to his minister's choices and policy suggestions. He left Richelieu the role of patron and protector of the Arts and letters, helped him to build a fortune for himself and his family and, often, left him to enjoy the pomp that accompanied authority. The King also supported his adviser during times of depression or danger for he was not short of enemies and adversaries, especially as there was serious political uncertainty for a long time. The royal couple had no children and Louis' most likely successor, until 1638, was his brother, Gaston d'Orléans, an attractive, light-hearted prince in whom all the Malcontents placed their hopes. Plots against Richelieu became increasingly numerous. In 1626, the King reacted by having his half-brothers, the Vendômes, imprisoned. He had the Prince de Chalais brought before the Court because he was involved in Court intrigues of which the Queen, Anne of Austria, was fully aware.

Strengthening Royal Authority Inside France

Richelieu worked to strength royal authority. There had been no constable beside the king since 1626. Nor had there been an Admiral of France. It was the cardinal who became Grand Master of Navigation and he launched an ambitious policy of coastal defences, naval presence and overseas expansion. The demolition of the fortresses in the interior of the kingdom and the 1626 edict outlawing duelling were seen as a determination to hold down a disobedient, quarrelsome nobility. Louis XIII refused to grant a pardon to an impenitent duellist, an example of this turbulent youth, Montmorency-Bouteville, who was beheaded despite the prayers of all his family. As to the reforms recommended by the Keeper of the Seals, Michel de Marillac, in an order known as the Michau

Code, they remained, for the most part, without effect. This suggested that the time was not ripe for reforms and that the main preoccupations were law and order within the kingdom and war outside it.

The Siege of La Rochelle

Louis XIII took action against the Protestants. La Rochelle had become the capital of Protestantism in France and the base for all Protestant uprisings. The town had established close links with the English who were worried by France's determination to built up a powerful Navy. An English fleet, commanded by Buckingham, landed on the Island of Ré in 1627 but was unable to retain the island. Since the people of La Rochelle supported this operation, a royal army came to lay siege to the town. Louis XIII was present at the siege but it was Richelieu who took control of the operations and had the siege reinforced by a totally watertight maritime blockade. The town capitulated on 27th October 1628. The King and his minister entered it a few days later. Louis XIII granted a general pardon but La Rochelle would not be the «Huguenot Republic of the Atlantic Coast» (Yves-Marie Bercé). This campaign sealed the union between the King and his minister. New revolts broke out in Languedoc and military campaigns were again launched. Eventually, in 1629, the monarch signed the Peace of Alais. He upheld the religious tolerance established by the Edict of Nantes but put an end to places of safety and, therefore, to the political power of the Protestants.

Undercover Warfare

At the same time, France was drawn into the European conflict arising from the succession of Mantua. Northern Italy became the stage for the confrontation between leading powers. Major negotiations took place in Ratisbonne in 1630. In Italy, a miraculous ceasefire was obtained between the Spaniards and the French thanks to the intervention of a papal emissary named Jules Mazarin. The Emperor finally recognised Charles de Nevers as Duke of Mantua and this ended the complex Italian struggle. It also removed the threat of direct war with France, just when the country was being forced into a confrontation with the Lutheran King Gustavus-Adolphus of Sweden, who was supported by French diplomacy and funding.

The Great Storm or the Day of Dupes

During these dramatic events, Richelieu had appeared to support the war against the Catholic princes. On 11th November 1630, the queen mother railed against the man who had been her protégé and she was doubtless speaking on behalf of the party with a strong religious background which the cardinal's policies worried and terrified. This «great storm» led people to hope that the cardinal would be disgraced and he himself believed he was lost. It was Louis XIII who took the final decision. He assured Richelieu of his continuing confidence. He had his adversaries arrested and punished, among them Marillac, Keeper of the Seals. This was the «Day of Dupes» for those who had hoped to see the cardinal dismissed. It took Marie de Medicis into voluntary exile and she never returned. Gaston also left the kingdom. Although Richelieu's position left him with greater freedom to act, he did not win over his enemies and although Louis XIII's confidence was long-lasting, it was never total and remained open to doubt for the King kept a jealous hold on his royal authority and freedom of decision-making. As to the negotiations with the Duke of Savoy after the crisis in Northern Italy, they brought France the fortress in Pignerol on the Piedmont side of the Alps. At the time, it was a «gateway», providing access to Italy for the purpose of military campaigns.

The fact that Richelieu remained in power meant that the same «undercover warfare» policy was being extended with the aim of intervening indirectly in Europe. Swedish successes weakened the situation of the Emperor and the Catholic camp within the Empire. The approach of war made military preparation necessary, incurring heavy expenditure and, consequently, heavier, more numerous taxes. It met with some resistance and the opponents placed their hopes in Gaston d'Orléans. It was for him that Maréchel de Monmorency, who deemed himself ill-rewarded by the King and Richelieu, fomented rebellion in Languedoc. He was defeated in Castelnaudary and taken prisoner. He was then taken to Court and sentenced to death. Louis XIII refused to grant a pardon to the rebel who was beheaded on 30th October 1632 despite being the youngest son of one of the kingdom's grandest families.

Declaration of War

In 1634, after several years of dazzling victories, the Swedish army was defeated in Nördlingen and the imperial cause seemed to have gained the upper hand. Gaston d'Orléans fomented an increasing number of plots with the Spaniards who captured the Elector of Trier, one of France's protégés. On 19th May 1635, Louis XIII had a declaration of war carried, in feudal fashion, to the Cardinal-Infant who was governing the Spanish Netherlands from Brussels. War broke out and it was to last until 1659. The entire life of the King and his realm was to be dominated by this major conflict. French offensives in 1635 resulted in a rout. In 1636, France was attacked from all sides. The Spanish army advanced as far as Corbie, only 120 km (75 miles) from Paris and panic seized the capital. The King and Cardinal had to flee to Compiègne from where they directed military operations and, eventually, the Spanish attack ran out of steam. Meanwhile, imperial troops raged through Champagne and Burgundy.

Popular Uprisings

The situation within the country was difficult because there were increasing numbers of popular uprisings. Fiscal pressures weighed heavily on the people who took up arms to fight tax collectors. The «Croquants» revolts affected towns and country districts throughout south-western France. Sometimes the rebels took minor noblemen as their leaders. In 1637, the rebels were dealt a crushing defeat by the army in a battle that resulted in one thousand deaths.

In the summer of 1639, the government had to withstand the Barefoot Revolt which began in Avranches. Originally, it stemmed from a rumour that the government wanted to introduce the salt tax in parishes in which it did not exist. In these parishes, salt was obtained from the saltpans in Mont Saint-Michel Bay. The revolt spread to Rouen and throughout Normandy. Salt tax collectors were killed in Rouen in August and Richelieu decided to put down the revolt. Colonel Gassion, who commanded foreign mercenaries, re-established law and order in Lower Normandy by crushing the rebels at Avranches on 30th November 1639. Spectacular reprisals showed Richelieu's determination to make an example of the rebels.

The Final Conspiracies

In 1642, the Cinq-Mars conspiracy came to the fore. It was Richelieu himself who had encouraged Cinq-Mars, the son of one of his faithful followers, to seek the King's friendship for the solitary monarch was in need of affection. Louis XIII heaped the most sumptuous charges on the young man – he was Monsieur le Grand (Equerry). There had been other favourites before him but Cinq-Mars was different in that he wanted to play a political role and rid himself of Richelieu, the man who had made his fortune. He envisaged a coup d'état against the minister, with the backing of Spain. Was he encouraged by Louis XIII to try and establish contact with Madrid in his attempt to counterbalance the cardinal who was continuing to prolong the war? The young man let himself become involved, going so far as to sign a treaty. The aim was to chase out Richelieu and call on Gaston d'Orléans who would be appointed Lieutenant General of the Kingdom and make peace with Spain, as he had already promised to do, through the reciprocal return of conquered land. Queen Anne of Austria may have been aware of the plot and may have revealed its existence in order to retain custody of her sons at a time when there were moves afoot to take them away from her.

Louis XIII travelled to the south of France and laid siege to Perpignan. Richelieu, who was ill, had to stay in Narbonne. Soon, he had in his hand a copy of the treaty which Cinq-Mars had signed with Spain. This was an indication of the remarkable network of informers that Richelieu had succeeded in setting up all over Europe. The evidence convinced the King, who was by that time tired and aggravated by the capricious behaviour of his Grand Equerry. Cinq-Mars was arrested on 13th June 1642. His friend, François de Thou, who came from an illustrious family of magistrates and historians, knew of the conspiracy but had not revealed its existence. The two young men were taken to Court, sentenced to death and executed in Lyon. The Duke de Bouillon, who had been involved in the plot, only saved his own head by assigning his principality of Sedan to Louis XIII.

Victory on the Horizon

Despite these internal struggles, France's situation was strongly established. The Spanish armies had been defeated to north and south. The Swedish army had survived and, at the end of December 1641, France and Sweden planned to open two peace conferences, one in Münster for the Catholic powers and the other in Osnabrück for the Protestants. On 4th December 1642, Cardinal de Richelieu died. Mazarin had replaced Father Joseph as Richelieu's confidant. He had shown his talent as a negotiator in Europe. When Richelieu died, Louis XIII called the Italian to the Council. He permitted the return of a few of the cardinal's adversaries, such as Gaston d'Orléans. On 21st April 1643, the Dauphin was christened and the King chose Mazarin as his godfather. On 14th May 1643, Louis XIII died.

An invasion force of 28,000 men then tried to overrun France from Flanders. It suffered a decisive defeat at Rocroi on 19th May 1643. This victory, led by the Duc d'Enghien, Louis XIII's young cousin, showed that the much-feared Spanish footsoldiers grouped in tercios were no longer invincible. It was a dazzling success resulting from the policy implemented by Louis XIII and Richelieu.

LOUIS XIV

For later generations Louis XIV was the perfect embodiment of a monarch, admired by some, detested by others. Yet the judgments passed on the king and his long reign have been contradictory. For many years, historians had an ambiguous attitude. Although they were quick to condemn costly wars, the policy of royal glorification and religious persecution, they were sensitive to the way in which he strengthened the role of the State and the grandeur of the nation. After the Second World War, a more disdainful attitude came into being. The Great King was frequently compared unfavourably with his subjects whose life was often difficult, especially as they had to pay for the insane ambitions of their sovereign. A sombre view of the reign emphasised the constraints imposed upon society, the economic difficulties and the ridiculous nature of life at court. More recently, there are those who have recalled that the decisions of the King of France, which were severely criticised by historians, were in fact a reflection of the normal reactions of princes of the time.

Anne of Austria's Regency

Louis XIV was born on 5th September 1638 and was five years old when he mounted the throne on 14th May 1643, on the death of his father, Louis XIII. Anne of Austria, in order to circumvent the decisions taken by her deceased husband, needed the support of the parlement of Paris which gave her full authority to govern France. The parlement was both a Court of Justice and a court of peers; it was a «sovereign» court with a special place compared to the other parlements in the provinces, especially for the size of its judicial district. The parlements were required to record royal edicts and, where appropriate, propose the corresponding «remonstrances». The King could, however, ignore them and could even break up any resistance by holding a «bed of justice». Since the parliamentarians owned their positions within the justice system which were, therefore «monetary» but which had become hereditary, they also enjoyed a large measure of independence from royal authority.

Mazarin's Government

Although Anne of Austria was the sister of the King of Spain, she continued to implement the policies of Louis XIII and Richelieu which meant, first and foremost, war against the Hapsburgs of Spain and Austria. This was why, in order to govern the country, she had kept a Roman cardinal among her closest courtiers, Giulio Mazarini, whose name had been given a more French consonance and turned into Jules Mazarin. The papal diplomat appeared to be irreplaceable because he knew Europe well. He was well acquainted with its many courts and the complexities of its political map. Despite torments and strife, he succeeded in maintaining Queen Anne of Austria's trust and friendship. His style of government was quite different to that of Richelieu. The subtle Italian showed amazing flexibility while revealing an iron will when necessary. There were, however, many who were discontent, wishing to put an end to the brutal politics and climate of constraint that had been prevalent since the days of Richelieu and remove the obedience which was imposed upon the court and the nobility.

The Fronde Revolt was an indirect consequence of France's international undertakings. Like Richelieu, of whom he was a follower, Mazarin believed that the kingdom could and should pay for the costly politics of war. Yet just as tangible results were about to be achieved (peace appeared to be possible in the Holy Roman Empire and France was to act as arbitrator), the country ran out of steam. The parlement expressed this exhaustion by refusing to ratify the financial decisions taken by the government.

The Old Fronde

Early in 1648, the Regent came to the law courts to hold a «bed of justice» in order to ensure the ratification of a series of fiscal edicts prepared by Superintendent Particelli. However, on the next day, the parlement declared the « bed of justice» to be null and void. The sovereign courts of Paris then sent members of parliament to meet in the Saint-Louis Chamber in the law courts and prepare a text including 27 articles. Among other things, they asked that no taxes should be levied without the consent of the sovereign courts, a condition which placed control on the crown. The Regent gave in.

Barricades

Mazarin was waiting to take his revenge. The French armies enjoyed success on all fronts at that time. When Condé's fine victory in Lens against the Spanish army (20th August 1648) was announced, Mazarin decided to strike at the parliamentarians' opposition by having the leaders arrested. In particular, he sought to imprison an old parliamentarian named Broussel, on 26th August 1648. Riots broke out in Paris. The town's middle classes took up arms. The rioters fought the King's guards. The co-adjutor to the Archbishop of Paris, Gondi, an ambitious man who wanted to replace Mazarin and who had the support of parish priests in Paris, did nothing to calm things down; in fact, quite the contrary. On

27th August, barricades covered the streets of Paris. On 28th August, Broussel was freed and the parlement asked that the barricades be taken down but the troubles continued. Calm returned only very gradually, over the following days.

The Queen settled, with the court, in the Château de Rueil near Paris. But she was forced to begin discussions and, on 22nd October, a royal declaration ratified all the articles drawn up by the Saint-Louis Chamber. A limited form of monarchy was instituted, in theory at least. The King returned to Paris. Paradoxically, it was at this moment that the Treaty of Westphalia was signed, ending the war in the Holy Roman Empire (24th October 1648). France was to obtain a presence in Alsace and the right to monitor «German liberties».

The First Fronde Revolt

After giving in to popular wrath, the Regent and Mazarin called the German mercenaries from Condé's army to the outskirts of Paris. The court, having pretended to celebrate Epiphany, left the capital on the night of 5th/6th January 1549 and settled in Saint-Germain-en-Laye. Condé installed a blockade around Paris with 8,000 to 10,000 men. On 8th January, Mazarin was declared by the supporters of the Fronde Revolt to be an «enemy of the King and his State» and a disturber of public rest. At the same time, in England, King Charles I was beheaded – an event which stupefied continental Europe.

The «Mazarinades»

An intense pamphlet war was waged against Mazarin. Later on, the texts became known as the «mazarinades» after the title of the work by Scarron, La Mazarinade (1651). More than 5,000 of them were listed. Mazarin was blamed for his foreign origins, his power over the King and his ties with Anne of Austria, the taxes he had created, his taste for luxury and Italian opera and his personal enrichment. He was the «priest with twenty chapters», or the «lord with a thousand titles». The writers were in the employ of princes, parliamentarians or Gondi. Parisian printers had full order books for five years. The people of Paris were tired of the blockade. Appeasement during the spring of 1649 proved to be of short duration and internal tensions led to a break in relations between Condé, who wanted to wield political power, and Mazarin. The cardinal wanted a show of strength. He therefore had Condé arrested with his brother, the Prince de Conti, and his brother-in-law, Longueville (18th January 1650).

The Union of the Frondes

The revolt flared up again, encouraging the «Union of the Frondes». The royal troops then set off to reconquer the provinces in which revolt had been fomented by the princes and their followers. Campaigns took place in Normandy, Burgundy and Guyenne and the court travelled the length and breadth of the land. Yet the political conflict remained. Mazarin decided to withdraw and he left on the night of 6th/7th February 1651. He travelled via Le Havre where the princes had finally been imprisoned and set them free. The Parisians went to the Palais-Royal on the night of 9th/10th February 1651 to see whether the young king was still resident there or had left the capital. The Queen Mother asked Louis XIV to go to bed fully clothed and pretend to be sleeping. This humiliation left the young sovereign with bitter memories. The royal family was unable to leave Paris; Mazarin continued to direct the Regent's actions from abroad.

Condé and the Fronde

By September 1651, Louis XIV had been declared to have reached the age of majority and the Regency was coming to an end. Condé then took a vital step. This time, it was a personal revolt on the part of a prince of royal lineage. Condé was in favour of strong royal authority and he did not want it under the control of the States or the nobility. However, he wanted to guide the young King, thereby replacing the Queen Mother and her Italian adviser. He sought support in Bordeaux and Guyenne and backing from the Spaniards. Anne of Austria recalled Mazarin who had recruited a small army at his own expense and he joined the sovereign in Poitiers in January 1652. It was Turenne who, having rallied to the royal cause, led the fighting against Condé. Paris fell prey to rioters in the spring of 1652. Condé's troops and the King's army under the command of Turenne were encircling Paris. On 1st and 2nd July, during the battle fought in the suburb known as Faubourg Saint-Antoine, the Grande Mademoiselle had the cannons in the Bastille turned against the troops of her cousin, Louis XIV, and she saved Condé who was able to enter the town. On 4th July, Paris suffered a particularly bloody day known as «Condé's reign of terror». 1652 was also the most terrible of all years for the ordinary people in the Paris area.

Calm Returns

Exhaustion was obvious. Mazarin was skilled enough to withdraw again, in order to calm the situation. Condé left France and entered the service of Spain. The monarchy now seemed to be the country's only guarantee of a return to peace. On 21st October 1652, Louis XIV triumphantly entered the capital. Today's historians believe that the Fronde did not end in 1653 and that the following years were marked by brief and sudden reoccurrences.

Education for a King

Louis XIV was crowned in Reims on 7th June 1654. Throughout these years, Cardinal Mazarin, the young King's godfather who had been responsible for his education since 1646, introduced him to his work as a sovereign and taught him about European politics. However, he was careful not to let him take even the smallest decision. The young prince also learnt from his mother the manners and lifestyle of the court. The Franco-Spanish War was ended by the Treaty of the Pyrenees (7th November 1659), in which one of the main clauses was the marriage of the young King with Philip IV's daughter, the Infanta of Spain, Maria Teresa. This was a wager for the future. One day, the King of France might be led to claim part of the Spanish empire or a right to the throne of Spain, on behalf of his wife. Louis XIV met his father-in-law on Pheasants' Island at the Franco-Spanish border and the marriage with Maria Teresa was celebrated in Saint-Jean-de-Luz on 9th June 1660.

Taking Power

The most essential date in Louis XIV's reign is the year 1661. Mazarin's death on 9th March led the King to take a major decision which was announced on 10th March – he would no longer have a prime minister. This meant that the sovereign was both reigning and governing and this strengthened the image of the monarchy since all power was in the hands of one and the same person. However, it also deprived the sovereign of a convenient shield since any discontent could no longer be deflected towards the prime minister. This «seizure of power», which has often given rise to extensive commentary, was followed by another major decision i.e. to remove from office the Superintendent of Finances, Nicolas Fouquet, who was arrested on 5th September 1661 in Nantes where the court was residing.

Fouquet's Trial

Fouquet had worked with Mazarin to find the necessary financial resources that would enable them to end the war and fund peace. He had also enabled the cardinal to amass a huge fortune and he himself was not forgotten in the process. When he hosted a visit from the King to Vaux-le-Vicomte amid dazzling luxury in the summer of 1661, he angered the sovereign who believed that only he could enjoy such splendour. The King had already privately condemned the Superintendent because he controlled the finances and that gave him a power which the monarch did not have. It was, then, the entire financial organisation and the world of financiers that Louis XIV and, through him the State, wanted to monitor and control. Finally, as Marc Fumaroli states, Fouquet represented a moderate tradition through his friendships and loyalties and this had not been the tradition in royal eyes since the days of Richelieu and «reasons of State». The policy of reconciliation and dialogue was not supported by the young, authoritarian King. Louis XIV would have liked Fouquet's trial to have ended in a death sentence but the judges were content to banish him from the realm. The King then changed this to imprisonment in the citadel in Pignerol.

Kingship

These decisions taken in 1661 revealed Louis XIV to his subjects. In future years, he would respect his commitment and devote his energies to the job of monarch, a job which he enjoyed and held in the highest esteem. This meant constant work throughout his life, listening to his ministers and generals, studying business and projects, and taking decisions. He brought to the task great personal majesty and a political sense which brought sparkle to the royal function. He took over his predecessors' determination to obtain exact and perfect obedience and he instigated fear. Louis XIV wanted to bring luxury to all public ceremonies such as the audiences granted to foreign ambassadors. On such occasions, he had a liking for sumptuous clothes and jewellery. He expressed himself clearly and forcibly. In order to strengthen the prestige of the French monarchy among the French people and other European countries, the royal personage was celebrated throughout his reign. There were poems praising his merits, medals recalling his most outstanding successes, portraits immortalising his person, and equestrian statues erected in the kingdom's towns to underline his glory.

Colbert in Business

Jean-Baptiste Colbert had managed Mazarin's huge fortune and had been recommended to the King by the cardinal. With his in-depth knowledge of the financial system on which Fouquet based his actions, he had prepared the Superintendent's downfall. He was then ordered to replace him, but without the title. Since Louis XIV wanted to take over the position of Superintendent himself, Colbert, who was a minister in 1661, was only Controller General in 1665. He raised this function to the foremost in the land despite the fact that, since the Middle Ages, it had been the Chancellor who had enjoyed the leading role. Michel Antoine saw this as a revolution for the monarchy which was then based on finance and no longer on justice, especially as Colbert had charge of numerous other sectors e.g. Water and Forestry, the King's Buildings, the King's Household and the Navy. Colbert worked to find out more about the State's income and expenditure and tried, with no little measure of success, to find the resources required to pay the armies, prepare a Navy for warfare and build royal palaces.

Ministerial Dynasties

Mazarin's assistants, with the exception of Fouquet, kept their positions. Le Tellier, who was responsible for military affairs, increasingly sought support from his son, Louvois. Hugues de Lionne had charge of French diplomacy. Louis XIV, right until the end of his life, gave a great deal of his time to affairs of state which were discussed at council meetings. The most important council for general political affairs and foreign affairs was the upper council or council of ministers and anybody asked to join it became a minister of state. The King had only a handful of ministers but he placed his trust in them, often throughout their lives, although he was not averse to reminding them, sometimes rather brusquely, of the weight of his authority. He demanded constant loyalty, absolute secrecy and an immense amount of work. He chose his counsellors from among a small number of families in the wealthy middle classes and not from the nobility. Among them were Colbert, Le Tellier or Phélypeaux.

The Structure of the Monarchic State

Affairs were dealt with in detail by the Council of State which ruled on litigation in the King's name. This was the old form of monarchy. To it was added a new administrative structure with added powers which centred on the Controller General and Secretaries of State (for War, Foreign Affairs, the Royal Household and Navy, and Affairs of the Reformed Religion). Only some of these men were ministers. They were supported by civil servants of various ranks and it was they who set up the details of the decisions taken by the King. Louis XIV often chose to work with them on a one-to-one basis. In the provinces, royal power was increasingly dependent on the Intendants who were subject only to the King. The scope of their work continually increased; they were responsible for justice, the police and finances. They were increasingly successful in their dealings with other local forms of authority such as provincial governors, bishops, gentlemen, judges and town councils. Royal authority was, by definition, absolute i.e. not bound by any ties. The way in which Louis XIV exercised this power is, with the wider-ranging administration, the source of the concept of absolute monarchy which many historians have highlighted, at the risk of making a mistake. It is preferable to talk, like Roland Mousnier, of an administrative monarchy which is no longer content to act merely as arbitrator and monitor but which implements enterprise, management and control.

Politics of a Great Power

Louis XIV's policies were, from the outset, aimed at a strengthening of France's position in Europe and the King followed the line set by his father and the two cardinal-ministers. France was in a favourable position. It was no longer threatened by the Hapsburgs who had been severely weakened by long years of warfare and by the Treaties of Westphalia and the Pyrenees. The kingdom of France had the largest population in Europe and it had shown that it was capable of funding huge armies. Louis XIV, a young monarch, was determined to gain fame and, in the 17th-century world, glory was first and foremost based on military prowess so there was a need to wage war and win it. The peace in Europe enabled Louis XIV to plan and prepare for war without being subjected to it. The period of preparation covered the first years of his personal government. Hugues de Lionne was ordered to undertake negotiations throughout Europe in order to establish solid relationships. He was to sign the treaties that would give France allies in case of conflict. Le Tellier was to reorganise the army and his son, Louvois, succeeded in increasing its size without compromising on discipline or coherence. Finally, Colbert succeeded in giving France, a country with no real maritime tradition, a fleet ready for warfare, capable of rivalling the Navies of England and the United Provinces.

Second Only to the Emperor in Europe

At the same time, Louis XIV maintained political tension in Europe by using diplomatic incidents abroad to obtain reparations and, in doing so, confirm his leading role on the continent. In the symbolic hierarchy of kings, he was second only to the Emperor. After the death of his father-in-law, the King of Spain, he emphasised the rights of Queen Maria Teresa despite the fact that she had undertaken, in solemn waivers, to abandon all claims to the Spanish throne. Legal experts used, as an argument, a right existing in the Spanish Netherlands, the right of devolution, and this provided the excuse for war. It was an easy conflict but it worried England and the United Provinces which threatened to enter the fray. This led Louis XIV to end his military operations but not before he had won from Spain a number of fine towns in the north such as Lille and Douai.

The Dutch War

This, though, was only a temporary peace. Louis XIV had understood that he needed further alliances in addition to the one negotiated secretly in 1670 with King Charles II of England. The enemy chosen by the King this time was Holland which had dared to stand in the way of the conqueror. War broke out in 1672 and resulted in dazzling victories. The United Provinces were invaded; they had not actually capitulated. A political revolution brought William of Orange to power in The Hague and he was thereafter Louis XIV's permanent enemy. The King of England, who had entered the conflict on the French side, was forced to withdraw for the alliance with the very Christian King seemed suspicious to the English. The Emperor then entered the fray and waged war on the King of France. However, Louis XIV's generals won a number of fine successes, the most outstanding being Turenne's victory at the Battle of Turckheim (1675). The royal navy under the command of Duquesne also won a number of outstanding victories on the coasts of Sicily (1676) in the face of the redoubtable Dutch fleet. The peace treaty signed in Nijmegen in 1678 ratified the new conquests in northern France (Cambrai, Valenciennes and Maubeuge) and resulted in the acquisition of Franche-Comté. The royal policy found coherence by pushing the northern border back far from Paris and making it more linear by abandoning enclaves in foreign territory. To make any invasion of the country more difficult, Vauban, the famous engineer, was ordered to build or rebuild fortresses right round the edge of the realm. This created the «iron belt» that was to provide the defence of the capital and guarantee French territory against any enemy incursion.

Although the quest for personal glory, the strengthening of the French presence in Europe, territorial expansion and the fortification of the kingdom were the main preoccupations during this early part of the reign, they were not the only ones.

Social Submission

Public law and order was also a priority. Louis XIV had lived through the Fronde uprising and he worked to prevent it happening again. He forced his close family to respect the utmost obedience. He monitored the nobility which had, for a long time, been rebellious and quarrelsome. The parlement in Paris had had its knuckles rapped in 1655 and it, too, felt the weight of royal authority bearing down on it. In 1673, Louis XIV prohibited the pre-registration remonstrances and this prevented the parliamentarians in Paris from expressing opinions on royal decisions. Instead, they had to be content with their judicial role. In Paris, a new post was created – Lieutenant-General of Police, again in an attempt to ensure law and order while improving everyday life in the capital. La Reynie, who was the first person to hold the post, won general esteem for his work. There were still a few rebellions in the kingdom, resulting from resistance to taxes. There was also the Lustucru War in the Boulonnais area in 1662 or the Stamped Paper Revolt in Brittany in 1675. However, these uprisings ceased after 1680 and, again, France produced an image of a society subject to royal authority.

The Grand Ordinances

Thanks to this relative tranquillity in the country and thanks to the tenacity of Louis XIV and his ministers, the government was able to implement major reforms in order to adapt French law and give it greater uniformity. This quite naturally followed on from the efforts made by the monarchy since the early 16th century. It was a long-term project which led to the publication of grand ordinances relating to civil proceedings (1667), criminal proceedings (1670), Water and Forestry (1669), trade (1673), the navy (1681) and the colonies (1685). The legislative system was not liberal in inspiration; on the contrary, it strengthened controls. However, it had the advantage of clarifying the situation and avoiding more obscure points which often led to arbitrary decisions.

Royal Factories and Trading Companies

The encouragement for economic activity was also very ambitious. Colbert encouraged the setting up of factories which would supply high-quality goods in large quantities in order to limit the imports of products manufactured abroad, especially as the balance of payments deficit was offset by precious metal and this was considered at the time to represent a country's wealth. Factories were therefore set up to supply the King and his court – the Gobelins factory for tapestries and furniture and Saint-Gobain for mirrors. Overall, even if luxury production was encouraged, the success of the policy remained limited. The same applied to the trading companies that aimed to imitate, in France, the Dutch East India Company which earned fabulous profits. Many of these enterprises failed but the French East India Company survived despite many difficulties. Also worth remembering are the initiatives taken to extend, populate and organise distant areas within New France in North America. In 1682, Cavelier de la Salle travelled down the Mississippi and gave the King's name to the new American territory that he discovered – Louisiana.

The Court

Louis XIV is, perhaps, easier to understand through life at court and his taste for the Arts. The idea of building up, around the person and daily existence of the King, a strictly-regulated court life which, as Saint-Simon so aptly remarked, gave importance to things that had none, dates back to very ancient times. Henri III had wanted to establish a strong etiquette which would have put distance between the monarch and his courtiers. The presence in France of queens who were Spanish Infanta encouraged a change that had been delayed by civil and foreign wars, as well as by the personalities of Henri IV and Louis XIII. Louis XIV, on the other hand, turned his full attention to this unusual social life. It goes without saying that it took time to achieve the immovable mechanism that regulated life in Versailles and enabled the entire universe to know what the King of France was doing every minute of the day and night. The court remained itinerant for a long time, with a marked preference for Saint-Germain-en-Laye. However, it was in Versailles that the fine series of festivities and entertainments known as the Plaisirs de l'île enchantée was held. Court life required courtiers to attend the monarch assiduously, especially those who held one of the many charges in his household. This turned a leading aristocrat into little more than a lackey even if his main task was to supervise royal servants. However, for Louis XIV, this society was to provide the background for every form of delight and, if ritual existed, it was to be the ritual of every form of pleasure whether music, gaming, theatre, hunting, dancing or banqueting.

The King's Closest Courtiers

At various times in his life, Louis XIV was more or less successful in providing leadership for court life. His youth was remembered as a time of luxury and entertainment, especially as the young King was not known for his marital fidelity, even though he was respectful towards Maria Teresa. He set an example of an eventful, even libertine, love life. After numerous mistresses, some well-known, others less so, he fell in love with the imperious, elegant, quick-witted Marquise de Montespan who was a good example of youth at court. The monarch was surrounded by his closest family – Anne of Austria whom Louis XIV removed from power and who died shortly afterwards; Maria Teresa who lived in the shadow of her august husband; the Dauphin, or Monseigneur, the only surviving child born to the royal couple and, later, his sons; the King's brother, Monsieur and his two wives, Henrietta of England then, after her death, Princess Palatine. The entire life of the court revolved around the King's day – his rising with a strict hierarchy in the «entrées» reflecting the degree of closeness with the monarch, Mass again with its distinctions, supper and retiral. As the life at court was a means of drawing the King's attention, it was an ideal way of discreetly regulating the life of the nobility since aristocrats awaited favours from the monarch in the form of bishoprics or abbeys for younger sons, governments, embassies or military commands for elder sons. By remaining far from the prince, in Paris or in the provinces, entire families closed the door on royal favour and, in some cases, sentenced their dynasty to decline.

Arts, Letters and Sciences

The same attitude prevailed as regards the arts where Louis XIV, having studied with Mazarin, remembered what the Italian had taught him. Art could serve the image of the monarch who had a duty to protect and encourage artists. The King also had to be the only person to commission major artistic enterprises. Finally, the monarch had the same attitude to what we would now describe as «cultural institutions». He provided dazzling protection while indicating a desire for glory and exercising discreet surveillance. Louis XIV agreed to act as patron of the Académie Française et he gave his opinion on the choice of future members. New academies were set up i.e. the Académie des Inscriptions (1663) and the Académie des Sciences (1666). The royal academy of painting and sculpture had already existed since 1648. Louis XIV was fond of music. It accompanied every moment of his life when he was not working. In his youth, he enjoyed taking part in ballet productions and he encouraged French opera (lyric tragedy) in its early days. He also kept a close eye on all the architectural projects undertaken during his reign and built up super art collections, especially paintings. He supported Molière against the fanatics and brought Racine and Boileau to court.

Maturity

Even if the official celebration of the King and his glory may seem rather overdone and, therefore, misleading to us today, most French people at the time were in favour of a policy which guaranteed law and order within the country and gave the French monarchy a high degree of prestige. After Nijmegen, Louis XIV was encouraged to extend and harden the policies implemented in the early days of his reign. However, they proved to be more dangerous.

The Revocation of the Edict of Nantes

Within the country, there was a determination to re-establish religious unity. Louis XIII and Richelieu had maintained the tolerance granted to the Protestants by the Edict of Nantes while removing their political and military might. Louis XIV's reign, on the other hand, was a time of persecution. It seemed possible to obtain the conversion of members of the Reformed Religion, through threats if necessary, or by garrisoning in their areas soldiers who would make increasingly oppressive demands. The «dragonnades» as they were called proved effective. There were more and more conversions and Louis XIV allowed himself to be convinced that it was time to go one step further and consider that there were almost no Protestants left in France. In this case, the Edict of Nantes served no useful purpose and it was therefore rescinded in October 1685. The decision was praised by fervent Catholics as a triumph for the true religion. In fact, numerous Protestants preferred to leave France and settle in other countries. A few people, among them Vauban, raised their voices in protest at the time of the Revocation, deploring the departures that were weakening the country and giving added strength to neighbouring nations. The Protestants who remained in France concealed their religious convictions. Later, at the beginning of the 18th century, the Cévennes area was the scene of a Protestant uprising and the «Camisards», as the rebels were called, even succeeded in defeating regiments of the King's army in 1704. The Revocation also annoyed the Protestant princes in Europe who, since the 16th century, had often been allies of France. This fed the attacks on the tyrannical policies of the King of France who was described as a danger for all Protestants, throughout Europe. The same severity was evident in the royal attitude to Catholics who moved away from the doctrine of the Church. The Jansenists, for example, suffered alternating periods of persecution and tolerance. At the end of his reign, Louis XIV dispersed the last nuns from Port-Royal Abbey (1709) and had the abbey buildings demolished (1710). Finally, he obtained from the Pope a further condemnation of Jansenism in the papal bull Unigenitus (1713).

The Court in Versailles

This new stage in the King's life was also the moment at which the court moved to Versailles (1682). Louis XIV, who was fond of hunting and walks in the fresh air, had decided to effect alterations to the small lodge where his father liked to stay. The King decided to abandon the constant movement of the court, although it continued to go to Marly or Fontainebleau every year. It was a means of recognising that the sheer weight of the new administrative system made the erstwhile itinerant nature of court life more difficult to organise. The result was the creation of a political and administrative capital for the kingdom. And it was not Paris. It has sometimes been said that, since the Fronde revolt, the King mistrusted the large, restless town. It is true that the King no longer lived in the midst of the Parisians and this was doubtless of no little importance. The palace was not finished when the court moved in and the work continued for some considerable time for the King had a noticeable liking for his «buildings» and he enjoyed continuously changing the luxurious surroundings in which he lived. Louis XIV had taken into his service the artists who had worked for Fouquet i.e. Le Vau (architecture), Lebrun (painting) and Le Nôtre (landscape gardening). Hardouin-Mansart extended the palace with buildings overlooking the gardens, then added the wings and stables. Louis XIV had learnt from Mazarin to respect Art, to seek beauty and to pay attention to opulence. His residence was to be more outstanding than any other in the kingdom, or even in the world. One of the projects which amazed his contemporaries was the Hall of Mirrors. Quite apart from its impressive proportions and silver furniture, it had a set of paintings created in honour of the King of France alone. The presence of the court required that premises be provided for the administration of the kingdom, for the horses and carriages, and for everyday life. A new town grew up around the palace. It was at this time that Louis XIV, the widower of Maria Teresa decided to lead a life that complied with the precepts of the Church's teaching. In 1683, he secretly married Madame Scarron, the widow of a legless poet, who had raised the King's illegitimate children and who had, thanks to royal favour, become the Marquise de Maintenon. She was an intelligent woman who led a discreet, withdrawn life at the court but there is no doubt that she must have influenced the monarch.

Reunification

Louis XIV wished to prolong his military and diplomatic successes by strengthening the kingdom's system of defence. To this end, new estates had to be acquired round the borders. Legal experts and historians were therefore required to study the archives and trace documents recalling old feudal rights under which lands located outside France were dependent on any estates recently acquired by the country. If the lord did not recognise this tie and the authority of Louis XIV, the land was confiscated. These «reunification processes» allowed for countless annexations during a time of absolute peace. In the same way, Louis XIV occupied the town of Strasbourg (1681), without reason and without resistance. These provocations angered many German princes whose rights were encroached by these procedures and who turned to the Emperor just when his imperial majesty was under threat from the

Turks. Thanks to the King of Poland, John Sobieski, he succeeded in freeing his capital, Vienna (1683).

The War of the League of Augsburg

Gradual mobilisation within Europe led to a new conflict, known in France as the War of the League of Augsburg (1688-1697). At this time, William of Orange landed in England in response to the discontent of the English with regard to James II Stuart who was forced to seek refuge in France. William of Orange mounted the throne in London. The war that was beginning therefore had a maritime dimension, with the French fleets supporting James II in his efforts to win back his kingdom. The French success at the Battle of Béveziers (1691) was not to last. In 1692, after a difficult sea battle, a large part of the French combat fleet was set alight in La Hougue. The war at sea, which was ruinously expensive, was replaced by privateering. Acting in the King's name, privateers from Dunkirk or Saint-Malo would attack enemy merchant ships, thereby damaging international trade. Jean Bart, a seafarer from Dunkirk, had many successes. On land, Louis XIV's armies «raged» through the Palatinate undertaking a combination of pillage and threats designed to obtain the payment of money. The systematic, pitiless character of these operations was to constitute a festering wound for Germany. France won numerous victories, showing that its armies were capable of withstanding a strong European coalition. However, Louis XIV appeared to be increasingly isolated in Europe. The results of the decade between 1680 and 1690 were ambiguous – there was a difficult war and religious tension within the country. In addition to that, there were serious economic crises as a result of climatic conditions, for example in the years 1693-1694. The end of the reign was therefore marked by a number of major changes.

Old Age

Although Louis XIV lived to the age of 77, he saw the deaths of his main assistants – Colbert in 1683 and Louvois in 1691. There came a new generation of ministers, doubtless with new ideas. The administrative system had expanded and was doing its utmost to find out more about the kingdom, its population, its resources and its diversity, as shown in the reports demanded from the Intendents for the benefit of the Duke of Burgundy (1697). Many reform projects were drafted. To fund the war, a capitation tax was created in 1695 and levied on all the King's subjects, even the nobility, in accordance with the wealth or social status of the person. Later, in 1710, a new tax, the tithe, was instituted with the same care to respect individual capacities and social justice. It is possible that a new society and economy had already been born. In particular, the harbours along the Atlantic coast began to turn their attention to colonial trade.

The Spanish Succession

It was for reasons of moderation that negotiations developed in order to put an end to the War of the League of Augsburg. Louis XIV agreed to recognise William III as King of England and to abandon the lands annexed during «reunification», with the exception of Strasbourg. It is true that this moderation can be explained by the recent death of King Carlos II of Spain, who had no direct descendent. Because of the family ties between the sovereign houses, numerous princes could lay a claim to the Spanish succession, among them princes from the House of France as well as the Emperor and his sons. This was a huge challenge for the Spanish empire was vast, in Europe and worldwide. Louis XIV and William III prepared diplomatic solutions allowing for the division of the empire but the Spaniards would not agree to other European powers dividing up their possessions and Carlos II wrote a will on his deathbed, designating as his successor Louis XIV's second grandson, the Duke d'Anjou. The King of France was the only person who could maintain the integrity of the many territories. After discussions in the upper chamber, Louis XIV accepted the will on 16th November 1700. A Bourbon, Philip V, set off to mount the Spanish throne.

A World War

The decision resulted in yet another war, known as the War of the Spanish Succession. The maritime powers, England and the United Provinces, who wanted to take over Spanish trade with the American colonies, stood up to this new international order. The Emperor intervened in the name of his rights to the crown of Spain and a grand alliance was formed against the King of France and his grandson. We shall not go into details but, instead, will highlight a few points. The encirclement of France by lands belonging to the House of Hapsburg had disappeared. Yet the French monarchy still had to make a large contribution to the defence of Spanish possessions in the face of its enemies. After a few years of uncertainty, it became clear that the Bourbons were in a difficult situation. Whole sections of the Spanish empire fell into the allies' hands and the Iberian Peninsula itself was partly occupied. The English Duke of Marlborough and the imperial general, Eugene of Savoy, inflicted several rousing defeats on Louis XIV's armies and Lille fell in 1708. Louis XIV wanted to negotiate and, through the discussions, it became obvious that the allies wanted Philip V to abandon the throne in Madrid. The King accepted the idea but refused to remove his grandson from his new kingdom. Yet the winds of change had begun to blow. The Spaniards had shown themselves to be loyal to the French prince and the allies were confronted by difficulties in Spain. The Bourbons were not totally defeated since they found the means of continuing the war despite the terrible, hard winter of 1709 during which the French suffered cruelly. The King of France, in a solemn, moving letter, appealed to his subjects' feelings of patriotism. In particular, the long war led to the gradual collapse of the anti-Bourbon coalition. England declared itself ready to negotiate at the end of 1710.

The Treaty of Utrecht

Just as the idea was gaining ground that Philip V would remain King of Spain while losing much of his empire, in Italy for example, Louis XIV suffered a number of deaths in his family and his own succession was thrown open to doubt. His son, the eldest of his grandsons, and the eldest of his great-grandsons all died in 1711 and 1712. Philip V moved nearer to the crown or a possibly regency and, with him, came the spectre of a major worry for Europe – the union of Spain and France. However, after an unexpected French victory (1712) and after solemn waivers imposed upon the Bourbons by English diplomats to guarantee the separation of the two realms, the peace treaty was signed in Utrecht in 1713 then in Rastadt in 1714. Despite his grief and mourning, the King retained his energy for a long time. He took increasing precautions to prepare the reign of his heir, a child born in 1710. He continued to work diligently and illness still left him enough time and energy to take leave of his closest family and courtiers, with a sense of majesty. He is believed to have said to his courtiers, «I am leaving you but the State will last for all time… I hope that you will do your duty and will sometimes remember me». The dimension that Louis XIV gave to the function of monarch, the scope of the achievements of his reign, especially in the artistic sphere, the incipient administrative system, the resources that it succeeded in drawing from the kingdom and, finally, the extension of national territory aroused admiration in 18th-century princes, many of whom sought to imitate the King of France. On the other hand, during the days of Louis the Great, actions were taken which changed the face of the monarchy. There was more marked, more restricting royal authority, close monitoring of society as a whole and a political removal of traditional elites. Gradually these characteristics were less well accepted by the French people who began to look at ways to achieve greater liberty.

THE END OF PRE-REVOLUTIONARY FRANCE

Over the centuries, France had acquired a structure that was referred to, during the French Revolution, as the «ancien régime». The cohesion of pre-revolutionary France lay firstly in its spiritual characteristics.

The Christian Faith

Christianity was the King's religion and, theoretically at least, the religion of the entire French people. It formed the basis of the monarchy and of society as a whole. Any creation and all authority came from God. Roman Catholicism was the main religion in France. Louis XIV called into question the rights that had been granted to the Protestants by the Edict of Nantes and the Jews were merely tolerated in the realm. It was not permitted to declare oneself an atheist or simply uncommitted. Sacraments, religious feast days and prayers marked the lives of everybody in France. The clergy enjoyed an eminent place in the kingdom because its members undertook the essential task of directing and confessing people. It was maintained through the receipt of tithes. The Church of France had, over the years, acquired an efficient organisational structure. Through the Concordat, it depended greatly on the King of France and the proclamation of Gallican liberties had enabled the Church to acquire a large measure of independence from Rome and the papacy.

Respect for the Past and for Freedom

This spiritual order implied respect for religious, ethical, political or intellectual authorities. The written or spoken word was subject to more or less close scrutiny. Censorship was commonplace, denouncing anything that appeared to be an insult to God, the King or good morals. Heterodox or new ideas were difficult to defend for, in addition to the above, there was a respect for the past, for tradition and custom. The Ancien Régime was further complicated by the fact that the implementation of new edicts did not necessarily remove existing realities but, instead, added to them. By defending rights acquired in the past, a province, town, village, community, trade or craft often defended privileges or rights that others did not enjoy such as exemption from taxes, municipal «franchises» or provincial «liberties». Although the Ancien Régime allowed little space for individual freedom, it was the guardian and protector of all forms of liberty.

The King and his Subjects

The Ancien Régime was, first and foremost, a political order based on a monarchy of divine right. The French people were the «subjects» of the King and this word on its own indicates that they owed him obedience. All authority had a single source, the King, who had been considered as an emperor in his kingdom since the Middle Ages and who recognised no greater power except God. His authority was further strengthened by the building of the State i.e. a more structured form of administration that was as large as it was effective, and by the confirmation of royal sovereignty after the difficult period of the Wars of Religion. The King was the supreme arbitrator, the dispenser of all justice, the creator of all laws and the defender of the realm. Although there was no written constitution, there was nevertheless a constitution based on the past, on fundamental laws derived from history.

The Action of the Monarchy

Public power was delegated in a very large measure. Firstly, official posts had been created and, over time, had become monetary and hereditary. Precise, temporary commissions had led to the installation of Intendents in the provinces. They became the prince's eyes and ears, thereby amplifying the unification, modernisation and centralisation of the realm. The monarchy was the driving force behind vast enterprises. It attempted to define, simplify and give uniformity to the law. It encouraged people to become more mobile, encouraged the transport of goods and the circulation of news by creating roads and bridges, establishing the corresponding engineering trade and setting up a post office. The King's agents modernised towns and undertook urban planning. Measures were taken to stimulate trade, especially international trade, in order to encourage production in State factories and avoid famines, poverty and epidemics. Monarchic power encouraged artistic creativity and scientific research. The State occupied a central position and weighed heavily on the life of the kingdom, making it unique in Europe. This was the specific characteristic of the French «model» of administration.

The Burden of Royal Taxation

The State gathered strength through wars which had required the build-up of a regular army and, by extension, of a permanent tax. The incessant conflicts of the 17th century had led to an enormous leap in royal taxation and this had not been accepted without rebellion and tensions. It had been collected within the traditional framework that spread its effect and with the assistance of financiers who saw their own interests in the system. In turn, this had given the monarchy freedom of movement. Yet over the years, the monarchy showed itself to be incapable of changing the tax system on a sustainable basis because of the system of privileges and it did not have at its disposal the methods and financial institutions that existed in Holland or England.

The Birth of a Nation

The existing political organisation was gradually eroded. The idea that all powers could be combined, whether executive, legislative or judicial, became intolerable. On several occasions, the monarch recalled that the nation and its King were one and the same and that the country could not be defined separately from the sovereign. Yet the nation gradually appeared to be the source of all legitimacy. There were those who sought to express themselves in its name, in particular the members of the parlements, the courts of justice that registered royal decisions. In the country as a whole there were few opportunities for dialogue and negotiation between the King and his subjects. Although a few provinces had Provincial States, the States General were not convened after 1614. In the final analysis, the nation confirmed its existence alongside and against the King. The Revolution then put an end to the monetary nature of official functions, before turning against the monarchy itself.

Legal Inequality

Society was traditionally divided into three «orders», of differing sizes. The clergy and nobility had a function in society – the defence of the realm for the aristocrats and prayer for the men of God. This provided justification for the privileges that they enjoyed. The nobility was defined less in terms of a clear status than through its impression of belonging to a race apart, thanks to its way of life and values. This social group remained open to families who acquired fame in the service or the King or who purchased public functions. The inequality between subjects was a legal fact. It was marked by a taste for «rank», for ancient hierarchies that were occasionally recalled in ceremonials. This indicated, in church, at the royal court, in towns and in rural areas, just what traditional order was. Although these honours produced a natural respect for these elite groups, they also upheld, among those wielding power, a disdain that was equally natural. Sometimes this led to a cascade of contempt which was not necessarily softened by Christian charity and which gradually became unbearable. Social inequality was evident in direct taxation since it was not paid by either of the first two orders. The monarchy had created indirect taxes or new direct taxes to which everybody was subject but this approach was a failure, generally speaking. In addition to this, there was common inequality between men and women, although this was seldom called into question.

Feudal Rights and Seigniorial Rights

Feudality was no more than a memory but a few specific characteristics of the system remained and were considered as annoyances. The last traces of servitude and «mortmain» had doubtless disappeared but the man-to-man ties still existed, albeit often in a symbolic manner and associated with the payment of feudal duties. The seigniorial system bound a peasant to land under the protection of the lord to whom the land belonged. This meant that the peasant was not the full owner of the land. Instead, he enjoyed «useful ownership» and was required to pay duties to the lord of the manor, e.g. the recognitory rent payable to the lord. In addition to the ownership rights, the lord had other rights such as a monopoly on hunting and this was subject to a great deal of criticism at the end of the 18th century. He also enjoyed the right of banality under which peasants were required to use the lord's mill and oven. Finally, although royal justice was prevalent almost everywhere and all subjects could have recourse to it, the lords also retained rights of justice. The work carried out by craftsmen and tradesmen was usually organised in a vertical structure, running from journeyman up to master, although there were a number of «free» trades and Turgot had tried, in vain, to establish freedom of work. Pierre Goubert wrote that the Ancien Régime was «a sort of immense, muddy river carrying in its waters dead, cumbersome tree trunks, weeds and grasses torn away from the river banks, living organisms of all ages and all sizes…» Pierre Gaxotte saw it rather as «a very great and very old construction» and concluded that «… overall, it was a rich construction with a luxurious façade, a construction in which people lived better, and in larger numbers, than elsewhere». The entire 18th century was marked by these contradictions.

The Regency
In 1715, Louis XIV's nephew, Philippe d'Orléans, became Regent and governed in the name of Louis XV, the great-grandson of the deceased monarch, who was only 5 years old. He replaced the middle-class ministers by councils of leading aristocrats and decided to reside in Paris rather than Versailles. He preferred to replace the austerity of the previous reign by a light-hearted lifestyle, with peace in place of warfare as a foreign policy. The Regency marked a break in the policies of the Sun King. However, in 1718, for reasons of efficiency, the Regent returned to the traditional institutions and practices of the monarchy.

Prosperity
There was no doubt that the Europe of the 18th century was prosperous. The French population rose, in just a century, from 22 to 29 million. People lived longer; the death rate decreased because there were fewer epidemics and famines. However medical progress was slow until the introduction of the vaccination against smallpox. Birth rates, on the other hand, remained very high although demographers have observed advances in contraception within families even though it was firmly condemned by the Church. The increased population was better fed, doubtless thanks to slow improvements in agricultural output even if it is no longer acceptable to describe this as an «agricultural revolution» as it was in days gone by. The system whereby land was left to lie fallow, was

beginning to be ignored but it was often necessary because of a lack of fertiliser. Animal husbandry provided manure and the sector expanded, enabling the French to eat more meat.

Trade

Trade within the country was encouraged by a good road network set up by the «Roads and Bridges» engineers and made possible by the statute labour owed to the monarchy (the people gave their labour from time to time for the «king's highway»). On the other hand, the Customs & Excise duties and tolls implemented within the country continued to restrict the circulation of goods since the merchandise then became more expensive. Economists began to demand free circulation of commercial goods, in the same way that they demanded freedom for industry in order to arrive, through competition, at a drop in prices and, therefore, increased consumerism. International trade enjoyed development because the products from the colonies (coffee, sugar and rum) were increasingly becoming a part of everyday life. This led to spectacular prosperity for the islands in the West Indies and the main harbours along France's Atlantic coast. Trade also included the transport of black slave labour from Africa to the Americas and the slave trade was one of the factors in French prosperity throughout the Age of Enlightenment.

Law's System

The Regent encouraged the experiment implemented by a Scotsman named Law. A royal bank issued paper money which could be converted into gold and silver at any time, and a commercial company offered shares which met with resounding success because people hoped for a huge return on their investment. The system was based on trust. When the first alarm sounded, in 1720, everybody wanted to rid themselves of their bank notes and shares and Law was forced to flee abroad. For a long time thereafter, France mistrusted bank notes. Shareholders were ruined while those who had sold in time had become rich. However, the State was able to pay, with paper money, the huge debts that Louis XIV had incurred in order to fund his wars. Law's system had provided for a quicker circulation of money and this whipped up the economy.

Louis XV

In 1723, Louis XV was declared to have attained the age of majority and the Regent died. The King's cousin, the Duke de Bourbon, was minister for a short time and he encouraged the monarch's marriage to Maria Leszczinska, the daughter of a King of Poland who had lost his throne. The King then asked his former tutor, the aged Cardinal Fleury, to hold the reins of government. The cardinal tried to maintain peace at any price and, when forced to agree to war, he tried to limit its scope. One of the main results of this policy was the handing over of Lorraine to Stanislaw, the King's father-in-law. After Stanislaw's death, it was to return to France. Stanislaw prepared for the gradual annexation to French territory which consequently acquired new coherence since the Duchy of Lorraine was an enclave within it. Louis XV was an intelligent but hesitant man who gave the impression of being only periodically interested in serious matters. Yet he was enthusiastic about military life and European affairs and had no hesitation in directing secret diplomacy himself.

Victories and Defeats

France was drawn into long wars. The War of Austrian Succession (1740-1748) had a happy outcome thanks to the fine victory at the Battle of Fontenoy, won by the Maréchal de Saxe. Louis XV was present at the battle but it more especially benefited France's ally, King Frederick II of Prussia. These conflicts also enabled the installation of two branches of the House of Bourbon in Italy, one in Parma and the other in Naples. In addition to tension within Europe, there was an on-going confrontation between France and England in the Indian sub-continent and in North America. In this respect, French diplomacy implemented a «revolution» by moving closer to Austria which, since the days of Charles V, had been a hereditary enemy. England and Prussia then became allies and were the victors of the Seven Years' War (1756-1763). Louis XV gave Canada to England and retained only the sugar-growing islands in the West Indies which were so important for French trade.

The Age of Enlightenment

The 18th century has been described as the Age of Enlightenment, when light was to triumph over darkness i.e. prejudice, traditions and fanaticism. A secret organisation, freemasonry, developed this opposition of light and shade. Masonic lodges brought together men who wished to reflect on major social, ethical and philosophical issues. Their solidarity was emphasised by ritual and this went some way towards smoothing out any social differences. For a long time, the provincial academies, of which there was an increasing number, served the same purpose. Finally, the literary salons, held especially in Paris, with Madame de Tencin, Madame Geoffrin, Madame du Deffand, Mademoiselle de Lespinasse or Madame Necker symbolised the alliance of fine minds and writers, in short the elite of society and culture.

The Encyclopaedia

The spread of knowledge and new ideas was undertaken through the written word which benefited from progress in the printing sector. The press also enjoyed rapid development. Although censorship still exercised control over all the books printed, forbidden works still circulated in France. A major editorial enterprise (1745-1772), the Encyclopaedia, drawn up under the leadership of Diderot, was to include every form of knowledge, in particular trade techniques, but many of the articles had a philosophical or controversial slant and the project was faced with countless difficulties, the first being its completion and the second the achievement of a quite remarkable distribution. Numerous «philosophers» wrote articles for this dictionary.

The Philosophers

This was the title given to writers and journalists who had no hesitation in criticising the most archaic traits of society, the monarchy and the Church. Their reflection led to the emergence of new principles such as the separation of power and political freedom in Montesquiou's work, tolerance and optimism from Voltaire, or the social contract and general determination in Rousseau's writings. The texts written by these philosophers made political discussions particularly lively in the country as a whole and led people to hope for audacious reforms.

Political Conflicts

Wars had again weakened royal finances. Machault, Controller General, created a new tax which was to be levied on all incomes, including those of the privileged orders. The clergy protested, the king effected a U-turn and the Church was not liable for the tax. The financial difficulties were aggravated by a political crisis. Opposition to government policy was being vigorously expressed, especially in the parlements which, during the Regency, had regained their right of remonstrance. They used it to great effect. The confrontations took on a religious dimension for the parliamentarians were magistrates sensitive to Jansenist concepts, loyal to Gallican ideas and hostile to the influence of Rome. They did not accept the condemnations that the monarchy had obtained in Rome with regard to Jansenist ideas. An atmosphere of religious fervour enveloped the controversy and the fires were further stoked by a clandestine paper called Nouvelles ecclésiatiques published from 1728 onwards.

Louis XV's reign was marked by a ministerial instability that reflected the uncertainties of the sovereign and the depth of the attacks on his ministers.

The Damiens Attack

The King's image was in decline. He had been described as the «Beloved» when he fell seriously ill at the beginning of his reign. Gradually, he became the target of criticism, especially regarding his private life for he had numerous mistresses and he let one of them, the Marquise de Pompadour, acquire a certain amount of influence. The quarrels relating to Jansenism made things worse and eventually Damiens, who had been a servant to parliamentarians, stabbed the King on 5th January 1757. The wound was not serious but Damiens was quartered for high treason. The attempted murder showed that part of public opinion had been aroused against Louis XV.

Choiseul

Military difficulties during the Seven Years' War did not improve the situation. The King ordered the Duke de Choiseul to end the conflict and prepare revenge by reorganising the army and weaponry. Choiseul was a great nobleman, an officer and a diplomat and he completed the task that had been set for him. He also «purchased» Corsica from the Republic of Genoa; the island was conquered with some difficulty. Choiseul was a man of war who placed little importance on the wheeling and dealing of the parlementarianss. They, however, scored a point when they obtained the suppression of the Company of Jesus which had close links with the papacy and was the target of Jansenist attacks (1762-1763). This measure disorganised secondary teaching where the Jesuits played a vital role. The King was tired of the attacks led by the parlements against the decisions taken by his council or against his representatives in the provinces. On 3rd March 1766, he reminded the Parlement, in the so-called «Flagellation Session», that as far as the French monarchy was concerned sovereign power lay with his person and his person alone and that «the rights and interests of the nation, which certain have dared to separate from the monarch, are necessarily one with our own and repose in our hands only». Knuckles were rapped but this was not sufficient.

The Maupeou Reform

At the end of 1770, Louis XV dismissed Choiseul who wanted to wage war on England in revenge while Louis XV was primarily concerned with solving the interior crisis. He decided to strike a resounding blow by changing the organisation of the justice system and he entrusted the energetic Chancellor Maupeou with this reform (23rd February 1771). The magistrates would no longer purchase their posts and would no longer receive spices (originally, a perquisite but later they became a mandatory tax). They would be appointed and paid by the monarch. They would therefore lose their independence and their role which they had worked hard to render political. The Parlement de Paris retained its right of remonstrance. The former parliamentarians would receive reimbursement for their posts and would be replaced by new magistrats. Father Terray, who was appointed Controller General, launched a reform of the tax system. Louis XV, however, who had supported the Maupeou reform, seeing it as a means of giving the monarchy strength and vitality, died in 1744.

Louis XVI

His grandson, Louis XVI, was a pious, upstanding young man. He let himself be convinced that the Maupeou reform was too brutal and he recalled the parlements as they had been before 1771. The Chancellor concluded, «I won, for the King, a trial that had been lasting for three centuries. If he wants to lose it again, it's up to him. He's the master». However, Louis XVI listened to Maurepas' advice and built up a brilliant government team which proposed a wide range of reforms.

Turgot's Reforms

Turgot belonged to the world of «Philosophers»; indeed, he was its main element. His programme was simple. «No bankruptcy, no increase in taxes, no borrowing, and savings....» This policy was designed to solve the financial difficulties. However, Turgot then went further and proposed a number of major changes. He was in favour of free trade and, in 1774, he established the free circulation of cereals in order to avoid shortages and speculation. The measure was deemed, on the contrary, to have caused supply problems in 1775 after a poor harvest and riots broke out. This was the «Flour War» and Turgot had to use force to re-establish law and order. He also removed the mandatory work demanded of peasants on royal roadways in 1776 and replaced it by a tax levied on all landowners which was to be paid to the Bridges and Highways department. He removed the «jurandes», now better-known as corporations (5th January 1776) and established the freedom of work. This upheaval, however, was regarded anxiously by master craftsmen who lost their monopolies and by the work force who lost collective protection. The measures were neither understood nor accepted; they aroused criticism from every sector. Louis XVI, the only person at court to have made financial cutbacks, could no longer support his minister and he dismissed him on 12th May 1776. Malesherbes also withdrew but before leaving public office he had time to prepare reforms that would render the prison regime less harsh and grant Protestants the right to figure in civil registers (this came into effect in 1787).

The War of American Independence

Affairs inside the country then took a back seat for France had an opportunity to take revenge on England. It was Vergennes, Minister of Foreign Affairs, who prepared for the conflict. The English colonies in America were rebelling against the home country and, in 1776, they declared their independence. France began by providing secret aid through the playwright, Beaumarchais. A number of high-minded noblemen such as La Fayette set off to fight for freedom on the other side of the Atlantic. Louis XVI was reticent as regards assistance for the rebels who were revolting against their legitimate sovereign. He allowed himself to be convinced, however, and, after a clear victory on the part of the Americans, a treaty of friendship and alliance was signed between the young United States and the King of France (6th February 1778). France supplied large amounts of aid. An expeditionary force was sent to America and fleets operated along the American seaboard and in the Indian Ocean. Washington was able to encircle the English in the Yorktown Peninsula and obtain their capitulation (19th October 1781). A peace treaty was signed on 3rd September 1783 putting an end to the war and recognising the independence of the United States.

The Approach of the Industrial Revolution

The 18th century was marked by intense technological research even though it did not bear fruit immediately and even though many of the innovations came from England. Machinery, for example, was to facilitate the production of fabrics. Ironworks which had, until then, been built in forests where they were fired with charcoal now used coke and the metalworking industry gradually moved into the coalfields. Machinery was expensive and required large amounts of capital, as well as a large, skilled work force. And in order to ensure that the product sold was not expensive, salaries had to be low. France was entering the industrial era. Unusual inventions were appearing. The steam engine was being perfected but Cugnot's steam-powered carriage, the ancestor of the automobile, was a failure. On the other hand, crowds flocked to see man conquer air travel when the Montgolfier brothers had the idea of building a canvas balloon covered with paper and blown up using hot air until it became lighter than the ambient air. In 1783, the first hot-air balloon rose to a height of 500 metres. The monarchy was also interested in exploration of the world. Louis XVI, an admirer of Captain Cook, wanted French explorers to be equally present in the Pacific and he personally prepared instructions for La Pérouse, a seafarer who disappeared during his great voyage of discovery.

The Financial Crisis

Necker, a banker from Geneva, had replaced Turgot as Controller General and, during the war, he had contracted loans. After publishing his budget in 1781 (the first time such an event took place), he was forced to resign because his figures were criticised. However, public opinion retained an image of a man capable of working miracles. The military engagement had simply increased the debts of a State which did not know where to turn to find the necessary resources. Any fiscal reform was rendered impossible by the hostility expressed by the parlements. They were supported by the nobility which refused fiscal equality and by the Third Estate which was against any new tax.

Calonne

In 1783, Calonne, who was leading the government, counted on economic prosperity to solve the monarchy's financial problems, rendered even more serious by the loans that had been contracted. An incipient economic crisis after 1785 dashed his hopes and discontent spread. Calonne then tried to propose a fiscal reform which would involve taxing all income from land, without exception, and imposing the tax by a meeting of an assembly of wealthy landowners. They, however, defended the privileges that were under threat from this «territorial grant». The assembly was dismissed but opposition then came from the Parlement de Paris which demanded a meeting of the States General.

Public opinion played an increasing role in public affairs and was only too happy to take, as its target, Queen Marie-Antoinette whose name was mentioned, quite wrongfully, in 1785 in connection with a fraud known as the «case of the queen's necklace».

A Meeting of the States General

Louis XVI handed the government over to the Archbishop of Toulouse, Loménie de Brienne, who launched a huge programme of reforms for the civil service, public finances, justice and army. The States General were to be convened later once the financial situation had been stabilised. The King announced it to the parlement on 19th November 1787. His cousin, the Duke d'Orléans, declared it to be illegal but Louis XVI recalled his royal prerogative, «It is legal because I wish it». Resistance spread. In Rennes, there was public disorder and, in Grenoble, the crowd threw roof tiles at soldiers when the government wanted to force the town's parliamentarians into exile. Loménie de Brienne was unable to cope and, on 8th August 1788, he announced that the States General had been convened. He then resigned, leaving Necker to take over.

THE REVOLUTION AND THE KING

The States General

Louis XVI and his ministers, unable to resolve the financial difficulties besetting the monarchy, decided in 1788 to convene the States General which had fallen into disuse since the last meeting was convened in 1614. The King decided on this meeting to facilitate the adoption of new taxes, those who enjoyed privileges hoped for a confirmation of their rights, liberal noblemen and enlightened middle classes saw this as an opportunity for reform and the peasants expected relief from the financial burdens to which they were subjected. The States carried with them so many hopes and, therefore, became the source of many a misunderstanding. They also enabled the Third Estate to become more aware of the situation, marvellously summed up in January 1789 by Father Sièyes in the following terms, «What is the Third Estate? Everything. What has it been until now in the political system? Nothing. What is it asking for? To become something.» Books of complaints were drafted, proclaiming the subjects' love for their King but demanding, at the same time, that everybody should be fiscally equal with no regard for «orders» and «privileges». Some of them demanded the freedom of the press, the abolition of lettres de cachet (orders from the King for internment without trial) and equal justice for all. Elections were held for each Estate. There was direct suffrage for the clergy (the lower orders, of landowning extraction, were predominant) and the nobility and indirect suffrage for the Third Estate. Electoral districts corresponded to bailiwicks. Representatives of the Third Estate were mainly middle-class i.e. landowners, lawyers and barristers, merchants, journalists etc. The sovereign had not reached a decision on voting rights. According to the regulation of 27th December 1788, there were twice as many representatives of the Third Estate as of each of the other two. If the system used per capita voting, the Third Estate would hold a majority; if it was a vote per Estate, the Third Estate would have only one vote and would be in the minority compared to the other two.

The Constituent Assembly

On 4th May 1789, the representatives were brought together in Versailles in the presence of the King but ceremonial highlighted the inequality between the Estates, in the order of procession and in clothing. This ancient custom was felt as a humiliation by the Third Estate. As the States were then left to their own devices, the representatives of the Third Estate met separately; they were joined by members of the lower orders of clergy and by a few liberal noblemen. On 17th June, further to a motion tabled by Sieyès, representing Paris, the representatives of the Third Estate declared themselves to be a National Assembly. They declared that they represented the nation and that only the nation could authorise the levying of a tax. This was the first revolutionary act. Since, on 20th June, the King ordered the closure of the chamber in which the Third Estate was meeting, they moved to different premises, a real tennis court, and swore that they would «never be separated and [would] meet wherever circumstances demanded until such time as the constitution of the kingdom be established». On 23rd June, in the chamber known as the Salle des Menus Plaisirs, the King declared that he was cancelling the decisions taken by the Third Estate and he asked the three Estates to sit separately. After his departure, and once the master of ceremonies, Dreux-Brézé, had requested, in the King's name, that the chamber be emptied, Mirabeau, a gentleman-adventurer and elected member of the Third Estate, is said to have replied, «Go and tell your master that we are here by the will of the people and that we shall leave only by the force of bayonets».

The Storming of the Bastille

Louis XVI pretended to give way and, on 27th June, he invited the clergy and nobility to join the Third Estate. On 9th July, the Assembly declared itself to be a National Constituent Assembly. In fact, the King had troops placed around Paris and he dismissed Necker who, as manager of the kingdom's finances, enjoyed great popularity. The Parisians who had been monitoring the events began to worry. Unrest spread and, in the Palais-Royal, speakers such as Camille Desmoulins aroused new energy. From 12th July onwards, riots occurred and the rioters began looking for weapons. On 14th July, after taking guns from the Invalides, they believed that they would find more in the Bastille, a fortress used as a detention centre for political prisoners. Shots were fired from the citadel. The rebels captured it, massacred the governor, De Launay, and murdered the Provost of the Merchants of Paris. Louis XVI, faced with the wrath of the Parisians, sent away the troops and recalled Necker. On 17th July, he went to the City Hall and accepted the three-coloured cockade – red and blue as the colours of Paris and white representing the monarchy. La Fayette, the hero of American

Independence, took command of the bourgeois militia which had become the national guard.

The Night of 4th August

The events in Paris, the rumours of conspiracies, and fear of brigands caused great anxiety in country districts; it was known as the period of «Great Fear». The peasants, who had taken up arms in order to prepare for all eventualities, attacked castles and archives to destroy the documents setting up feudal rights. This violence in rural areas convinced the National Assembly that it had to put an end to the remains of the feudal system. On the night of 4th August 1789, at the request of liberal-minded noblemen, the Assembly voted for the abolition of feudal and seigniorial rights, tithes and privileges. Later, it hesitated and declared simply that feudal rights could be bought back in return for harvests and farms. However, the basis of the old society disappeared i.e. judicial inequality between subjects. The new principles were explained in an admirable text that summarised all the ideals of the Age of Enlightenment, the Declaration of the Rights of Man and the Citizen (26th August 1789) which strongly recalled the «natural, inalienable and sacred rights of man» but also highlighted his duties. Article I proclaimed that «All men are born and remain free and equal before the Law; social distinctions can be founded only on common utility». Article II recalled that these rights were «liberty, property, security and resistance to oppression».

October Days

The Assembly was divided as to the position of the King. It granted him a suspensive veto for two years. Sieyès considered that this was «a lettre de cachet issued against the general will». Louis XVI then refused to sign the decrees that ratified the decisions taken during the month of August. Once more, popular anger came to the assistance of the Assembly. The Parisians were alarmed at the arrival of a regiment in Versailles and were indignant to learn that soldiers had trodden the three-coloured cockade underfoot in the presence of the Queen. A procession led by women reached Versailles on 5th October. La Fayette intervened to calm the crowd but, the next day, the royal family left the palace and was taken to Paris. The King settled in the Tuileries Palace.

Newspapers and Clubs

The Constituent Assembly completed a considerable amount of crucial work. Decisions were taken at a time when political debate was rife in Parisian salons, cafés, public places and «clubs» (like the Jacobins or Cordeliers clubs, so-called because they used premises in convents). The freedom of the press allowed for numerous new papers which compared and contrasted various political ideas. In the Assembly, too, disagreement was expressed between monarchists in favour of the royal veto and patriots who were hostile to the concept.

National Property

On 2nd November 1789, a major measure was taken against the Church whose property was placed «at the disposal of the nation» in order to reabsorb the deficit. The State was to provide «in appropriate fashion for the expenses of worship, the maintenance of its priests and the relief of the poor». In the short term, this compromised much of the work undertaken by the ecclesiastical world such as assistance for the sick or poor, and teaching. The nationalisation process placed «national property» on the market and it was purchased by the bourgeoisie. This also meant, in many cases, that buildings which had been masterpieces of mediaeval architecture were left to fall into ruin. The Constituent Assembly went even further by claiming that spiritual authority, like political control, depended on the country's citizens. This denied the Church its independence and subjected it to the will of the people. The bishops and priests would be elected by the same voters as political representatives. They would take an oath, swearing to be «loyal to the nation, the law and the king». This «civil constitution of the clergy» dating from 12th July 1790 was one of the essential breaking points in the Revolution for it removed from the spiritual domain if not its independence then at least a part of its pre-eminence. The obligation to swear an oath to the Civil Constitution, which was condemned by the Pope, divided the clergy. There were those who took the oath and those who refused («non-juring priests»). Around them there grew the first premises of opposition to the Revolution.

«Départements»

Wide-ranging administrative rationalisation was undertaken. When the departments (the equivalent of «counties») were set up, the new system removed the jumbled administrative network that had existed for centuries during the Ancien Régime. At the same time, economic life was cleared of its traditional restrictions such as interior customs & excise or tolls. The Allarde Decree (1791) removed the guild wardenships and masterships. In the name of freedom to work, workers were forbidden by the Le Chapelier Law (1791) to create «any gatherings of craftsmen, workers, journeymen or people roused to revolt by them against the free exercise of industry and work». Workers no longer had the right to defend their interests collectively, to strike or to form coalitions, which the corporations entitled them to do. Finally, the Assembly decided to issue bonds known as «assignats» which were guaranteed against national property; their use became mandatory. On 14th July 1790, the Assembly organised its first festival, the Fête de la Fédération, on the Champ de Mars in Paris. It created general reconciliation. After Mass, La Fayette took the oath, in the name of all the national guards set up in France, to be loyal to the nation, the law and the King and Louis XVI

114

swore in his turn to respect the constitution which would be decreed by the Assembly and accepted by him.

The King's Flight and the 1791 Constitution

In fact Louis XVI, troubled by the fate of the Church, felt himself a prisoner in the Tuileries Palace and, on the night of 20th June 1791, he fled towards Metz. He was arrested in Varennes and brought back to Paris under escort. The Assembly was embarrassed and it decided to forget the escape, claiming that the King had been kidnapped and ordering the dispersal of the Republican demonstrators on the Champ de Mars on 17th July. There were fifty deaths and the dramatic events showed the Constituent Assembly's determination to complete its project – it was aiming at a constitutional monarchy. The 1791 Constitution, the first in the history of France, provided for the election of a legislative assembly by landowning voters (who would require high incomes), themselves elected by so-called «active» citizens (who paid a contribution equal to at least three days of work). The Assembly voted in laws and public expenditure, controlled the ministers who were appointed by the King and left the King his suspensive veto. The new administrative system was to be highly decentralised. Active citizens would elect justices of the peace and mayors; voters would elect departmental judges (the parlements had disappeared in the political storms of 1790) and a jury consisting of active citizens would judge crimes.

The Legislative Assembly

The new Assembly, elected in September 1791, consisted of new men for the Constituents had decided that they could not be re-elected themselves. Political tendencies were coming to the fore with the Feuillants, Girondins and Jacobins. The financial crisis was marked by the rapid depreciation of the assignat. Economic crisis gripped the country and the social crisis led to peasants' revolts. The political crisis was reflected in the resistance of the non-juring priests and in the first operations planned by noblemen who had sought refuge abroad, some of them as early as July 1789. They were the «émigrés». For a long time, European sovereigns such as the King of Prussia, the Empress of Russia and the Emperor had been busy with a third division of Poland and they preferred to see France occupied with its internal problems. The Revolution and the ideas that it defended and wanted to spread began to worry them. International tension arose from the German princes, referred to as the «landowners of Alsace», who considered that they had suffered loss as a result of the end of feudal rights on their lands in Alsace.

War

The idea of a war began to gather momentum. The King and Assembly had, according to the Constitution, a joint right to take the decision. Louis XVI considered that an unfortunate conflict would enable him to regain his lost power; the Legislative Assembly believed that victories would reveal the traitors and provide a permanent basis for the Revolution. It would also provide an opportunity to spread the benefits of Revolution through all the countries in Europe where the people were still the victims of tyranny. The King chose Girondin ministers, who were popular with Madame Roland. On 20th April 1792, war was finally declared on the King of Bohemia and Hungary, i.e. the Emperor, Marie-Antoinette's nephew.

10th August 1792 and the End of the Monarchy

The campaign began with defeats for the armies were poorly organised and badly commanded. The people of Paris were both worried and vigilant. The government decided to arrest non-juring priests but Louis XVI opposed his veto. In order to oblige him to yield, the Parisians overran the Tuileries on 20th June. The King drank the good health of the nation but did not budge. On 11th July, the Assembly declared the country to be in danger and volunteers arrived in huge numbers. On this occasion, the men of Marseille sang the «Song of War for the Rhine Army» written by Rouget de l'Isle; it became La Marseillaise. The advance of enemy armies spread panic. The Duke of Brunswick, the commander-in-chief, wanted to protect the royal family from popular wrath and threatened, in a «manifesto», to let «total subversion» take hold of Paris and condemn the rebels to «torture» if any outrage was committed against the King, Queen or their family. This threat led to a further uprising on 10th August 1792. Parisians and volunteers attacked the Tuileries Palace which was being guarded by Swiss guards. Louis XVI sought refuge in the Legislative Assembly which, under pressure from the crowd, voted in favour of the arrest and demise of the King. It also decided to introduce elections, by universal suffrage, for the new assembly known as the Convention. Executive power was entrusted to a provisional council which was soon in the sway of Danton, a former barrister, who had founded the Club des Cordeliers.

September Massacres

A Commune had seized power in Paris and carried out large numbers of arrests among non-juring priests, aristocrats, former ministers etc. They had been thrown into improvised prisons, often convents. The announcement of the Fall of Verdun, which opened the way to Paris, led to the massacre of the prisoners from 2nd to 6th September 1792. Trials which were no more than mere mockeries took place in the prisons and ended with the death sentence or release. The authorities left well alone. More than one thousand people died as a result. These deaths aroused fright and fear.

THE FIRST REPUBLIC

On the day on which the Legislative Assembly members went their separate ways, on 20th September 1792, the French army won a victory beside the mill at Valmy. By winning this modest victory against the Prussians, Generals Dumouriez and Kellermann showed the scope of French determination and they saved both Paris and the Revolution. On 21st September 1792, France was proclaimed a Republic and symbolically, to mark this new era of liberty, all public deeds would henceforth be dated Year I. The initiative now lay with the French forces who, after the victorious outcome to the Battle of Jemmapes (6th November 1792), were able to go on and conquer Belgium.

The King on Trial

The Convention, which had proclaimed France a Republic, had been elected by universal suffrage but only one-tenth of voters actually cast a vote. The Girondins held a majority in the assembly and were classified as right-wing. Opposing them were the Montagnards, who were further to the left. They included Danton and Philippe d'Orléans, Louis XVI's cousin. Between the two groups were the centrists, forming «la Plaine».

The first major affair was the trial of Louis XVI. His defenders, including Malesherbes, pleaded that the monarchy was inviolable, this having been included in the 1791 Constitution. They also denied the agreements established between the King and foreign sovereigns but certain documents seemed to suggest the opposite. Robespierre, a lawyer from Arras who was elected to the States General and re-elected to the Convention by Paris, summarised his position as follows, «You have not to pass sentence for or against a man; you have to take a measure to ensure public salvation». The members of the Convention voted in favour of the death penalty by a small majority (387 in favour, 334 against). Louis XVI was guillotined on 21st January 1793 (on the former Place Louis XV renamed Place de la Révolution and, in 1795, Place de la Concorde). The guillotine had been designed by Dr. Guillotin and may have been improved by the King himself in order to shorten the suffering of those who died in this way. After the execution of the monarch, there was no turning back for the members of the Convention, who were regicides.

The use of capital punishment broke with a monarchic tradition that had been in existence since the very earliest days of France and it constituted a challenge for European princes who formed a coalition.

A Country in Danger

The coalition represented a danger for the country. The decision to raise 300,000 men caused resistance which, in Vendée in the west of the country, led to a veritable civil war. On 11th March 1793, Vendean rebels took Machecoul and massacres occurred. In their next moves, they captured Cholet then Saumur. Dumouriez, defeated at Neerwinden (March 1793) passed over to the enemy. The Montagnards then had the Convention adopt a number of emergency measures (April 1793) including shorter delays before suspects were brought to Court, confiscation of émigrés' property, sums of money forcibly borrowed from the wealthy, and the sending out of representatives on missions in various departments. A Committee of Public Safety was set up to apply Assembly decisions immediately and pitilessly. The Girondins were worried by the attacks on individual liberties and private property. They tried to resist. Marat, a journalist, was arrested but acquitted triumphantly. The man in the street chose between the factions in the Convention. The Parisian «sans-culottes» who monitored its actions were craftsmen or small shopkeepers from the suburbs. They detested the «silk breeches» worn by the nobility and demanded equality for all citizens. On 2nd June, the Convention bowed to their pressure and voted in favour of the arrest of the Girondins. The Montagnards seized power.

The Committee of Public Safety

Called by the Girondins, entire towns and regions revolted against the Parisian dictatorship. Toulon and Corsica called on the English for assistance. To the west of the country the «Whites» had taken control of the countryside and towns in various departments (Vendée, Loire-Inférieure, Maine-et-Loire, Deux-Sèvres) where aristocrats and non-juring priests added fuel to the fire in the fight against the Revolution. In July 1793, Marat was assassinated by a young royalist, Charlotte Corday, in his bath where he was treating a skin infection. The Committee of Public Safety, with Robespierre and Saint-Just, was ordered by the Convention to govern a country threatened from inside and out. The arm used by the Committee was Terror. Surveillance committees affiliated to the Club des Jacobins issued «citizenship certificates» or designated the «suspects» who were brought before revolutionary tribunals. In all 20,000 death sentences were passed. Marie-Antoinette, the Girondins and many others were sent to the guillotine. In order to win popular support, the revolutionary government proclaimed the abolition of feudal rights without any indemnity (17th July 1793), the imposition of maximum prices as demanded by the sans-culottes (1st October 1793), the abolition of slavery (4th February 1794), the distribution of suspects' property to the poor and the right to an education, work and assistance. To replace the spiritual influence of the Church, Robespierre wanted to develop a civic ethic, create a revolutionary calendar (October 1793) that would lead people to forget Christian feast days, institute the celebration of martyrs of the Revolution, and finally create the worship of the Supreme Being.

In particular, this dictatorship meant mass mobilisation in August 1793, resulting in an army of 800,000 men. Young generals such as Jourdan and Hoche achieved great feats and by autumn 1793 the borders of France had been cleared of foreign troops.

The Vendean Uprising

The Republican Army (the «Blues») marched through Western France from autumn 1793 onwards. The Whites were defeated in Cholet (17th October 1793). After the victory at Savenay (23rd December 1793), the Republican General Westermann wrote, «Vendée no longer exists. It died beneath the sabres we pulled from their scabbards… I crushed children beneath the hooves of horses and massacred women…» Turreau's «infernal columns» marched this way and that across Vendée from January 1794, implementing a scorched earth policy. In Nantes, the duty representative Carrier had almost 3,000 prisoners drowned in the Loire. In all, the Vendean Uprising produced some 400,000 victims - 180,000 Whites and 220,000 Blues.

9th Thermidor

Elsewhere in France, the towns were recaptured and a young Corsican named Napoleon Bonaparte took Toulon back from the English. As a result he was appointed to the rank of brigadier. These successes had not put an end to political constraint. Robespierre, with the backing of Danton, had managed to overcome the Enragés then he turned against Danton and the Indulgents, all of whom were sent to the guillotine. A new Law on Suspects (22nd Prairial, Year II / 10th June 1794) instigated the Reign of Terror. However, on 26th June, Jourdan won a decisive victory at Fleurus and opened the way for the reconquest of Belgium. Robespierre's dictatorship became unbearable. On 27th/28th July 1794 (9th Thermidor Year II), representatives who feared for their lives and the representatives with the «Plaine» succeeded in eliminating Robespierre and his friends who were immediately sent to the guillotine.

Reaction

This marked the beginning of a period of relief after years of dictatorship. The prisons were emptied of their inmates and the émigrés were gradually able to return to France. «Merveilleuses» and «Incroyables» drew attention to themselves by their extravagances, a means of forgetting fear. The Jacobins were pursued, in their turn, and in the south-east of the country royalists implemented a veritable reign of royalist terror. Military successes continued – Belgium was occupied and, later, annexed, and Holland was turned into the Batavian Republic. These military successes made it possible to sign peace treaties (Basel, April and July 1795). England and Austria remained at war. The Vendeans laid down their arms under the terms of agreements signed in La Jaunaye (17th February 1795) and the return of freedom to worship appeased religious conflict, although guerrilla warfare continued in the west of France until the country became an empire. Major work was undertaken in the educational sector. There were central schools to replace secondary schools (one per département) and a number of leading colleges were set up, including the Ecole normale supérieure (30th October 1794), Ecole centrale des travaux publics (later renamed Ecole polytechnique, 28th September 1794).

13th Vendémiaire

The question facing those who had supported 9th Thermidor was the future of the Régime. How could the Revolution be stabilised? How could they save fundamental rights already acquired and protect those involved without encouraging a return to the monarchy? A new constitution was drafted, preceded by a declaration of rights and duties. It provided for two assemblies – the Council of the Five Hundred and the Council of Elders, elected by landowning voters. «We must be governed by the best; they are the most educated and have the greatest interest in maintaining laws», declared Boissy d'Anglas. The two councils designated a Directoire which had five members. When the royalists wanted to instigate an uprising on 5th October 1795 (13th Vendémiaire, Year IV), Barras, member of the Convention asked the young General Bonaprte (who had been connected with Robespierre and his faction) to help him put down the riot. Bonaparte had cannons brought in to protect the Convention and became one of the saviours of the Republic. He married Joséphine de Beauharnais and soon received the command of an army that was to be sent to Italy. On 26th October 1795, the Convention broke up after voting in a general amnesty.

The Directoire

The Directoire was dominated by Barras who came from an aristocratic family in Provence. He had twice saved the Convention, in Thermidor and Vendémiaire.

The financial situation was catastrophic; the assignat had lost much of its value and was abandoned in February 1796. Eventually, on 30th September 1797, the State went bankrupt. As the war had restarted, the regime became increasingly dependent on its generals who conquered new areas and sent back to Paris the booty that they then acquired. Bonaparte won several outstanding victories in Northern Italy, using daring innovative tactics. He administered his conquest with authority and talent, replenished the State's coffers and signed a peace treaty with Austria in October 1797. A Cisalpine Republic was set up around Lombardy.

The financial difficulties also led to an ethical and social crisis for quick fortunes were being made thanks to the black market, illegal dealings and speculation. It was then that the Equals' Conspiracy broke out. François (alias Gracchus) Babeuf proposed an egalitarian, communist society, «No more private property. The Earth belongs to no-one; its fruits are the property of all». The conspirators were denounced and arrested in May 1796, taken to Court and executed and this would have been no more than a passing event if the programme had not frightened property owners and if it had not been seen as a foretaste of the collectivist systems of the future.

Coups d'Etat

The Directoire was engaged in an on-going struggle to combat twofold opposition from royalists and Jacobins. As the elections were favourable to the royalists and General Pichegru supported their cause, three directors, supported by Bonaparte who was in Italy at that time, unhesitatingly implemented illegal action on 4th September 1797 (18th Fructidor, Year V) by denouncing the elections and deporting the political representatives and two other directors. Then, on 11th May 1798 (22nd Floréal), action had to be taken on the left wing and the Jacobin representatives were removed. Bonaparte was becoming too cumbersome as a result of his successes in Italy. The directors therefore decided to send him away and they suggested a campaign to conquer Egypt, thereby cutting England's trade route with the East Indies. By failing to uphold the constitution and the elections, the Directoire brought discredit on itself.

THE CONSULATE AND EMPIRE

By 1799, the French were tired of ten years of political uncertainty and general disorganisation within the country. They no longer trusted the Directoire, which had become very unpopular.

External affairs had weighed heavily on the life of the nation since Belgium and the left bank of the Rhine had been annexed by France and there was a need to defend sister republics (in Holland, Switzerland and much of Italy). The army was therefore important in France, especially as it had intervened on several occasions to re-establish law and order and support the government.

The Coup d'Etat of 18th Brumaire

Bonaparte, basking in the glory of his victories and his Egyptian adventure, was seen as a solution. After his return to France, he joined Sieyès, who had become a Director, in preparing a coup d'état. On 18th Brumaire, Year VIII (3rd November 1799), a false conspiracy was announced. The assemblies were transferred to Saint-Cloud, Bonaparte was placed in command of the armed forces in Paris and the Directors were neutralised. On the following day, Bonaparte went before the members of parliament who gave him a hostile reception and wanted him outlawed. Lucien Bonaparte, however, who was chairing the Assembly of the Five Hundred, reacted quickly. He declared to the troops that a plot was threatening the Republic and General Bonaparte. The grenadiers entered the meeting room and forced the parliamentarians to leave. The coup d'état had succeeded.

Bonaparte removed Sieyès, became First Consul and selected two other consuls. One, Cambacérès, was a regicide; the other, Lebrun, a royalist. This marked the birth of a new regime, the Consulate, based on a system prevalent in Antiquity, and Bonaparte showed, from the outset, his determination to reconcile the old and the revolutionary France.

The First Consul

Bonaparte imposed a constitution (the so called « Year VIII Constitution») which gave him all powers. He appointed ministers and drafted laws which the Council of State was then required to prepare and draft. There were three assemblies – the Tribunat discussed the drafts of law but had no voting rights, the legislative body voted on laws but could not debate them, and the Senate monitored compliance with the constitution. Universal suffrage was skilfully re-established but was used only for referenda in which the voters answered by «Yes» or «No». The members of the Tribunat and legislative body were selected by the Senate from a list of leading names and the members of the assemblies were, for the most part, men who had gained fame during the Revolution. This ensured political continuity. Bonaparte had to redress the military situation, which had become difficult. To do so, he launched the second Italian Campaign (Marengo, 14th June 1800) while General Moreau won decisive victories in Germany (Hohenlinden, 3rd December 1800). The regime depended on success beyond its borders. An attempt on Bonaparte's life in Rue Saint-Nicaise in Paris, on 24th December 1800, showed that the regime was dependent on Bonaparte's continuing existence.

England was alone in continuing the struggle against France because it refused to accept the annexation of Belgium, a permanent threat for London. However, it agreed to the Treaty of Amiens (27th March 1802) and the general peace after ten years of warfare was welcomed enthusiastically, especially among the working classes. It was to last for only one year.

The 1801 Concordat

The First Consul did his utmost to reconcile all the people of France. A new Concordat was negotiated with Rome and signed on 15th July 1801, laying down the framework for relations between the French State and the papacy. The bishops were appointed by the First Consul and received canon appointments from the Pope. This was a return to the balance of the Ancien Régime. However, all the clergy were paid by the government to which they swore an oath of allegiance. Bonaparte found strong support among the clergy and the French people were satisfied with the reorganisation of the Church. Negotiations with the royalist rebels and the return of the émigrés were offset by the granting of jobs and honours to former revolutionaries.

Administrative and Monetary Reorganisation

The search for national agreement required a major shake-up of the country's administration in order to complete the work begun during the Revolution. Although the administrative divisions drawn up since 1789 (departments, arrondissements, towns or villages) were retained, they were headed by men who were no longer elected but, rather, appointed by the government which could also dismiss them at will. These were the Prefects, sub-Prefects and mayors. Judges were also appointed by the government but they were declared immovable, and this guaranteed their independence. Twenty-nine Appeal Courts were created, as was a supreme court of appeal, the Tribunal de Cassation.

There was also fiscal and monetary reorganisation. A private bank, the Banque de France, was granted the right to issue bank notes (February 1800). Currency was stabilised. The franc corresponded to 5 grams of silver (17th Germinal, Year XI; 7th April 1803). The «Germinal» franc kept its value until 1914, which shows how successful, and necessary, the stabilisation was.

Set in Granite – Legion of Honour, High Schools, Civil Code

Bonaparte also invented a distinction, the Legion of Honour. Originally, it was to bring together the social elites, possibly creating a nobility with ties to the First Consul. It was merely a token of honour, a Cross, which Bonaparte liked to pin personally on the chests of brave soldiers or talented civilians. The Directoire had tried to rebuild secondary education through central schools; they were replaced by high schools (lycées) in which discipline was military in nature. The pupils wore uniforms and gathered to the sound of a drumbeat.

French law, which had been thrown into disarray by the Revolution, found new expression through the Civil Code published in March 1804. The rules on liberties, property, inter-personal and intra-family relations were written down and applicable throughout France, unlike the customs of the Ancien Régime. Clear principles were laid down, «.. Good fathers, good husbands and good sons make for good citizens». The results of the Revolution were acknowledged e.g. the equality of all in law or the right of each individual to access any employment depending on his or her skill. The Code also insisted, under Bonaparte's influence, on the father's authority within the family. «The husband shall protect his wife and the wife shall obey her husband». It emphasised the intangible nature of property, «Property is the right to enjoy and dispose of things in the most absolute manner…» To facilitate the control of the world of craftsmen and tradesmen, the 18th-century concept of a «worker's logbook» (carnet ouvrier) was re-established. Employers were required to enter all periods of worker employment in the log.

The Execution of the duke d'Enghien

Peace abroad; peace at home! In August 1802, Bonaparte asked the French people to decide on the following question, «Shall Napoleon Bonaparte be a Consul for life?» The response was unambiguous – 36 million in favour; 8,734 against. Peace, though, was merely an illusion. Conflict began again with England which could not accept French predominance on the continent. The royalists began to show signs of restlessness within the country and one of them, Cadoudal, came to Paris to assassinate Bonaparte but was arrested before he could do so. The First Consul then took a serious decision. He used the plot as an excuse to order the arrest of the Duke d'Enghien, a Bourbon who was close to the border but still outside France. After a mockery of a trial, the prince was executed by firing squad (21st March 1804). This marked the final break with royal blood and Bonaparte showed that he did not want the return of the Bourbons. He reassured all those who had benefited from the Revolution (politicians or owners of national property) and who did not want a return to the Ancien Régime.

Napoleon I

However, the regime required a stable foundation and an assurance of law and order. A new monarchy seemed to be the best solution. In May 1804, Napoleon Bonaparte was proclaimed Emperor by the Senate under the name, Napoleon I. On 2nd December 1804, he was crowned. The Pope had agreed to attend the ceremony but it was the Emperor himself who placed the crown on his own head before crowning his wife, Joséphine. Napoleon's power was initially military, based on a strong army which he had inherited from the Revolution. The Empire also needed victories over the European coalitions and this was to drag France into a never-ending spiral of war.

From Boulogne to Austerlitz

After the Treaty of Amiens, Napoleon considered landing in England and he took another look at the many projects which had been drawn up since the end of the 17th century. A fleet was prepared in Boulogne, ready to cross the Channel. However Admiral Villeneuve was unable to hold off the British fleet under the command of Admiral Nelson for any length of time and this posed a threat for any operation. The conquest of England was not feasible. As England brought Austria and Russia in its wake (this was the Third Coalition), Napoleon acted very quickly, built up his Grand Army in Boulogne and used forced marches to take it to Germany. The town of Ulm capitulated (20th October 1805). On the following day, Villeneuve left Cadiz where he had sought refuge and engaged Nelson near Cape Trafalgar. It was a terrible defeat which left England total control of the sea, although Nelson was killed during the battle. Napoleon continued to advance towards Austria, entering Vienna and confronting the Russian and Austrian armies near Austerlitz on 2nd December 1805. This victory was a strategic masterpiece and it forced Austria to make peace. It was then Prussia's turn to enter the war (Fourth Coalition). The victories in Jena and Auerstadt (14th October 1806) enabled the French to enter Berlin then, after the difficult Battle of Eylau against the Russians (8th February 1807) and the Battle of Friedland (18th June), the Czar agreed to negotiate. Napoleon and Alexander of Russia met in Tilsit, on a raft in the middle of the Niemen, in July 1807.

The Continental Blockade

In order to force England to its knees, Napoleon decided to institute a continental blockade which would prohibit all imports of English goods. By ruining English trade and industry, it might be possible to force London to sign a sustainable peace. The alliance with the Czar of Russia seemed to suggest this would be a possibility. However, the blockade required coastal surveillance and a fight against smuggling, and it led to new conquests, in Spain and in the Papal States. Napoleon felt himself carried along by his talents as a strategist and by his armies and he wanted to dominate the continent. However, English hostility never faltered. The country prepared and funded coalitions against France whose geographical expansion it refused to accept, especially in Belgium, and whose economic competition was also seen as unacceptable. The European monarchies remained opposed to anything reminiscent of the Revolution and Napoleon was heir to this period. Finally, in most defeated countries, national reactions came to the fore as people prepared to take revenge. Philosopher Fichte addressed the Germans in the following terms, «If you take up your courage again, you will see around you a race which will provide the most glorious of memories for Germans».

The Spanish Affair

Despite the docility of the Spanish sovereign, Napoleon forced him to abdicate in Bayonne in 1808 and set his own brother, Joseph, on the throne. The Spanish people remained loyal to their former monarch and Madrid rebelled on 2nd May 1808. On 3rd May, there were terrible reprisals. The Spaniards' resistance led to the capitulation of General Dupont in Baylen. For the first time, one of Napoleon's armies had been shown not to be invincible. The English took advantage of this new front to land troops in Portugal under the command of Wellesley, the future Lord Wellington. In order to continue his offensive, Napoleon was forced to leave a large army in Spain. Meanwhile, to improve the continental blockade, and counting on the weakness of the Pope, Napoleon invaded the Papal States. The Pope excommunicated him but was then arrested and deported. This conflict led many Roman Catholics to turn their backs on the imperial regime.

Marriage with Marie-Louise

Napoleon's difficulties encouraged Austria to take up arms again in 1809 (the Fifth Coalition). The Battle of Wagram (6th July 1809) enabled Napoleon to force the Emperor of Austria into submission and, in 1810, Napoleon married the Emperor's daughter, Marie-Louise, having repudiated Joséphine. The King of Rome was born in March 1811 and the future of the Napoleonic dynasty seemed assured. Napoleon had given Europe a new face. The kingdom of Holland had been entrusted to his brother, Louis, as Spain had to Joseph. The kingdom of Westphalia was created and attributed to another brother, Jérôme. Napoleon occupied the kingdom of Italy, with Milan and Venice, and his stepson, Eugène de Beauharnais, was its viceroy. In

Naples, Joseph had been replaced by Joachim Murat, the husband of Caroline Bonaparte. Another sister, Elisa, was Queen of Etruria. Poland enjoyed a revival, having been turned into a Grand Duchy. The Holy Roman Empire had been replaced by the Confederation of the Rhine. The Austrian sovereign had waived the elective title of Emperor and had taken on the now hereditary title of Emperor of Austria.

Despotism

The never-ending war brought changes to the imperial regime which became increasingly despotic. Napoleon governed by senatus-consult or by decree. Civil liberties were restricted and the press put under surveillance. Censorship was reintroduced and even the theatre was monitored. Under Fouché, a former college teacher and supporter of the Convention, the police played an increasingly important role and arbitrary detention reappeared. The government wanted to direct minds by keeping close control on education and by controlling writers deemed to be too independent. In 1806, the imperial catechism was introduced for «the defence of the country and the throne».

Meanwhile, the imperial administration worked to introduce new crops (sugar beet and potatoes), facilitate industrial innovations (e.g. the use of the Jacquard loom for Lyon's silk industry) and improve networks of communication. Despite the blockade and short-lived crises, and thanks to France's military domination and the opportunities that this provided, the Empire was a period of economic growth.

Napoleon was tempted to give the Empire the trappings of a monarchy like any other, by creating imperial nobility, setting up his own court (where etiquette was rigid and everybody was bored) and instituting high-ranking positions such as imperial field marshal, Arch Chancellor, Grand Chamberlain etc. The Emperor also drew support from «dignitaries», all those who had risen to a certain social rank thanks to the Revolution or thanks to their commercial or financial talents.

The Napoleonic Army

The army had a place of its own within a system in which war was all-important. National service was mandatory for all Frenchmen between the ages of 20 and 25 but recruitment was effected by the drawing of lots and men with enough money to pay for a replacement could be exempted. The veterans were responsible for training new recruits, thereby combining experience and young talent. Promotion was always based on valour in combat. Over time, needs changed these basic rules. Dependent countries were required to supply military contingents which did not remain constantly loyal. As supplies did not always arrive when needed, the soldiers lived off the countries they conquered, committing pillage. Yet a military career remained an enviable possibility and field marshals built up huge fortunes. All the soldiers worshipped the Emperor whose familiar form, grey frock coat and bonhomie aroused great enthusiasm.

The Retreat from Russia

Since the Czar of Russia remained his rival on the continent, Napoleon decided to invade Russia in 1812. The army of twenty nations was badly commanded and the Russians waged a national war against it, implementing a scorched earth policy. Napoleon directed his troops towards Moscow and entered the town but it was ravaged by a gigantic fire. The Czar did not seek peace and, with winter imminent, the decision had to be taken to retreat. It was to be dramatic for there was a lack of food and clothing. The crossing of the River Beresina in November was the most dramatic episode of all. Of the 600,000 men who had entered Russia, only 100,000 returned to Germany. It was a total disaster.

German Campaign, French Campaign

The sovereigns, although under Napoleonic domination, began to regain their confidence. The German Campaign in 1813 was marked by the Emperor's defeat in Leipzig by the coalition forces. Napoleon pulled out of Germany, Spain and Italy. This was the end of the Grand Empire. The allied armies entered France. Napoleon then recovered his talents as a strategist and moved his armies of young recruits quickly, winning a number of fine victories – against the Prussian Blücher in Champaubert and Montmirail and against the Austrian Schwarzenberg in Montereau. The allied generals decided to avoid doing battle and, instead, to advance on Paris which capitulated. The Emperor, in Fontainebleau, wanted to continue the fight but he was faced with the refusal of his field marshals and he abdicated on 6th April 1814. The allied powers left him his title of Emperor and the sovereignty of the tiny island of Elba. As a result of the first Treaty of Paris, France lost near all the lands that it had conquered.

The First Restoration and the Hundred Days

Talleyrand, who had long directed Napoleon's diplomacy and had had no hesitation in betraying him, persuaded the allied sovereigns to call upon Louis XVI's brother, who had become the heir to the House of Bourbon after the death, in 1795, of his young nephew in the Temple prison. He mounted the throne under the name Louis XVIII but the new King knew nothing about the new France. He granted his kingdom a liberal charter and accepted the social advantages resulting from the Revolution. However, he replaced the three-coloured flag by a white standard, dismissed the army veterans and left the royalists to strike fear into the hearts of the holders of national property. Napoleon, who was bored on his island, watched as discontent with the Bourbons grew. He decided to land in France in March 1815. All along the way, he was given an enthusiastic welcome and the regiments sent to stop him rallied to his cause. The Allies, who were negotiating in Vienna and redefining the map of Europe, went back to war. On 18th June 1815, Napoleon was defeated at Waterloo by Blücher and Wellington. This was the end of the Hundred Days. Napoleon asked England for asylum and was deported to the island of St. Helena, off the coast of Africa, where he died in 1821. The Napoleonic legend was born when, in 1823, Las Casas published his Mémorial de Sainte-Hélène, a text inspired by Napoleon who created in it the image that he wanted to leave to posterity.

THE RESTORATION AND THE JULY MONARCHY

After the Emperor's defeat, the European monarchs worked to rebuild a Europe that had been totally changed by the French Revolution and the Empire.

The Congress of Vienna

Metternich, Chancellor of Austria, wanted to re-establish the balance of powers that existed on the continent before 1789 and institute collective security in order to maintain peace and suppress all revolutions. The victors met at the Congress of Vienna where Louis XVIII was represented by Talleyrand. He defended the idea that France had, in spite of everything, remained a royalist nation and he took advantage of the divisions between the allies who wanted to remove any notions of revolution and conquest still prevalent in France. The country was occupied by more than one million soldiers from all over Europe who committed rape and pillage. On 20th November 1815, after Waterloo, the second Treaty of Paris redrew the borders of France, returning to the 1790 situation. The conquests (Belgium and the left bank of the Rhine) were lost but France lost none of its own territory even if the succession of wars had left it particularly weak. The country lost the border fortresses it had retained in 1814 and the coalition countries were granted high levels of indemnity.

Facts and Figures

Losses in terms of human lives had been high, approximately 1.4 million deaths during the Revolutionary and imperial wars. Rural life had been radically changed by the ending of seigniorial and feudal rights and by the sale of national property, which led to the development of smallholdings and small estates. The wars and the Continental Blockade had upset international trade relations whereas the 18th century had based its prosperity on long-distance trade. Industrialisation had progressed but France entered the industrial era with the impression that it was far behind England and suffering from economic inferiority. The French people remained strongly divided after the dramatic political events. Those who had once held privileges were in favour of the return of the monarchy and Western France and the Rhône Valley remained royalist. In 1815, only a few working-class groups regretted the disappearance of the Emperor.

The Charter

After the errors of 1814, Louis XVIII adopted a more skilful attitude by upholding the concept of an uninterrupted, absolute monarchy with all the forms of the Ancien Régime (e.g. the court) and the white flag while, at the same time, guaranteeing the liberties acquired during the Revolution. He did not accept the imposition of a constitution. Instead, he granted his people a «charter», finding the tradition in a rather mythical account of the history of France. The King held executive power and shared legislative power with two assemblies – a chamber of peers appointed by the monarch, who skilfully combined lords and dignitaries from pre-revolutionary France with members of the new elite, and a chamber of deputies elected by a land-based suffrage – only the richest landowners, some 90,000 in all, were entitled to vote. The Chambers did not control the government.

The Lost Chamber

In 1815 and 1816, reprisals against former Jacobins became increasingly commonplace. Sometimes, they were spontaneous; sometimes they were legally organised. They included massacres in the South of France, the removal from office of certain civil servants, imprisonment and deportation. The regicides, including Cambacérès, Fouché or the artist David, were forced into exile. This was the White Reign of Terror, encouraged by the election of a «lost chamber» to use the words of the King himself, a chamber consisting of hard-line royalists who had a passionate hatred for the Revolution. Maréchal Ney, who had promised to bring Napoleon back as a prisoner after his return from Elba and who had rallied to the Emperor's cause, was sentenced to death by the Chamber of Peers and executed by firing squad. Louis XVIII, frightened by such excesses, dissolved the unmanageable Chamber on the advice of Richelieu who was directing the government and Decazes who had won the sovereign's confidence.

The Murder of the Duke de Berry

A more liberal Chamber paved the way for a moderate policy of reforms which, in particular, gave a degree of freedom to the press. Decazes wanted «to «nationalise» the King and «royalise» the nation». In 1820, the assassination of the Duke de Berry, the King's nephew, by a worker named Louvel was interpreted by the Ultras as a consequence of this liberal attitude. Decazes was dismissed. The Duke de Berry had a posthumous son who later became the Bourbon heir in this elder branch of the dynasty.

The influence of the Ultras and a secret royalist society, the Knights of the Faith, could then be felt in a law which suspended individual liberties.

Anybody suspected of conspiracy could be held in detention for three months without the intervention of a judge. The freedom of the press was curtailed in 1822. The opposition sought refuge in secret organisations such as the Charbonnerie, which originated in Italy and which fomented uprisings or instigated plots that were quickly repressed. The 1824 elections were a landslide for the Ultras.

France was reintegrated into the monarchies. European governments even asked the French army to re-establish the absolute monarchy in Spain where the sovereign's powers were limited by the liberals.

Charles X and the Ultras

When Louis XVIII died in 1824, his brother, Louis XVI's last surviving brother, acceded to the throne under the title Charles X. He decided to have himself crowned in Reims to establish, rather anachronistically, a link with ancient rites. During his reign, the Ultras held full sway. In 1825, the government voted in a law which provided indemnities for former émigrés whose property had been confiscated during the Revolution (the «billion for émigrés» law). The Church regained its position within the State through its hold on education. The law of sacrilege imposed capital punishment on anybody who stole a liturgical artefact. Villèle, under whose direction the government took these measures, seemed to be re-establishing the Ancien Régime and discontent spread. After requesting the dissolution of the Chamber and noting the mediocre results, he was forced to resign.

The Four Ordinances

Martignac then attempted to introduce liberal policies but Charles X preferred violent, authoritarian methods. In August 1829, he appointed Prince Jules de Polignac to head his government, a man who symbolised the Ancien Régime and the court at Versailles. The King hoped that the expedition against Algiers would give the regime back some of its prestige – in fact, it took almost twenty years to conquer Algeria. As the 1830 elections were a failure for him, the King decided to use force and four ordinances were published on 26th July 1830 – the freedom of the press was suspended and censorship re-established, the new Chamber was dissolved, the electoral law was modified and elections were scheduled for September.

The Three Glorious Days

Led by Thiers of the National, a new paper sponsored by Talleyrand, journalists protested and decided that the newspapers would be published on the following day. The Prefect of Police had the printing presses destroyed and a riot broke out on 27th July. On the 28th, the three-coloured flag was flown from City Hall. Marmont's small detachment was unable to restore order. On the 29th, barricades were built and the capital was in the rioters' hands. The government withdrew to Saint-Cloud. These three days have been referred to as the «Three Glorious

Days». In Paris, liberal deputies, led by banker Lafitte, gave command of the National Guard to La Fayette. They were also in favour of an «Orleanist» solution.

The July Monarchy

The idea was to set up a monarchy that would be really constitutional, like the one in England, a monarchy that respected essential liberties and lent an ear to the new elite. One prince seemed an ideal candidate for the throne – Charles X's cousin, Louis-Philippe d'Orléans who was born in 1773. He was the son of Philippe-Egalité who had voted in favour of the death of Louis XVI and he had fought in the revolutionary armies before emigrating. The father of eight children, he had simple tastes, was unsophisticated in appearance and lifestyle and was well-known for his liberal ideas. He accepted the throne and went to City Hall were La Fayette reluctantly agreed to the solution. Charles X abdicated on 2nd August and slowly went into exile. Louis-Philippe agreed to be King of the French People and not King of France. He unreservedly recognised the Charter. He adopted the three-coloured flag and granted voting rights to a larger number of voters but the assemblies still did not control the government. Louis-Philippe was to embody the «bourgeois monarch», with an open-minded attitude to economic progress.

A Period of Riots

The beginning of the reign was difficult, with endemic uprisings in Paris and social riots. In Lyon in November 1831, silk workers took over the town which Maréchal Soult had to take back by force. The regime obtained greater stability with Casimir Périer in 1832 and immediately became conservative in outlook. The King embodied continuity and order; the government, with the backing of a majority in the Chamber, exercised power. However, the new system was faced with twofold opposition. The legitimists were in favour of the elder branch of the House of Bourbon, on the grounds that its «legitimacy» was greater, and the Duchess de Berry landed in France to defend the rights of her son, the Duke de Bordeaux. Eventually, she was arrested in conditions that resembled an episode in a novel (1832). The supporters of the Republic did not accept the «July Monarchy» and secretly organised themselves into the Society of Human Rights. During the funeral of General Lamarque, a riot was fomented by young republicans on 5th/6th June 1832; it was violently put down. Further riots broke out in Lyon and Paris in 1834 and it took 13,000 soldiers four days of bloody fighting to defeat the rioters. All the people living in an apartment block in Rue Transnonain, from which a shot had been fired, were massacred. Repression rained down on the republicans.

The Entente Cordiale

Despite their policies of repression, successive governments implemented a programme of reforms. An electoral law set up «county councils» (conseils généraux), the first stage in local democratisation. François Guizot, at the Instruction publique, tabled a major law on primary education in 1833, obliging every town or village to maintain a school and leaving anybody with the capacity to do so the right to teach (whether a lay person or member of the Congregation), although he insisted on the presence of religion in teaching. Louis-Philippe worked to break the isolated position in which France found itself after the Three Glorious Days. He was particularly prudent when Belgium became independent and, on this occasion, moved closer to England. Thiers implemented a bellicose policy again in 1840 because of the situation in Egypt but he was dismissed by Louis-Philippe who, through Guizot, brought in a policy of peace and entente cordiale with England, during the reign of Queen Victoria.

Guizot

Guizot, a historian and lecturer at the Sorbonne, was to impose his ideas from 1840 to 1848. He refused to countenance absolute monarchy or absolute democracy and this meant that political immobility was inevitable in internal affairs. However, it facilitated peace with foreign countries. In particular, he hoped that social and economic development would improve the everyday life of the French people, hence his statement in 1843, «Seek enlightenment, seek wealth, and improve the ethical and material condition of our country, France». The government counted on the middle classes to lead the country into industrialisation. A new change in the transport system arrived with the building of roads and canals and the French railway network began to take shape, gradually revolutionising travel for goods and people alike.

The Banquet Campaign

The July Monarchy, however, failed to react when a serious economic crisis appeared in 1846-1847 and the diffuse sense of discontent added to the demands of the middle cases who wanted an extension of political rights, especially voting rights. Since the regime had forbidden meetings, the prohibition was avoided by arranging a major series of banquets at which the speeches were political in nature. Another banquet was scheduled for 22nd February 1848 but was banned by the government. However, there was a demonstration of students and workers and the National Guard fraternised with the crowd. Louis-Philippe then realised the extent of popular anger and dismissed Guizot. On the evening of the 23rd, when the demonstrators, having celebrated the political U-turn, attacked a guard post, shots were fired and 16 people killed. Throughout the night, the bodies were carried through Paris and there was a general revolt. When the rebels attacked the Tuileries Palace, Louis-Philippe decided to abdicate in favour of his grandson. His elder son had been killed in an accident and the child was still young. This meant that there would be a regency.

FROM SECOND REPUBLIC TO SECOND EMPIRE

Crowds had overrun the Palais-Bourbon where the Chamber sat and the Republicans took control. They were firmly of the opinion that the monarchy had to go. A provisional government was acclaimed. The best-known of its members was the great poet, Lamartine.

The spirit of 1848

Through his lyrical speeches, Lamartine was a fine embodiment of the new republic which wanted to establish fraternity between men and instigate the «spirit of 1848» which was spreading throughout Europe and reminding people of the Revolution of 1789. The Republic was imposed by the people of Paris and was, on the surface, accepted by all. In a climate of unanimity and in the presence of the civil and religious authorities, «liberty trees» were planted all over the country. This agreement concealed tension among the Republicans. Some were in favour of political liberty but did not want to change the social order; others wanted wide-ranging social reforms in order to improve the dreadful lot of the working classes. It took all Lamartine's eloquence to ensure that the three-coloured, and not the red, flag won the day.

Liberties

Once the Republic had been proclaimed, the government implemented a daring set of political measures. It proclaimed universal suffrage and France was the first democracy to try out this system. Slavery in the colonies was abolished, thanks to the work of the republican writer, Victor Schoelcher. The death sentence was abolished. The freedom of the press, the right to hold meetings and freedom of religion were established and this led to great political effervescence, especially in the clubs. The political liberalism was completed by the decree of 25th February which was drafted by socialist Louis Blanc, a member of the provisional government, and which proclaimed the «right to work». In the same context, the government set up National Workshops, an extension of the traditional charity workshops, which provided higher wages.

The Constituent Assembly

It was planned to elect a Constituent Assembly and the Parisian revolutionaries realised that universal suffrage might take over the revolution. France was still a rural country and the peasants were willing to follow recommendations from their priest or local landowner. The nobility had regained some of its influence in country areas, even though republican ideas were gradually spreading in villages. The conservatives, who opposed the Republicans, soon recreated a united front, a «party of law and order». Elections were held (23rd/24th April 1848). It is true that the liberal Republicans won but there were large numbers of monarchists and the socialist Republicans were beaten. The new Assembly feared the threat being posed by demonstrations in Paris and they decapitated the movement by having its leaders arrested (Raspail, Barbès, Blanqui and Albert, a worker who had been a member of the provisional government).

June Days

Since the National Workshops were deemed unproductive and dangerous (the 115,000 unemployed had nothing to do and were subject to all types of propaganda), the executive committee, which acted as a government, decided to close them down (21st June). Riots immediately broke out. The east of the capital was covered with barricades. The fighting lasted for three days and several thousand people were killed. General Cavaignac, a convinced Republican, re-established law and order and, having become President of the Council, was then seen as the strong man in the liberal and conservative republic. The Assembly was able to turn its attention to the constitution inspired by that of the United States; it was passed on 4th November 1848. In addition to a single assembly which held legislative power, there would be a President of the Republic elected for four years, also by universal suffrage. He would not be re-eligible.

The Election of Louis-Napoleon Bonaparte

Although the Republicans' candidate was Cavaignac, the situation was reversed by one man – Louis-Napoleon Bonaparte, one of the Emperor's nephews. He had twice attempted a coup d'état and been imprisoned. He had defended social ideas by publishing a work entitled Extinction du paupérisme. His name also recalled a prestigious foreign policy which would make people forget the humiliations of 1815. The Conservatives, anxious to defend social order in the face of the «red peril», supported the candidate whose name was well known in rural districts – «to you, my name is a symbol of order and security», declared the «uncle's nephew». He was also favourably welcomed by those who believed that «moral order» could provide protection against social revolution and that the Church had a role to play in politics. Bonaparte was elected on 10th December 1848.

Conservative Policy

In May 1849, the elected legislative assembly revealed the triumph of the monarchists, as well as the deep roots laid down by the Republicans in a few rural departments. The anxiety aroused among the majority by this Republican force explains the conservative measures taken by the assembly. The Falloux Law of 15th March 1850 broke the monopoly held by the University over education. The «freedom» of teaching enabled all, and in particular the Church, to open primary and secondary schools. The law also gave the Roman Catholic Church control over education. The law of 31st May 1850 restricted universal suffrage by requiring that electors be resident for at least three years, as proven by the payment of a tax on assets. This excluded a large number of workers who travelled around in search of employment and the poor who were not liable for tax.

The Emancipation of the President

Louis-Napoleon Bonaparte was clever enough to distance himself from this policy. He began travelling through the provinces, calming the people, reassuring the middle classes and glorifying the army. Latent conflict had arisen between the President and the Assembly. It was clear that the President had not wished to stand down when the constitution stated that he was not eligible for re-election. The Assembly would have agreed to a revision of the constitution if the president had accepted its conservative programme but this he refused to do, preferring instead to curry favour with the people through social ideas, through the revolutionary origins of the Bonapartes and through his foreign policy which was favourable to nationalities.

The Coup d'Etat of 2nd December

As the constitution had not been revised, all that remained was a takeover by force. This was carefully and meticulously prepared. Louis-Napoleon succeeded in appointing one of his loyal supporters as commander of the military forces in Paris. Everybody could see a coup d'état coming, which it did on the night of 1st/2nd December 1851, a symbolic date in the imperial tradition. The National Assembly was occupied and 78 people arrested, including Thiers. Conservative parliamentarians who tried to react were arrested in their turn. The unrest continued. On 4th December, the «Boulevard Shootings» resulted in several hundred deaths among unarmed civilians, many of them members of the middle classes.

Unlike the coup d'état instigated by his uncle, the one fomented by Louis-Napoleon Bonaparte had resulted in bloodshed. It had ended the republic run by the Conservatives. As uprisings then took place in the provinces, in small towns and even in country districts, in the name of Republican legality, the Republicans were hit by Bonapartists ideals which were said to constitute protection against the «red peril». The difficult birth of this new regime weighed heavily on its future. One example of this would be the unwavering hatred of Victor Hugo who went into exile. Repression was widespread throughout the country, leading to a string of extraordinary Court hearings, deportations to Cayenne and Algeria and banishments.

The Ideas of the Prince-President

By a crushing majority, a plebiscite approved the coup d'état. This enabled Bonaparte to draft a new constitution and remain President for ten years. Louis-Napoleon, an intelligent and ambitious man, enjoyed secrecy and he remained difficult to understand. He was proud of being a Bonaparte and had always been convinced that he would succeed in restoring the Empire. He had no hesitation in recalling the principles rife in 1789 and the first article of the new constitution (14th January 1852) recalled that it was the «basis of the public law of the French people». The «Prince-President», as he was called, worshipped the «people», who were willingly idealised, but he retained strong disdain for any representative institution giving the people an opportunity to express their views. Dialogue between the population and the head of state had to be direct, undertaken through plebiscites. Although Bonapartism was neither right-wing nor left-wing, it was forced to govern with conservative forces.

Napoleon III

The Prince-President set up a personal dictatorship. He had command of the army, made war and peace, appointed people to every conceivable post and ensured that justice was meted out in his name. Although universal suffrage was re-established, the legislative body, whose members were elected, had only a consultative role. At election time, the Prince-President proposed official candidates and gave them his full support. It was the Council of State which drafted laws. All public liberties were suspended. The freedom to meet, the freedom of association and the freedom of the press no longer existed. Finally, the slide towards an Empire was completed with a senatus-consult of 7th November 1852, «Louis-Napoleon Bonaparte is Emperor of the French people under the name of Napoleon III».

An Authoritarian Empire

Although the population was closely regimented and monitored and although any opposition was muzzled and tracked down (this was the period of the «Authoritarian Empire»), the regime remained popular. Napoleon III was determined to boost the economy again and encourage development and modernisation through the railway network, banks and farming. He was also careful to improve the lot of the working class. He wanted to conceal the political constraints behind a brilliant court life led by his wife, the beautiful Eugénie de Montijo, and known as the «imperial festivities».

An Ambitious Foreign Policy

The Emperor instigated an ambitious foreign policy. He wanted to turn France into a great power again. Colonial expansion continued in Senegal, Algeria, Cochin-China where Saigon was occupied and, later, Cambodia. Napoleon III wanted to act as an arbitrator between European powers. He intervened in Crimea, siding with the United Kingdom against Russia who wanted to establish a veritable protectorate over the Ottoman Empire. The fall of Sebastopol in September 1855 marked this new French presence in Europe. The peace conference was held in Paris in 1856 and constituted revenge for the Congress of Vienna. In the name of the various nationalities, Napoleon III signed an alliance with Piedmont reigned over by Victor-Emmanuel II but which Cavour wanted to use to achieve Italian unity. To succeed, Italy had to shake off Austrian control. In 1859, the Austrians, who had declared war, were defeated by the French and Italians at the battles of Magenta and Solferino. Worried about reactions elsewhere in Europe, Napoleon III abandoned Piedmont, his ally which obtained Lombardy but not Venetia. France retained its lands on the other side of the Alps i.e. Nice and Savoy. In particular, Napoleon was anxious about the reactions of French Catholics to the threats weighing on the papal States.

Discontent

The Empire's international policy was a source of discontent for part of public opinion. A free trade agreement signed with the United Kingdom in 1860 annoyed the business community. The Catholics feared that Italian unity might be detrimental to the interests of the Pope and, in 1867, French troops had to protect Rome against attempts by Garibaldi to take it over. The Chassepot rifle was used for the first time and the despatch from the French commander stated, «The Chassepots have worked wonders». This added to the indignation of French patriots. Finally, an economic crisis in 1866-1867 increased difficulties for French people.

The Empire as a Social State

Napoleon III tried to find a political response. He began by taking initiatives in the social field, asking Victor Duruy to modernise and develop the education system. The Emperor also tried to win the confidence of the working classes by granting workers the right to strike in 1864. This daring «social» policy met with little success and caused very few to rally to the Empire. Napoleon therefore tried to liberalise the regime gradually by increasing the powers of the legislative body but, although from 1867 onwards parliamentarians were entitled to call upon the government to take action, the latter had no real responsibility. In 1868, law partly re-established the freedom of the press and the freedom to hold meetings. The liberal bourgeoisie was not overly impressed by such a discreet overture. However, Republican opposition was gaining ground, as was confirmed during the 1869 elections. Unrest continued to develop among the working classes.

A Liberal Empire

One last step towards a liberal empire was marked by a reform which gave the legislative body new powers. The initiative for laws was shared between the Emperor and the legislative body but the ministers were deemed to be «liable». A plebiscite held in May 1870 approved this liberal change which had been enabled by Emile Ollivier, a Republican who had rallied to the imperial cause. The Empire seemed to have been consolidated.

The Capitulation of Sedan

Defeat swept through the Empire. The Emperor had defended the principle of nationalities and German unity but soon he had to face up to Prussia which, having defeated Austria in Sadowa in 1866, was carving out a position for itself as a great military power and preparing for German unity with itself at the centre. Tension increased further when a quarrel broke out with regard to the Spanish crown to which a Hohenzollern, a relative of the King of Prussia, had laid claim. France obtained full satisfaction in this matter but, as it was demanding assurances for the future, Chancellor Bismarck drafted a despatch (the «Ems Telegram») in terms which aroused the wrath of the French and led Napoleon III to declare war (19th July 1870). The Prussian forces were well armed and well commanded; they were victorious. Maréchal Bazaine was blocked in Metz and the French army encircled in Sedan on 1st September. The Emperor was taken prisoner. Only Belfort resisted, with Denfert-Rochereau.

THE THIRD REPUBLIC

As soon as news of the capitulation of Sedan reached Paris, on Sunday 4th September, crowds overran Palais-Bourbon. Gambetta made a speech proclaiming the fall of the Empire and the Republican parliamentarians went to City Hall to proclaim the Republic. A government of National Defence was set up. Military defeat had annihilated a regime which, though based on a coup d'état and strengthened by international prestige, had never been popular in hearts and minds.

The Siege of Paris

The German army encircled Paris on 19th September and bombarded the city. The government wanted to remain in Paris and continue fighting. Gambetta left the capital in a hot-air balloon to lead the resistance from the provinces. He was a «radical» Republican who, when standing for election in Belleville in 1869, had proposed the so-called «Belleville programme» which was politically advanced and socially prudent. He tried to galvanise energies and win the French people over to Republican ideas. He organised new military forces but they were unable to liberate Paris, especially as Bazaine had capitulated with the army intact. All attempts to break through enemy lines failed. The siege of the city was terrible. The population suffered extremes of hunger (they ate rats and the animals in the zoo), cold (it was a dreadful winter and there was a fuel shortage), fear and despair. The city was also the scene of a struggle between Republicans and revolutionaries.

The Loss of Alsace-Lorraine

Negotiations became vital and, on 28th January 1871, an armistice agreement was signed. This followed the proclamation of the German Empire in the Hall of Mirrors in Versailles on 18th January 1871. The elections held in February 1871 took place in dramatic circumstances and resulted in the appointment of 400 monarchist parliamentarians, who wanted peace but were unable to agree on the candidate for the monarchy, and 250 Republicans who wanted the installation of a Republic but could not agree as to the continuation of the war. This highly conservative assembly designated Thiers, Louis-Philippe's former minister who had been hostile to the declaration of war, as «chief of the executive power of the French Republic» and the word «Republic» was used even though the majority was preparing for the restoration of a monarchy. Thiers was asked to negotiate and, on 1st March 1871, the conditions imposed by Bismarck were accepted. Alsace and part of Lorraine were transferred to Germany and a war indemnity amounting to five billion gold francs was to be paid. The government was to sit in Versailles, Louis XIV's town.

The Commune

The capital, which had withstood the siege despite extreme suffering, saw the capitulation as a terrible humiliation and an act of treachery. Thiers and the Conservative parliamentarians feared an uprising. He wanted to disarm the Parisians, in particular the National Guard, a total of 500,000 men who had been armed during the siege. On 18th March, the government tried to retake the guns placed on the hill at Montmartre. Two generals were killed and riots broke out. The Parisian rebels organised themselves and set up the Commune of Paris on 26th March 1871. The Commune has been variously described as a model, a forerunner of the Communist revolutions of the 20th century, or the last of the many uprisings of the 19th century. Symbolically, it adopted the red flag. It declared the separation of Church and State, abolished conscription and permanent armed forces and adopted the principle of free, non-religious and mandatory education. In the final analysis, however, social reform was limited.

The Bloody Week

Thiers' government and the Assembly decided to recapture Paris by force and the moderate Republicans, wishing above all to give the Republican regime a sold grounding and avoid panic, decided not to stand in their way. The retaking of Paris resulted in the Bloody Week (22nd May / 28th May 1871). Faced with the advance of the regular army under the command of Mac-Mahon, the «Communards» executed hostages including the Archbishop of Paris and set fire to public buildings such as the Tuileries Palace. The conflict ended in the Père-Lachaise Cemetery, at the «Federates' Wall» and the «Versailles» army implemented fearsome reprisals thought to have resulted in 20,000 summary executions, 45,000 arrests and 13,500 guilty verdicts with many of the condemned being sentenced to hard labour in New Caledonia. The Republic had a bloody beginning but law and order had been re-established in its name and this reassured those who still feared the concept of a Republic. For the Socialists and the working classes, however, the Commune represented a missed opportunity for a popular revolution.

Restoration of the Monarchy – an Impossible Dream

Thiers assumed responsibility for the reprisals and was seen as the saviour of social order. The monarchist parliamentarians, however, were divided between legitimists who supported the Comte de Chambord, Charles X's grandson, and orleanists who favoured a descendent of Louis-Philippe. On 6th July 1871, in a public manifesto, the Comte de Chambord declared his loyalty to the white flag, «the standard of Henri IV, François I and Joan of Arc». The restoration of the monarchy was impossible in the immediate future. In the meantime, Parliament designated Thiers as President of the Republic (31st August 1871, Rivet Law). The Republicans were also divided. Jules Ferry and his friends were in favour of political liberalism; Gambetta preferred a more authoritarian approach to power while working hard to provide a solid basis for the republic. Between 1871 and 1875, Gambetta was the «Republic's travelling salesman», speaking at countless political rallies throughout France. As to Thiers, he reorganised the country and succeeded in paying the war indemnity. The last Prussian soldier left France in July 1873. Thiers himself was beginning to consider the concept of a republic and the monarchists, worried by this change, deposed him on 24th May 1873. He was replaced by Maréchal de Mac-Mahon.

Moral Order

In fact, the head of the political arena was Duke Albert de Broglie and the main policy was one of «moral order», giving the Roman Catholic Church a vital position as regards the conservation of society. The summer of 1873 was again given over to discussions between monarchists. The Comte de Paris, the orleanist candidate, agreed to stand down in favour of the Comte de Chambord who had no descendent. Because of this, the Comte de Paris saw an opportunity to become his heir. The prince's intransigence with regard to the flag and his refusal to accept the principles of 1789 again caused the failure of a restoration project which would doubtless have been difficult to achieve. Mac-Mahon's powers were therefore extended for a period of seven years and the seven-year presidency of the Republic remained a French tradition.

The Wallon Amendment

It was time to overcome the uncertainty and ambiguity, for the Assembly elected in 1871 had constituent power. A compromise between orleanists and moderate Republicans led to the first stage of this process and, on 30th January 1875, the Wallon Amendment specified that the President of the Republic would be elected by majority vote of the Senate and Chamber of Deputies. The existence of a Senate, reminiscent of the Chamber of Peers, pleased the orleanists while the word «Republic» was finally introduced in institutions. Constitutional laws were passed in 1875, giving the President of the Republic wide-ranging powers. He was elected for seven years by both Chambers meeting as the National Assembly. He was eligible for re-election and appointed the President of the Council. Like the two chambers in the Assembly, he could initiate laws and dissolve the Chamber of Deputies with the agreement of the Senate. He was, in some respects, almost a constitutional monarch and the constitution allowed for the restoration of an orleanist sovereign. The Senate, which included 75 life senators and others elected by universal indirect suffrage, lay at the centre of the institutions of which it was the guardian. The ministers were jointly responsible to both Chambers.

16th May

In 1876, the senatorial and legislative elections favoured the Republicans. Mac-Mahon, who still supported the restoration of the monarchy, refused to appoint Gambetta as President of the Council even though he seemed to have won election victory. Instead, he tried to take interim measures. Gambetta attacked him on the role of the Church in politics. «Clericalism is the enemy», he declared. On 16th May 1876, Mac-Mahon used his right to select counsellors who thought along the same lines as himself and, as the Chamber did not trust a ministry directed by de Broglie, the President decided to dissolve the Chamber, with the agreement of the Senate. The electoral campaign was decisive. Gambetta aptly described it in the following terms, «When France has spoken with its sovereign voice... the only solution will be to submit or resign». The elections held in October 1877 upheld the Republican majority. Mac-Mahon submitted and finally resigned in January 1879.

The Real Birth of the Third Republic

Republican Jules Grévy was immediately elected and he appointed a Republican government. The Republic had been established, with the Marseillaise as its anthem and the 14th July as its national day. The political upheavals resulted in changes to the institutions. The President of the Republic no longer dared to make use of the right of dissolution used by Mac-Mahon to prevent a Republican victory. The role of the President of the Republic was severely curtailed after the crisis of 16th May. It was the President of the Council who led government policy and he needed the confidence of the Chambers. The Chamber of Deputies, which was elected by direct universal suffrage, lay at the centre of political life; the Senate played only a moderating role.

Within this constitutional framework, a number of laws were passed guaranteeing public liberties. In 1881, there was a law on the freedom to hold meetings and the freedom of the press (this removed censorship); in 1884, freedom was granted to professional and workers' associations, leading to the development of a powerful trades union movement (the same freedom, however, was not extended to religious congregations). Mayors were thereafter elected by universal suffrage and no longer appointed by the government, except in Paris where the Prefect also exercised the functions of Mayor (1882).

Jules Ferry and Education

Jules Ferry, a barrister from Lorraine who constantly held power either as Minister of Public Education or as President of the Council, continued his work on schooling and, in particular, on the development of education, which was designed to reduce inequalities between people, train responsible citizens within the Republic, produce patriots capable of fighting for their country and, finally, give France a qualified work force. In 1881, all primary schools became free. In 1882, education became mandatory for children between the ages of six and thirteen and one day's holiday was scheduled, in addition to Sundays, to leave time for religious teaching «but outside school buildings». This marked the beginning of a non-religious State education system. Religion was no longer part of the system and the State controlled more than 80% of primary teaching. Jules Ferry proposed a tolerant form of secularity, «Ask yourself whether any father of a family, and I repeat any father of any one family attending your class and listening to your words, might, in all good faith, refuse his consent to anything he might hear you say».

In other sectors of education, the Republican influence was less marked. State secondary education was set up for young girls but the Roman Catholic Church was predominant in this respect. Only State faculties could issue diplomas. The results of this effort in the field of education were undeniable and illiteracy almost totally eradicated. This policy, emphasising secularity, did not call into question the concordat which allowed the State to have its way in the religious services which it funded.

Political Forces

Although the Republic and republican ideas were taking root, the Republicans lost their unity as the monarchist threat moved away. Moderate Republicans were referred to as «opportunists» since they took account of realities in order to introduce the reforms that they deemed «opportune». The differences became even clearer when the social question arose. New political sensitivities appeared, especially on the left wing which demanded more decisive action in order to provide assistance for the most deprived. This was initially the attitude of the radicals led by Clemenceau, a doctor from Vendée who was Mayor of Belleville. They were followed by the Socialists who were further to the left and, in some cases, influenced by the system designed by Karl Marx. These movements or men gradually became an integral part of the political system or even of government, setting aside some of their radical or revolutionary ideas. In this way, they led to the development of the entire political world which assimilated these left-wing and extreme left trends.

On the right, too, royalist movements gave way to an antiparliamentarian and authoritarian form of nationalism of which the first example was the Patriots' League founded in 1882 and led by poet Paul Déroulède. This nationalism took on anti-Semitic overtones, accusing the Jews of weakening national identity. Men of letters assisted this ideology, among them E. Drumont and his France juive (1886). In 1899, Charles Maurras used the Revue de l'Action française to restore the monarchic idea to its former glory by linking it with the strength of the family, local or regional diversity, the religious dimension and the principle of authority. Inversely, Roman Catholicism was developing and increasingly integrating social issues while opening its doors to modern society.

General Boulanger

The Republic took root despite serious crises. In 1886, General Boulanger was appointed Minister of War and he quickly gained popularity by turning his attention to the life of soldiers. They were entitled to wear beards, they had a plate and fork for their meals in place of the traditional mess tin, and the sentry boxes were painted red, white and blue! The General's fine appearance strengthened his popularity still further. In 1887, after a border incident with Germany, he was seen as the man likely to give France its «revenge» while the government was busy settling the incident through negotiation. The General became a dangerous nuisance. He was removed from the government and appointed to Clermont-Ferrand but crowds gathered at the station in Paris (Gare de Lyon) in an attempt to prevent him from joining his new post. Boulanger acted as a federating force for all those who felt no ties with the opportunist Republic, from Déroulède's nationalist right-wing to the radical left-wing. Boulanger had declared, when discussing a strike, that the army was not at the service of the bourgeoisie. He even received financial support from royalist circles.

The Strength of Republican Institutions

The Republicans who held the reins of government were then embarrassed by the «medals scandal» when the son-in-law of President July Grévy became involved in illegal wheeling and dealing. Grévy was forced to resign. Jules Ferry's candidacy was set aside and Sadi-Carnot was elected President of the Republic. Boulanger, who had been retired, took advantage of the situation to stand at numerous partial legislative elections in 1888 and the campaign ended with a triumphant election in Paris in January 1889. Boulanger, however, did not dare or did not want to attempt a coup d'état. Meanwhile, the government had now realised the scope of the Boulanger movement. The Minister of the Interior succeeded in frightening the General by threatening him with legal action in the High Court on grounds relating to State security. Boulanger fled to Belgium. His movement collapsed and the Republicans won a landslide victory at the 1889 elections. Boulanger committed suicide on the grave of his mistress, in Brussels in 1891.

The crisis also revealed the strength of the Republican institutions. The Catholic Church accepted this development. Pope Leo XIII, who had shown his preoccupation with social issues through his encyclical Rerum novarum (1891), encouraged French Catholics to «rally» to the Republican form of government, much to the disappointment of the royalists.

The Panama Scandal

Another crisis, the Panama Scandal, broke out in 1892. The Panama Canal Company had attempted to avoid bankruptcy by bribing members of parliament and the scandal revealed links between the world of business, journalists and politicians. Clemenceau, who had received money for his newspaper, was removed from public life.

Then, from 1892 to 1894, anarchists attacked public figures throughout Europe. E. Henry declared to the assizes that the anarchists were waging «pitiless war» on the middle classes and that anarchy was «a violent reaction against the established order». President Sadi-Carnot was assassinated in Lyon in 1894. Again, the government reacted and took advantage of the weariness of the anarchists themselves.

The Colonial Empire

After France's humiliating defeat in 1870, the Republican government worked to give it back its place as a leading power in Europe by providing it with a worldwide colonial empire. Jules Ferry was an ardent supporter of this policy which was not always well understood or accepted. He considered that it was necessary to find new markets for French trade and ports for the French fleet. The French turned Tunisia into a protectorate (1881) and built up French West Africa, starting from Senegal. From 1883 to 1885, Jules Ferry began the conquest of Annam and Tonkin. In 1885, he lost power further to a false rumour on the evacuation of Langson during the Tonkin War. This showed the degree of natural mistrust with regard to the colonial adventure.

Franco-British Rivalry: Fachoda

After the move into Laos, French Indochina came into being with a colony (Cochin-China) and four protectorates (Tonkin, Annam, Cambodia and Laos). France had built up a vast colonial empire second only to that of the United Kingdom. The rivalry between the two colonial powers soon became evident. In Africa, in particular, the French posed a threat to the Nile Valley where the British had settled. A British Army moved up the river and, in 1898, came face to face with a small French expeditionary force in Fachoda where it was garrisoned. When Captain Marchand refused to evacuate the area, the decision was despatched back to the capital cities and the Minister of Foreign Affairs, Delcassé, was tempted to order resistance, which would have meant war. In the end, Marchand was called back and conflict was avoided but the withdrawal was a deep humiliation for the French.

Colonisation

Colonial expansion had been achieved with limited resources and, for many years, the Chamber considered it to have been too expensive. However, a «colonial party» gradually grew up, involving numerous parliamentarians. The nationalist right-wing, which had initially been hostile, rallied to the idea of colonial expansion. The French empire covered an area of eleven million kilometres but was only thinly populated (50 million inhabitants). Its enhancement remained limited. Heavy-handed use of a cheap labour force, the confiscation of the best land, the suppression of any resistance, and a disdainful attitude towards local populations which were considered as inferior were common characteristics of this colonisation. Yet there were those who saw their mission in terms of high ideals, among them daring explorers such as Savorgnan de Brazza in Congo, missionaries such as the White Fathers led by Cardinal Lavigerie, doctors and officers such as Gallieni and Lyautey in Madagascar, or administrators like Paul Doumer in Indochina. They were careful to equip the colonies, encourage education, farming and crafts and raise the standard of living.

The Sentencing of Captain Dreyfus

Politicians and men of war were obsessed by the need for revenge over Germany. Action had to be taken against anything that might weaken the army. There was huge anxiety when, in September 1894, the authorities learned that one of the staff officers was supplying information to the Germans. An anonymous handwritten text, a «list» indicating the secret documents that had been forwarded, had been found in a wastepaper basket by a German Embassy cleaner who was a member of the French secret services. Because of the anti-Semitic climate, suspicion fell on one of the few Jews to be a staff officer, Captain Alfred Dreyfus, and experts recognised his handwriting. Dreyfus constantly protested his innocence but he was court martialled and, since the Minister of War had forwarded to his judges a damning «secret file» which was not revealed to the defence lawyers, he was found unanimously guilty and sentenced to be deported for life on 22nd December 1894. He was sent to Devil's Island in French Guiana.

The Affair

In 1896, Commandant Picquart discovered that a French officer, Esterhazy, was a traitor. Having obtained the «secret file», he was convinced that the list had been written by Esterhazy and that false documents had been drawn up by French counter-espionage and slipped into the file. He was then faced with opposition from the high command which did not want to admit that there could have been a miscarriage of justice, doubtless because the honour of the army was at stake. Picquart was appointed to a post in Tunisia and Lieutenant-

Colonel Henry forwarded an document that was damning for Dreyfus in November 1896.

During 1897, politicians alerted by Picquart realised that Dreyfus was innocent and, soon, controversy raged. The supporters of Dreyfus considered that the nation and its army could only be strengthened by the revelation of the truth; Dreyfus' opponents deemed that national cohesion and the army's reputation should not be damaged to support the personal interests of a single person, even if the man was innocent. As the suspicion regarding Esterhazy had been made public, he was brought before a court martial which acquitted him.

J'Accuse

The author Emile Zola published a resounding article entitled «J'Accuse» in Clemenceau's paper, L'Aurore, on 13th January 1898 and, because he was calling the military hierarchy into question, Zola was found guilty by the courts. In July, the Minister of War quoted in parliament the document forwarded by Henry but, shortly afterwards, it proved to be a fake. Henry admitted his offence and committed suicide on 31st August 1898. It was another year before there was a retrial. The Republicans themselves were divided as to the correct attitude to adopt. They reacted when they realised that anti-Semitism brought new unity and vitality to the nationalist right-wing which drew on it to maintain agitation and bring down the regime. The Roman Catholic press, in particular La Croix, supported this point of view. A trial was held in Rennes in the summer of 1899. Dreyfus was found guilty but with mitigating circumstances and he was eventually pardoned by the President of the Republic. The Captain was not reinstated until 1906. Picquart was appointed Minister of War in Clemenceau's government.

The Government of Radicals

The Dreyfus Affair helped the radicals and radical socialists to gain power in 1902. They had founded a political party in 1901 and it was to dominate French politics until 1940. They drew their support from lower middle classes, shopkeepers, craftsmen and minor property owners. They were in favour of very moderate social reform and were hostile to any upheaval or revolution. They sought alliances with the right or left wings of the political spectrum, as appropriate. Their political programme found its coherence in anticlericalism, since the Roman Catholic Church had been linked to the monarchy and Empire and remained close to the right wing. With Emile Combes, President of the Council from 1902 to 1905, they launched a regular offensive. France's diplomatic relations with the Holy See were broken off in 1904 and, on 9th December 1905, the law separating Church and State turned France into a secular country, «The Republic shall not recognise, employ nor make payment for the upkeep of any form of worship»

(Article 2). Since the Church was no longer recognised as a «corporate person», Church property had to be devolved to associations set up in accordance with the law of 1st July 1901 and it had to be subject to inventories. The Pope refused the setting up of these associations and the inventories led to a number of violent incidents.

The Socialists

Changes in industry and working patterns had highlighted the social question. Trades Unions had developed and 1895 saw the setting up of the left-wing Confédération générale du Travail. In the 1900's, strikes became increasingly common and lasted for a long time. Georges Clemenceau, President of the Council from October 1906 to July 1909, had no hesitation in sending the army out against the strikers. He also had to face agitation in the wine-growing areas of Southern France. Social difficulties and a policy of repression gave added impetus to the Socialist party which, in 1905, became the S.F.I.O. (Section française de l'Internationale ouvrière). Its main figure was Jean Jaurès, a philosophy teacher and great orator, who stated his opposition to Clemenceau, colonialism and war. He was assassinated on 31st July 1914.

Preparation for Revenge

War was threatening Europe. After the French defeat in 1870-1871, Chancellor Bismarck had succeeded, through an alliance between Germany, Austro-Hungary, Italy and Russia, in isolating France and, by doing so, in removing any possibility of revenge. Russia and Austria, however, were rivals in the Balkans. France therefore sought a rapprochement with Czarist Russia. French banks funded industrial development by launching loans on the French market. A political agreement was signed in 1891, followed by a defensive alliance against Germany. The United Kingdom, in turn, was worried by economic competition from Germany and began to seek allies. On 8th April 1904, the Entente cordiale was signed between France and the UK – Fachoda was forgotten. A Triple Entente was set up with France, the UK and Russia to oppose the Triple Alliance between Germany, Austria and Italy.

Conflict increased. Friction between Paris and Berlin over Morocco where France was establishing a protectorate almost led to war in 1905 and 1911. More especially, the collapse of the Ottoman empire during the Balkan Wars of 1912 and 1913, brought Austria and Russia face to face, the latter having afforded its protection to independent Serbia. Every European country was preparing for war and taking part in an «arms race». Nationalist sentiment was vigorously expressed. Sometimes this led great powers to lay claim to territories they had previously lost (Alsace-Lorraine for France); sometimes it led to a strengthening of minorities, for example in the Austro-Hungarian empire. In France, Raymond Poincaré was elected to the Presidency of the Republic in 1913 and he was determined not to yield further to Germany. He supported the three-year law which extended national service.

Faced with all these dangers, the left-wing parties united and a radical government supported by the Socialists voted in income tax in 1914. More particularly, it prepared for war.

THE FIRST WORLD WAR

The pretext for war was the assassination of Archduke Franz Ferdinand, heir to the throne of Austria-Hungary, on 28th June 1914 in Sarajevo in Bosnia. Vienna held Serbia responsible for the attack. Russia mobilised to defend its ally under attack (30th July). Germany, which was allied to Austria, declared war on Russia (1st August) and on France (3rd August). The UK entered the conflict on 4th August. The interplay of alliances had brought all the leading European powers into war. Italy remained neutral in 1914. France mobilised 3,600,000 men and Germany rather more. French soldiers wore red trousers, which were far too easily seen, while the Germans had chosen verdigris as the colour for their uniforms. Rifles were the main weapons. The German army had excellent heavy guns; France boasted good light artillery.

On 2nd August, the German army invaded Belgium, despite its neutrality, and entered France to encircle the allied forces in a vast pincer movement. Joffre organised the retreat and, taking advantage of the fatigue of the Germans who were near Paris, launched a counter-offensive known as the Battle of the Marne (5th to 12th September). One million men were taken to the front from the capital, by lorry and Parisian taxi. The chief of the German high command was then forced to send troops eastwards against Russia and, on 12th September, the Germans had to retreat. However, they wanted to take the harbours along the coast of Pas-de-Calais and the two powers then instigated a «race to the coast» which proved pointless. In the east, the Russian offensive had been halted at Tannenberg by Hindenburg. In December, the fronts stabilised without any decisive victories. Each camp declared that the war would be of short duration; in fact it continued, in difficult conditions.

In order to maintain their positions in the face of the enemy, the armies dug in, in trenches set out in parallel lines linked by narrow communication trenches. They were protected by mines and barbed wire. For attacks, equipment was to become increasingly important, with the use of mortars and guns that fired shells in a curving trajectory (the «crapouillot»), nerve gases and flamethrowers. Later, there were tanks. This meant mobilising all the economic forces of the nations involved and women often had to replace men in the fields and factories. Governments were forced to increase taxes and take out increasing numbers of loans. The war took on a worldwide scope. Japan and Italy entered the conflict on the French side. The Ottoman Empire and Bulgaria joined the powers of the central axis.

In 1915, four offensives were launched by France in Artois and Champagne but they met with total failure. The Front moved by only 4 kilometres and the fighting resulted in 400,000 deaths. In 1916, it was Germany's turn to launch an offensive on one point along the Front in order to wear France down. From February to July, Germany threw everything it had at Verdun. General Pétain held command during the fighting and was careful to maintain communication with Bar-le-Duc via the «Sacred Way». The battle killed 240,000 men on the German side and 275,000 among the French army. Verdun was not captured and was taken as a symbol of French resistance. The Battle of the Somme launched by the Allies was also an obvious failure.

In France, Poincaré called for a «Sacred Union» against the aggressor on 4th August 1914. The government included Socialists but, on the other hand, no parliamentarians from the Catholic right wing. Once the Front had stabilised, the parliament demanded control of government action which was increasingly subject to orders from General Headquarters and, in particular, from Joffre who was replaced in 1916.

Germany, which was subjected to an unbearable economic blockade, announced in January 1917 that it was about to launch all-out submarine warfare. Its submarines attacked ships heading for the UK which had, as its main commercial partner, the USA. The United States entered the war on 2nd April 1917. The American President Wilson declared that the war being fought by Germany was «against humanity». The Russian Revolution caused the abdication of the Czar in February 1917 but, although the Russian army was collapsing, the new government still intended to continue the war. As to the French army, it was undergoing a serious crisis. A new offensive prepared by Nivelle led to massacres on the Chemin des Dames in April. The soldiers' exhaustion resulted in mutinies and there were similar movements in Germany. One soldier wrote, «All the soldiers are shouting «Down with war»…» Repression was tough. There were 629 death sentences and 75 executions. Pétain, the new commander of the French army, withstood these movements with equanimity. He had no hesitation in punishing men as an example to others but he also did his best to improve the daily lot of his men, known as the «poilus». In the rear, strikes broke out and the movement was instigated mainly by women at work. Pacifist movements began to make their voices heard again and the Socialists left the «Sacred Union». Faced with this crisis, Poincaré appointed Georges Clemenceau President of the Council on 14th November 1917. The «Tiger», as he was known, imposed an authoritarian policy and fought against defeatism.

The situation had become exceedingly difficult. The Bolshevik Revolution had brought to power men who were seeking peace. On 3rd March 1918, it was signed in Brest-Litovsk; this marked the withdrawal of Russia from the conflict. The German army, freed on the eastern front, could launch major offensives in the west during the spring of 1918. The face of war had been changed by the introduction of tanks and by the use of planes for aerial combat and bombing raids. On 21st March 1918, the Germans managed to breach the Front in Flanders and Champagne. The Allies were initially overrun but the German advance was halted because the Germany army lacked reserves. Foch had been appointed by Clemenceau as Commander-in-Chief of the allied armies and he led the counter-offensive at the end of September, taking advantage of the assistance provided by one million American soldiers.

Germany found itself under threat of invasion and it sought an armistice, which was signed in Rethondes on 11th November 1918.

THE INTER-WAR YEARS

France was among the victorious nations and it recovered the provinces it had lost i.e. Alsace and Lorraine to which Poincaré and Clemenceau travelled in November 1918.

The Treaty of Versailles

Clemenceau was one of the main negotiators at the diplomatic conference held in Versailles and attended only by representatives of the powers that were victorious. President Wilson of the USA wanted to impose his own view of the world and a new form of diplomacy to be exercised through a Society of Nations. He came to France to take part in the negotiations. In fact, the victors wanted guarantees against future German aggression by imposing its disarmament (a reduced army and no combat fleet) and by occupying the left bank of the Rhine. Since Germany was deemed to be responsible for the war, it was to make «reparation» in the form of financial compensation. This question was to dominate international relations during the 1920's. The treaty was signed by the Germans in the Hall of Mirrors in the Palace of Versailles on 28th June 1919 but it satisfied nobody. The French considered that they had not been sufficiently rewarded for their efforts; the Germans dreamed of wiping out the humiliation imposed upon them. The Austro-Hungarian Empire had disappeared, leaving way for States with less power (Austria, Hungary), new States (Czechoslovakia, Yugoslavia around Serbia) or extended States (Romania). This change, the result of the victors' wishes, resulted in tension and instability. The Society of Nations set up on 28th April 1919 was to take decisions unanimously and this immediately deprived it of its efficiency.

A Costly Victory

The French victory celebrated on 13th and 14th July 1919 could not conceal the traumatism left by the war on its population. Losses were enormous in terms of human lives (1,322,000 within continental France) and the memories of this sacrifice were maintained by the building of war memorials in many French towns and villages to express the gratitude of the entire nation. Such a difficult period weakened still further a country in demographic decline. Added to this, there were large numbers of wounded and mutilated ex-servicemen and losses among the civilian population. The ex-servicemen, steeped in the prestige of battle, played a full role in public life. The country, too, had suffered with 565,000 houses demolished. Reconstruction took ten years.

To fund the war, the government had contracted increasing numbers of loans. This meant that the financial situation was very difficult and the entire world monetary system had suffered. While the franc's value against gold had remained unchanged since 1803, and while bank notes were convertible into gold, the war had led to the creation of paper money and, consequently, a rise in prices. Convertibility had been suspended.

The Sky Blue Chamber

Political life in the Republic was taken up again after the parenthesis of war. However, it was a right-wing and centrist majority, the «national Block», which won the elections in November 1919. This was the «sky blue chamber», an allusion to the colour of army uniforms, characterised by fear of bolshevism and a strong feeling of nationalism. As Roman Catholics held an important place, Clemenceau, who was an atheist, failed in his attempt to have himself elected President of the Republic. He left public life and died in 1929. Poincaré's successor was Paul Deschanel but, having shown signs of mental illness, he was forced to step down and, in 1920, he was replaced by Alexandre Millerand who wanted to make use of all the powers granted to a President of the Republic by the constitution.

The Occupation of the Ruhr

It was the question of war reparation which weighed most heavily on political life. Germany's payments were irregular and the national Block in France had as its maxim, «Germany shall pay». Aristide Briand, an independent Socialist and man of negotiation, was President of the Council from January 1921 to January 1922. He drafted a form of rapprochement with Germany but this was unacceptable to the Chamber. Poincaré, the former President of the Republic, returned to public life (January 1922 to June 1924) and proposed firmness by occupying the wealthy Ruhr area as a «productive guarantee». The German work force went on strike in an action of «passive resistance». They were replaced by French workers but not without some bloody conflict. Eventually, the new German chancellor, Stresemann, preferred to negotiate. The Dawes Plan prepared by an international commission organised a new schedule for payments by Germany. The Locarno Accords guaranteed the borders of France and Belgium. Germany, by acknowledging the loss of Alsace and Lorraine, was brought back into the community of nations. In September 1926, further to a proposal from Briand, it became a member of the Society of Nations. This was a symbol of reconciliation between erstwhile enemies and the beginning of strong hope for peace.

Totalitarian Temptations

The Bolshevik revolution of 1917 had destroyed the Czarist empire and resulted in a «Communist» regime in Russia. Thereafter, this model was to exercise strong fascination for the other countries in the world, for the political dictatorship and persecutions were not clearly visible and the egalitarian dream was embodied in a planned economy. The USSR became the country of universal hope supported by the celebration of Communist leaders such as Lenin then, later, Stalin. The Russian example had its followers. During the Socialist Conference in Tours in December 1920, a majority declared itself in favour of membership of the International Communist movement organised by Lenin. A new political practice came into being, with a highly centralised political party closely linked to the Russian Soviet regime which was developing a revolutionary programme. It sought its main support among the working classes but also held very real fascination for French intelligentsia over some considerable period. In 1930, Maurice Thorez became the Secretary of the political bureau.

Another temptation was running through Europe and, of necessity, had repercussions in France – Fascism. In Italy, Benito Mussolini had founded an ultra-national movement. Fascism (from the word «faisceau» meaning «cluster») was based on disappointment with the war. In 1922, Mussolini seized power and established a political dictatorship. His example was imitated. Based on a strong demand for nationalism, an ambitious man with skill in rousing the masses could very well be tempted to instigate action based on force.

The Left-Wing Cartel

The governments were unable to put public finances back on a sound footing after they had been weakened by the cost of the war, given that the reparation from Germany did not offset this expenditure. The decrease in the value of the franc against other currencies, especially the pound Sterling, was the most evident sign of these difficulties. Discontent led to the setting up of an electoral group known as the «Left-Wing Cartel» involving Socialists, Radicals and Radical-Socialists; it won the 1924 elections. The new majority obliged Millerand, who was deemed too authoritarian, to resign and he was replaced as President of the Republic by Gaston Doumergue. Edouard Herriot, for many years the on-going Mayor of Lyon and Chairman of the Radical party, became President of the Council. The Socialists gave him their support without being involved in the government and they proposed a tax on capital. Herriot returned to the anticlerical policies of old and tried to apply secular legislation to Alsace and Lorraine which were not French when the law separating Church and State came into force and in which the concordat was, and still is, valid. He also announced the closure of the embassy in the Vatican. These intentions led to uproar and strong hostility from Catholic associations. He was forced to make a U-turn. Herriot also failed to solve the financial problems and win the trust of bankers and those with savings. He was forced to resign and he attributed his failure to the «wall of money».

The Poincaré Franc

In the end, it was Poincaré who, from 1926 onwards, succeeded in organising financial stability. He formed a government of national union, sought support from the Radicals and Centrists and, thanks to his past record, reassured the Republicans and lay parliamentarians. By imposing spending cuts and an increase in indirect taxes, he also succeeded in reassuring savers and bankers. He was, however, unable to return the franc to its pre-1914 value, although he succeeded in stabilising it and its value was once again linked to gold with an exchange rate of 65.5 mg of gold for 1 franc i.e. 1/5 of a gold franc. This was the «fourpenny franc» (franc à quatre sous), the franc having traditionally been divided into twenty «pennies» (sous). The 80% devaluation represented a heavy loss for State creditors but it restored public credit and encouraged exports. After the 1928 elections, the new Chamber of Deputies in which the right-wing parties held a majority and supported Poincaré's action, voted in the legal stabilisation of the franc (June 1928).

Ministerial Uncertainty

Poincaré had been obliged to stand down for health reasons in July 1929 and the political situation then became confused. Centre right governments with André Tardieu and Pierre Laval at their head were unable to remain in power and ministerial instability reigned, especially because the Radicals, who were central to the political system, refused to accept the victory of the right wing. In 1930, however, the law on national insurance, which had been initially drafted by Poincaré, was voted onto the statute books to cover everyday risks through contributions from employers and employees. The system underlined solidarity within French society. Family allowances came into being in 1932. Political efforts to modernise the French economy in line with the economy of the USA through the concentration of businesses and rationalisation of work patterns, failed.

A Dream of Peace

Throughout this period Briand, who was often Minister of Foreign Affairs, maintained a policy of dialogue with Germany. To avoid the return of war, he worked to implement collective security. This led, on 27th August 1928, to the Briand-Kellogg Pact (Kellogg was the American Secretary of State) which was designed to «outlaw war». Briand even suggested to the general assembly of the Society of Nations, in September 1929, a «federal link» between the peoples of Europe, to create what might be called a United States of Europe. The generous enthusiasm concealed an inability on the part of French diplomacy to find its place in European politics. On the military front, it was decided to defend the country at all cost and the fortified Maginot Line was built during the 1930's, stretching from Switzerland to the Ardennes. Everything focussed on the stability of peace in Europe. The economic crisis, and international tensions, were to sweep away this dream of peace.

The Economic Crisis

On 24th October 1929, panic struck Wall Street, the New York Stock Exchange, and this crash was the clearest indication of the economic crisis affecting the entire world. Commercial and industrial activity went into decline; prices dropped and unemployment quickly rose. For a long time, France appeared to be a haven of prosperity, doubtless because the country remained largely rural and was protected by Customs barriers. Recession struck the country at the end of 1931. Many firms and people went bankrupt. Yet the crisis was more limited in France than elsewhere and unemployment less widespread (425,000 jobseekers in 1935) doubtless, and this is paradoxical, because of the archaic French economy.

In 1931, Briand failed in his attempt to be elected to the presidency of the Republic. Electors preferred Paul Doumer but he was assassinated shortly afterwards and replaced by Albert Lebrun. At the 1932 election, the left-wing majority won a victory. Successive governments from 1932 to 1936 had to face up to the crisis. They used expedients, trying to limit imports and increasing Customs duties. Central government also intervened to restrict production within the country and, by doing so, halt the drop in prices. Finally, as if in an attempt to comply with orthodox monetary thinking and for fear of inflation, the government refused to devalue the currency, which would have enabled the country to withstand international competition. Successive governments attempted to implement a deflationist policy by limiting public spending and decreasing salaries and the number of public sector workers. In fact, these measures merely weakened the French economy still further.

Political Crisis

The political world seemed to be incapable of finding solutions which would provide a means of overcoming the difficulties of everyday life. Discontent and despair strengthened nationalist leagues such as the Camelots du roi which had links with Action française or Colonel de La Rocque's Croix-de-Feu. They drew attention to themselves through street demonstrations and the wearing of uniforms, and they demanded institutional reforms. They also attacked the Republican regime which was held responsible for all evils. On 30th January 1933, Adolf Hitler became the Chancellor of Germany with the assistance of the National Socialist party, imposing the Nazi ideology and, soon, a dictatorship.

160

Italian fascism and German Hitlerism were not really imitated in France for there were no major national frustrations to feed patriotic and nationalist demands. However, traditional parties were shaken by discussions and internal crises. A reform of the constitution appeared to be increasingly necessary.

6th February 1934

The Stavisky Affair lit the blue touch paper. Stavisky was a fraudster who had enjoyed the indulgence of magistrates for some considerable time despite complaints filed against him. He also enjoyed support from politicians. He was about to be arrested when he was found dead and the suicide seemed suspicious. «Stavisky commits suicide with a gunshot fired at him at point blank range» read the headline in the Canard enchaîné, a satirical newspaper. The government was dragged into the affair, which aroused anger among the leagues and led to the resignation of Chautemps, President of the Council. Daladier was appointed to succeed him but the leagues called for a demonstration on the day on which the new team was sworn in (6th February 1934). Crowds filled Place de la Concorde and the violent confrontation with the forces of law and order who closed off the bridge leading to the Chamber left fifteen dead and almost 1,500 injured. Daladier, who had won the trust of parliamentarians, preferred to resign. The riot had toppled the Daladier government but not the Republican regime. The executive merely tried to free itself from the Chamber's grip by taking legislative measures in the form of decree-laws and by addressing the general public directly, over the radio. The former President of the Republic, Gaston Doumergue, was asked to appease the situation and he governed for several months.

The Birth of the Popular Front

The events in 1934 instilled a general sense of anxiety; people feared a violent Fascist takeover. After these events, left-wing political forces mobilised, beginning with the intellectuals on the Watchdog Committee for anti-fascist intellectuals. More importantly, encouraged by Moscow, the Communist party put an end to its isolation and its hostility vis-à-vis the Socialists and, in the autumn of 1934, Maurice Thorez called for a «popular front» which would include Communists, Socialists and Radicals. On 14th July 1935, a Group (Rassemblement) was set up and delegates even took an oath before a spectacular procession brought left-wing forces together. In September, the CGT, which had split between Socialists and Communists, was reunited. The programme presented to the French people by the parties remained moderate. It provided, for example, for the nationalisation of industries involved in the war effort. According to this programme, the Popular Front wanted to fight «against misery, war and fascism and in favour of bread, peace and liberty». Although certain projects were aimed at providing new rights for «workers», they also took over ideas applied by Roosevelt in the USA to encourage recovery by stimulating consumer demand.

Hitler's Initiatives

Political changes in Germany were a cause of increasing concern. In October 1933, the country left the Society of Nations. Hitler launched an ever-increasing number of initiatives e.g. an alliance with Poland and an attempted invasion of Austria which was halted by Mussolini. The French Minister of Foreign Affairs, Louis Barthou, drew up a policy of alliances to isolate Germany but he was murdered in Marseille in October 1934, with the King of Yugoslavia. In 1935, French diplomacy succeeded in negotiating a treaty of defensive alliance with the USSR. This did not prevent Hitler from ignoring the conditions laid down in the Treaty of Versailles and deciding to rearm Germany then remilitarise the Rhineland. France, caught up in its internal affairs, rendered fragile by ministerial instability and preoccupied by the forthcoming elections, did not react. The Society of Nations did not find any effective political solution in the face of Mussolini's attack on Ethiopia and let the situation develop.

Léon Blum's Government

On 3rd May 1936, the parties in the Popular Front won a landslide electoral victory. This success aroused great hopes. Strikes, most of them spontaneous and including sit-ins in factories, broke out in the middle of May and some 1.5 million workers took part. This popular pressure accelerated events. The leader of the S.F.I.O, Léon Blum, was asked to form the new government consisting of Socialists and Radicals but supported by the Communists even though they did not participate in it. Although women did not yet have the vote, three of them were appointed to the position of Secretary of State. Blum was a brilliant intellectual, with his roots in the bourgeoisie. He had become involved in politics at the time of the Dreyfus affair and had become a member of the S.F.I.O. He had to take swift action in the face of this dramatic situation. He personally arbitrated during the negotiations between employers and trades unions, led by the C.G.T. The Matignon Accord, named after Hôtel Matignon, the President of the Council's official residence, was signed on 7th June 1936. Salaries increased by 7 to 15%, the freedom of the trades unions was officially recognised and collective bargaining agreements were negotiated. «You have to know how to end a strike,» said Maurice Thorez. Social unrest gradually faded away.

During the summer of 1936, a number of laws entered the statute books. The working week was reduced to 40 hours in place of the previous 48, a point not planned in the electoral manifesto. Workers were entitled to fifteen days' paid annual holidays. Farm prices were supported by central government and, as foreseen, armaments industries were nationalised.

Central government also took control of the Banque de France which was still a private institution – thereafter the 200 largest shareholders representing the «200 families» could no longer direct the bank's policy decisions. Paid holidays enabled people to go on vacation and efforts were made to encourage sports and organised leisure. Léo Lagrange was appointed Under-Secretary for Leisure.

The Need for a Break

This social and cultural policy, which had been implemented at top speed during the summer of 1936, was soon to meet resistance as a consequence of the economic situation. Strikes followed by social measures worried the financial sector and the flow of capital weakened the currency, especially as the increased salaries caused a rise in prices. Léon Blum decided to devalue the Poincaré franc on 1st October 1936 but the devaluation, which was an unpopular measure, failed to right the economic situation for it was too little, too late. The law on the 40-hour working week had resulted in only a limited reduction in unemployment. On the other hand, it seemed to have obliged companies to cut production. The industrial structures were too old-fashioned to provide a rapid response to demand, which had been increased by the rise in salaries. There was, therefore, no economic recovery. On 13th February 1937, the President of the Council was forced to announce a «break» in the programme of reforms. This was made necessary by the worsening international situation. Blum decided to give top priority to the country's rearmament, to the detriment of social projects. By the end of 1936, military expenditure increased dramatically.

Attacks on the Popular Front

Threats were building up. The civil war in Spain following on from General Franco's coup d'état on 18th July 1936 was dividing supporters of the Popular Front. The Republicans asked France for aid but Blum preferred not to intervene, for fear that the conflict would engulf the whole of Europe since the dictators all supported Franco. This «non-intervention» was criticised by part of the left wing.

Attacks on the government by the press became increasingly virulent. They came in particular from the extreme right since the government had decreed that the Croix-de-Feu should be dissolved. An extreme right periodical, Gringoire, had already accused the Minister of the Interior, Roger Salengro, of being a deserter during the war and he committed suicide. Parties and organisations were set up to combat Communism and some of them, such as the P.P.F. (Parti populaire français) led by Jacques Doriot, himself a former Communist, was not too far from fascism.

The End of the Experiment

The Popular Front was shaken. The Communists opposed Blum on the question of the war in Spain; the Radicals opposed him on the subject of social unrest. In June 1937, the Radical senators overturned the government. The Popular Front survived the fall of Blum but, in April 1938, Edouard Daladier ended it by forming a radical government allied to the right wing. The experiment seemed to have failed. On the left, each of the parties accused the others while the right wing blamed Léon Blum's government for having divided and weakened the country. Paul Reynaud authorised an increase in the 40-hour working week and, by doing so, effected a U-turn on the social benefits acquired in 1936.

Hitler Attacks

The main aim of Hitler's policy was to unite all Germanic peoples with Germany then to give this great Germany a vast «living space». On 12th March 1938, the German army entered Austria which was then annexed to the Third Reich; this was known as the «Anschluss». Mussolini, who had initially opposed such an operation, did not react. The Führer then turned his attention to the three million Germans in the Sudetenland. They lived in Czechoslovakia, a state set up by the Treaty of Versailles forming the keystone of central Europe. Hitler's demands seemed to make war inevitable. The British leader, Chamberlain, and the French leader, Daladier, obtained a meeting in Munich, with Hitler and Mussolini (29th/30th September 1938). There, they yielded to German demands and Europe was swept by a sense of immense relief. Czechoslovakia had been sacrificed by the democracies. Prague was occupied by the Germans in March 1939. Later, those who had attended the Munich summit were blamed for their weakness, they who had wanted to safeguard peace at all cost. Hitler, moving on to a new stage in his plan, wanted to expand the country eastwards but he was faced by the USSR which agreed to sign a non-aggression pact with Germany. This signature stupefied the world at large but it also meant that the two powers had secretly provided for a new division of Poland. Hitler was convinced that the liberal democracies would not fight for Poland. On 1st September 1939, the German army entered Polish territory. On 3rd September, the United Kingdom declared war on the Third Reich, followed by France.

THE SECOND WORLD WAR

The Phony War

In September 1939, Hitler concentrated his offensive on Poland. The Blitzkrieg led to a German victory in just one month and the territory was shared with Germany's Soviet ally. In the west, there was a long period of waiting which was difficult for the soldiers to bear. They were demoralised by the «phony war». The French had a purely defensive strategy since the country seemed to be protected behind the Maginot Line and the country's army. The allies merely prepared the blockade of Germany and cut off supplies of Swedish iron passing through the Norwegian port of Narvik. The Franco-British expeditionary force took Narvik but was soon forced to withdraw because of the defeat of the French army.

The German Offensive

Having waiting until conditions were favourable, the Germans launched an offensive on 10th May 1940 on the western front. The military forces were more or less equal in number but Germany had given priority to its aviation and its tanks which, instead of being dispersed, were grouped in armoured divisions (Panzerdivisionen) that were to be used as «strategic battering rams» and carry the day. According to General Guderian, the main concept was to be a war of movement. Planes were to provide support for operations on the ground and strike at communication lines, general headquarters and troop garrisons.

The attack took place in the Ardennes where the system of defence was weak because the uplands were deemed to be impregnable. Having pushed through the lines at Sedan, the tanks headed for the coast. As the German troops had also invaded the Netherlands and Belgium, the allied armies had moved northwards. General Weygand, who replaced Gamelin at the head of the allied armies, tried to cut the German lines which stretched over a huge distance. He was unsuccessful. The armies were then caught in a trap in the north. The soldiers retreated to Dunkirk where, despite German shelling, a British fleet evacuated a large number of them (28th May/4th June). The others were taken prisoner.

Weygand did not succeed in stemming the advance of the German army and it entered Paris on 14th June. This military defeat led the civilian population to flee from the north of France and the Paris Basin. The «exodus» of almost eight million citizens, including old people and children, highlighted the fear and general panic and contributed to disruption in the country as a whole.

The Armistice

Daladier had been unable to establish a Sacred Union in the face of the enemy and propose a clear policy. In April 1940, he was replaced by Paul Reynaud who had a reputation for greater dynamism. Maréchal Pétain, the First World War hero, had become Deputy President of the Council in order to reassure the population and General de Gaulle, who had recommended the use of tanks in his books, was Under-Secretary for War. The government moved to Bordeaux and discussions got underway with a view to an armistice. Should the political authorities leave the country, as other governments or sovereigns had done in the face of the German advance, and establish themselves in North Africa to continue the war while the army was forced to capitulate and the country subjected to the lot that usually befell the vanquished? Or, on the contrary, should all fighting be halted under the terms of an armistice and negotiations begun with the enemy? On 16th June, Pétain was ordered by President Lebrun to replace Reynaud and form a new government. On the following day, he addressed the nation, «…I am giving myself to France in order to alleviate its misfortune…»

The Call of 18th June

On 18th June 1940, General de Gaulle, who had travelled to London, used the BBC to call on the French people to continue the struggle but his call met with little support at the time. «This war has not been decided by the Battle of France… whatever happens, the flame of French resistance should not, and shall not, be extinguished…» Pétain sought an armistice and it was signed in Rethondes, in the same place as the armistice of 11th November 1918. France was divided, by a «demarcation line», into a northerly zone occupied by the Germans, a no man's land, and a «free zone» in the south. Although France remained an independent country with diplomatic representation, it had been dismembered. What was to become of its armed forces and colonial empire? Thereafter, the UK bore the full brunt of the war and it feared that Germany might take over the entire French fleet. In Mers-el-Kabir, a naval base on the Algerian coast, a British squadron destroyed the French ships, causing the deaths of 1,300 sailors and creating tension between Pétain's France and the UK.

The Vichy Regime

Pétain set up his government in Vichy, carried along by immense popular support for the French saw him as their only means of defence against the Germans. With Laval, Deputy President of the Council, he instigated a constitutional process which put an end to the republican institutions and the Third Republic. It was replaced by the French State that was to guarantee the rights of Work, Family and Homeland. On 10th July, a large majority of parliamentarians voted in favour of granting Maréchal Pétain full power. He became the plenipotentiary head of state and carefully avoided convening meetings of members of the lower or upper house. A supreme Court of Justice was set up in Riom to consider, from 1942 onwards, the cases of ministers seen as responsible for the defeat. However, as Pétain himself had been involved in the decisions taken before the war, the trial was suspended.

National Revolution

Pétain was an old man of 84. The propaganda machine worked hard to praise his personality and actions with a hymn entitled, «Maréchal, nous voilà», and Labour Day celebrations were instigated on 1st May, the Feast of St. Philip. To the French people, overwhelmed by defeat, he offered and imposed a «national revolution» prepared by politicians who had survived the end of the Third Republic and who were in favour of peace. In many cases, they also supported dialogue with Germany. Other people involved in this strategy were supporters of Action française and «technocrats» who used the disaster to modernise France and central government. In fact, it was a traditionalist programme steeped in nostalgia for the past and highlighting the strength of rural civilisation («The land does not tell lies...»), training for young people through Youth Work Programmes (Chantiers de jeunesse), executive training at the Ecole d'Uriage, the celebration of family life and large families, and the organisation of work through trades and craft corporations. Although some of the ideas had an effect in the long term, the national revolution quickly proved to be a failure.

Persecutions

The regime soon took coercive measures. It suspended political parties and censored the press and radio. The Communists had already been the subject of law suits in 1939, after the Germano-Soviet pact. On 3rd October 1940, the regime drew up a status for the Jews, preventing them from working in a large number of professions; in 1941, the Commissariat for Jewish Affairs was set up. The regime also attacked freemasonry which was accused of being a State within a State. The military defeat and subsequent low morale enabled Pétain, who enjoyed great personal prestige, and a handful of other men to put an end to republican institutions, take over all power and prepare a political programme which took over the ideas of the extreme right wing and, therefore, led to the persecution of a section of the French people.

Collaboration

The other area of this political action was dialogue with the victor. In the eyes of Pétain's government, there was a need to resist the demands being made by Germany which used prisoners-of-war as a fearsome means of blackmail. Pétain met Hitler on 24th October 1940 in Montoire. In order to give France a place in the German Europe then in the planning stage, Pétain decided to collaborate with the Germans. However, annoyed by the power-sharing scheme imposed upon him by Pierre Laval, Pétain removed him from office on 13th December 1940 and replaced him, between February 1941 and April 1942, by Admiral Darlan who was designated as the Maréchal's successor.

The Occupation

Collaboration did not prevent the Germans from pillaging the country in economic terms, making everyday life very difficult for the French people. Food rationing was the commonest aspect, and rations varied depending on age and activity. In autumn 1941, all foodstuffs were rationed and food was scarce. These were the days of turnips and kohl-rabi, neither of which really calmed the pangs of hunger. Only country people were spared. A very prosperous black market developed and products that had become rare were sold at very high prices.

The Vel d'Hiv Round-Up

Since Darlan had lost the trust of the Germans, Laval became «head of government» on 18th April 1942. He gave new impetus to collaboration by claiming that the rapprochement between France and Germany was an essential condition for peace in Europe and that only a German victory would prevent the spread of Bolshevism. To facilitate the German action against the Jews, the government represented by René Bousquet decided to involve the French police and gendarmerie in the arrest of foreign Jews in the northern part of the country. The «round-up» organised on 16th and 17th July 1942 resulted in 13,000 people being brought to the winter cycle racing track (Vélodrome d'Hiver) in Paris before being taken to the camp in Drancy. From there, the Germans took them to the concentration camps by train. Foreign Jews in the southern part of the country who were already being detained in camps were also handed over to the Germans. Thereafter, Jews were required to wear a yellow star. Soon, deportations of Jews became systematic and they continued throughout the following years (in all 75,000 Jews were deported from France out of a total of 5,100,000 in Europe as a whole). This persecution was organised by Vichy and its government departments in advance of German demands. It shocked part of public opinion which loosened its support for the regime. Collaboration was also praised by writers such as Robert Brasillach and by politicians such as Doriot. A legion of French volunteers against Bolshevism was set up in 1941. Certain collaborators even enlisted in the Waffen SS in order to fight on the Russian front in German uniform. This active collaboration did little to soften the rigours of the Occupation.

Free France

In London, General de Gaulle was acknowledged by the British Prime Minister, Sir Winston Churchill, as the «leader of the Free French». Although the only people to join him in the early days were the fishermen from the Island of Sein and a few leading figures such as René Cassin and General Catroux, entire groups from the French Empire soon rallied to the cause of Free France. An operation in Dakar failed. In June 1942, Free French forces led by General Koenig won a victory at Bir-Hakeim in Libya, defeating the Afrika Korps and paving the way for the dazzling British victory at El Alamein. Gradually, Free France made its presence felt, albeit in a modest way, in military circles.

The French Resistance

In France, defeat was quickly followed by acts of resistance against the German occupation forces. Groups were gradually organised under the names Combat (Henri Frenay), Libération-nord (Christian Pineau), Libération-sud (E. d'Astier de la Vigerie) or Franc-Tireur (Jean-Pierre Lévy). After the deterioration of German-Soviet relations and the German attack on the USSR, the Communists also joined the Resistance movement. They attacked German officers and, in 1941, this led to terrible reprisals. The «Francs-Tireurs partisans» constituted the armed faction of this Communist resistance. Jean Moulin was the man who succeeded in federating the highly diverse movements by creating the National Council of the Resistance that recognised the authority of General de Gaulle in 1943. Five high school pupils from the Lycée Buffon in Paris were arrested, charged with membership of the Resistance and shot in 1943. While action remained limited in towns, the «underground» («maquis») grew up in rural areas. The German Gestapo fought the Resistance with the assistance of the French police and the Militia from 1943 onwards. Jean Moulin was arrested in Caluire near Lyon in June 1943 and died under torture.

In Vichy, after the occupation of the «free zone» at the end of 1942, Pétain's power was reduced to a mere shadow; real power had been seized by Laval with the backing of the Germans. From 1943 onwards, «obligatory work service» (S.T.O, Service du Travail obligatoire) required young people to go to work in Germany or in companies working for Germany. In all, there were 3.6 million such French workers. Those who refused to comply with their call-up for S.T.O. were tempted to join the Resistance. Pétain showed an inclination to call upon parliamentarians but the occupying forces were opposed to this. Soon, the country entered a period of «total collaboration» and political assassinations perpetrated by the Militia became increasingly common.

A World War

The war had taken on a global dimension. The United Kingdom had held out. Japan, an ally of Germany, had invaded South-East Asia. The attack on the naval base at Pearl Harbour on 7th December 1941 brought the USA into the conflict and, with them, their industrial might, scientific research and military power. Germany had also failed as regards the USSR. In 1941, Hitler ordered his army to attack his former ally but he was unable to achieve a rapid victory since Stalin implemented a scorched earth policy. Finally, the Wehrmacht capitulated on 2nd February 1943 in Stalingrad. The counter-attack could commence.

Giraud v. De Gaulle

The Anglo-American landing in Algeria, Operation Torch, in November 1942 was one of the signs of this counter-attack. Admiral Darlan, who was in Algeria at the time, wanted to seize power in Maréchal Pétain's name and with the agreement of the Americans. This maintained the idea that the head of State was running with the hare and hunting with the hounds. The Germans replied by invading the free zone. The French fleet in Toulon, which was intact, was scuttled to ensure that the ships did not fall into enemy hands. Darlan was assassinated in December 1942. Thereafter two men struggled for power – General Giraud, who supported Vichy and who was supported by the American President, Roosevelt, and General De Gaulle considered by Roosevelt as a future dictator but who enjoyed the support of the Resistance movement. During 1943, De Gaulle outstripped Giraud in the race for authority. This meant that a leading French figure could then impose on the allied powers the idea of a free France that was totally unconnected with the Vichy regime bogged down in its collaboration with Nazism and its unavoidable defeat.

The Allied Landings

After the Allied landing in Sicily (July 1943), the Allied troops landed in Normandy on 6th June 1944. For months, the offensive had been prepared by air raids in France. Despite the bad weather, Operation Overlord succeeded under the command of the American General Eisenhower and five bridgeheads were established along the coast. It took difficult fighting, with huge losses in human lives, to break through to Avranches by the end of July. A landing was organised in Provence and involved General de Lattre de Tassigny's men. Paris revolted and was liberated on 25th August 1944 by General Leclerc's second armoured division. It was many more months before the Allied armies finally overcame the German forces. They signed an unconditional surrender on 8th May 1945 – De Lattre accepted the capitulation with the other Allied commanders-in-chief. The use of the atomic bomb on Hiroshima and Nagasaki forced Japan to capitulate.

LIBERATION AND THE FOURTH REPUBLIC

The defeat of Hitlerian Germany with which the Vichy regime was linked and the victory of the Allies who had supported Free France produced a confused situation. On 9th August 1944, General de Gaulle re-established Republican legality and formed a government of «national unanimity» that included Christian Democrats (M.R.P, Mouvement républicain populaire), Socialists and Communists, as well as members of the Resistance movement. In 1944, women were given the vote for the first time.

Cleansing

Commissioners of the Republic were required to re-establish law and order throughout France for old scores were being settled and summary executions were on the increase. There may have been as many as 9,000 during the summer of 1944. Law Courts were set up to undertake legal «cleansing». In the following year, Robert Brasillach and Laval were sentenced to death and executed. Pétain was also sentenced to death but he was reprieved by De Gaulle and the sentence commuted to life imprisonment.

The New Constitution

Although De Gaulle embodied the continuity of the Republic, a referendum showed that the French people wanted a change of constitution. The projects drafted displeased De Gaulle, who was President of the Provisional Government and he preferred to resign on 20th January 1946. The constitution of the Fourth Republic, which was approved on 13th October 1946, was designed to avoid a return to an authoritarian regime and provide a guarantee of human rights. The National Assembly occupied centre stage among the new institutions. The President of the Council was required to obtain the support of an absolute majority of members of parliament. Since proportional representation was beneficial to small parties, they regrouped to form coalition majorities, many of them short-lived, and this led to great ministerial instability. Despite the best efforts of Vincent Auriol then René Coty, the President of the Republic played only a minor role in political life.

Governments found it difficult to define a coherent, continuous policy line but, more importantly, they were faced with a new international situation and, in particular, the emancipation of French colonies.

The Cold War

Victory over Germany and Japan left the two victors face to face – the USA, champion of the liberal, democratic system and the USSR which had built up a Communist society, a planned economy and political totalitarianism. Since there was a risk that any conflict could lead to nuclear war, the two powers confronted each other indirectly, in a very tense climate. This was the «cold war» which brought with it the arms race and an equilibrium based on terror. Soon, Europe and the rest of the world were divided into two camps. France belonged to the Union of Western Europe and to NATO (the North Atlantic Treaty Organisation), a military organisation involving the countries of Western Europe and the USA.

On-Going Opposition to the Regime

This had consequences in France where the Communists, who had taken part in the Resistance and the Liberation, had connections with the USSR. In May 1947, the Communist ministers who supported social demands were dismissed from the government by the Socialist Ramadier. Strikes, some of which degenerated into near-riots, paralysed the country from June to October, encouraged by the Communist Party and the C.G.T. They enabled the Communist party to recall its revolutionary vocation in the new climate of the Cold War, thereby arousing a new wave of anti-Communism. The strikes led to a division in the trades union movement. Force Ouvrière was created as a splinter group from the C.G.T. From then on, the regime had to face two groups in systematic opposition to its policies. On the one hand there was the R.P.F. (Rassemblement du peuple français) set up by General de Gaulle at the end of 1946 which criticised the weakness of the institutions and the regime based on political parties (De Gaulle had expressed a wish for a strong executive in his speech from Bayeux on 16th June 1946); and on the other hand, there was the Communist party which attacked the conservatism and anti-Sovietism of successive governments. It was the centre-right coalition, the Third Force, which then had to deal with the war in Indochina.

Colonial power had been called into question. Colonial empires (since 1946, the «Union française» included France and overseas countries) were contested both by the colonial elites who wanted to take control of their countries' destinies and by the two superpowers (USA and USSR) which disliked this globalisation of the European presence and which, in the name of liberty, supported the emancipation of people under colonial rule.

Reconstruction

The country had suffered as a result of the war. A total of 600,000 people had been killed and the economy had been pillaged by the Germans. The Liberation allowed for a rapid application of the programme drafted by the National Resistance Council – economic reforms, modernisation of the State, and generous social inspiration. This led to a string of nationalisations (Renault, Banque de France, the four main private banks, insurance companies, gas and electricity suppliers, coal mines, airline companies etc.). The State became a major force in the economy of the country in a system that expounded the virtues of a planned economy and was steeped in Socialist and Communist ideas.

The idea of planning the economy in the same way as the Soviet Union gradually took root and Jean Monnet, an economics expert who was appointed «Commissioner to Planning», was asked to draw up a plan that would modernise the economy and lay down economic priorities for the nation.

Administrators held an increasingly important place. In order to train leading members of the civil service, the Ecole nationale d'administration was set up in 1945. Further legislation set up the Social Security system to which all salaried workers were affiliated. Funded by contributions from salaries and employers and managed by representatives of salaried workers, it provided sickness and invalidity benefits and old age pensions. Central government organised unemployment benefits. In 1951, the minimum wage was introduced. This marked the birth of what is commonly called the «Caring State».

The Pinay Plan

In post-war years, France enjoyed continuous growth but the situation of the population remained difficult for a long time and rationing did not end until 1949. Reconstruction was accelerated by aid from the USA through the 1947 Marshall Plan; it ended c. 1952. Despite this, French economic growth remained slower than that of its neighbours. In particular, France suffered a budgetary deficit along with a weak franc and high levels of inflation. In 1952, Antoine Pinay, who described himself as an ordinary Frenchman and was referred to as the «man with the small hat», succeeded in improving finances by reducing public expenditure and increasing public borrowing. The loan, known as the «Pinay Loan», was index-linked to gold and it was, therefore, a resounding success. Although Antoine Pinay enjoyed great popularity among people with savings, who considered him as a particularly wise man, the benefits of his policy to the economy were short-lived.

The Common Market

The post-war years were also favourable to the construction of Europe, an idea of which Jean Monnet was one of the most fervent supporters.

173

Since the Cold War between the democracies and the USSR posed a threat, a union within Europe seemed to constitute a force in the face of the Soviet menace. A rapprochement between European countries that were erstwhile enemies required economic ties. Under the terms of a project drafted by Monnet and taken up again by Robert Schuman, the ECSC (European Coal & Steel Community) set up in 1951 was to harmonise production in France, West Germany, Italy and the Benelux countries. On 25th March 1957, these countries extended the economic cooperation by signing the Treaty of Rome that set up the European Economic Community, a Common Market in which Customs barriers would gradually cease to exist and which would draw up joint economic policies, initially in the farming sector.

In 1950, a project was also tabled for a European Defence Community. It aroused heated discussion in France.

Decolonisation – The War in Indochina

During the Second World War, Ho Chi Minh, who had been a militant member of the French Communist party, had set up a united resistance front, the Vietminh, and succeeded in integrating Communism into the national cause. In September 1945, he denounced the economic exploitation of his people and French oppression and pronounced the independence of Vietnam in Hanoi. France's military collapse and the occupation of Indochina by Japan followed by its defeat had stimulated this strong desire for liberty. For many years, the French government hesitated between negotiation and a policy of firmness. After the bombing of Haiphong, Ho Chi Minh went underground and war began in 1946. The Vietnamese made use of guerrilla tactics and, after 1949, received assistance from Communist China. The war in Indochina seemed to be one of the front lines in the Cold War and the USA, in their turn, provided support for France. The French troops, all of them regular soldiers, suffered many setbacks. Public opinion in France was little interested in this difficult conflict in a distant land. Finally, 12,000 soldiers were encircled in a dip at Dien Bien Phu and were forced to surrender on 7th May 1954.

The Mendès-France Experiment

Pierre Mendès-France, a radical Socialist who had been part of the Free French group in London, was appointed President of the Council because he had, for a long time, been seeking to end the war. As a supporter of a new form of political life, supported and praised by the magazine L'Express, he formed a government without negotiating with political parties and included a number of Gaullists. An international conference on Asia had been organised in Geneva and, as promised, Mendès-France succeeded, by July 1954 i.e. in just one month, in having the so-called «Geneva Accord» signed. The 17th parallel divided Vietnam in two. To the north was the Communist Democratic Republic; to the south a pro-American government since the USA had taken over from France, acting on behalf of the free world. Laos and Cambodia became independent.

On the other hand, Mendès-France showed great prudence with regard to the EDC and finally, on 30th August 1954, the project was abandoned, causing great anger among European countries which supported the idea. Despite a programme of modernisation of which one of the main features was the promotion of milk, and despite the undoubted confidence of public opinion, Mendès-France resigned on 5th February 1955 because of the opposition he had aroused in parliament.

Negotiations in Africa

At the same time, similar aspirations for independence were being expressed in Africa. Nationalism was embodied either by traditional authorities such as the Sultan of Morocco or by non-religious reformers such as Bourguiba in Tunisia. The French government granted Tunisia and Morocco independence in 1956. The same applied in Black Africa where moderates such as F. Houphouët-Boigny (Ivory Coast) and L. Senghor (Senegal) carried the nationalist hopes with them. The law drafted by Gaston Defferre in 1956 generalised universal suffrage and instigated assemblies to deal with local affairs. In 1958, a referendum was held but it provided only for autonomy within the French community. However, by 1960, the African States had gained their independence while retaining strong political, economic and cultural ties with France.

A National Drama – War in Algeria

In Algeria, however, a difficult war broke out in 1954. One million Europeans owned modern farms and they trained the urban middle classes. The Moslems, some 8.4 million people in all, were poorer and less well-educated. In 1947, Algeria's status upheld the political inequality, providing for the election of an Algerian assembly in which the Moslems would be represented by the same number of parliamentarians as the Europeans. Algerian nationalism was split between supporters of the reforms and supporters of revolutionary action. On 1st November 1954, a National Liberation Front (FNL) launched an insurrection, targeting civilian and military buildings and demanding recognition for Algerian nationality. The Mendès-France government, with F. Mitterand as Minister of the Interior, quickly took security measures and recalled the special links between Algeria and France, while at the same time proposing reforms. In August 1955, the rebels brutally massacred European and Moslem civilians; this led to a total breakdown of relations between Europeans and Algerians. The Army was called in to re-establish law and order.

A Situation with No Foreseeable End

In 1956, the elections brought to power a government described as a «Republican Front», under the leadership of Socialist Guy Mollet who implemented an active social policy (third week of annual paid holidays) and prepared for the creation of the EEC. Mollet had given Algeria priority in government policy. He travelled to the country and was faced with the anger of the Europeans there. Finally, the government decided to send in soldiers doing military service, and it also extended the period of national service. France was sinking into another war. In fact, the Algerians never had the capacity to build up an army and, instead, they used guerrilla warfare with skirmishes and bomb attacks. This was also a propaganda war aimed at appealing to international public opinion. The FNL mobilised the Moslem population, sometimes by means of intimidation. In October 1956, the French authorities hijacked a plane and arrested the nationalist leaders, in particular Ben Bella. The Suez expedition led by France and the UK and supported by the young state of Israel against Egypt under Nasser who had nationalised the Suez Canal, stretched relations between France and Arab countries almost to breaking point. France and the UK were forced to put a halt to the operation, under pressure from the USA and USSR. In 1957, a provisional government of the Algerian republic (G.P.R.A.) was set up outside the country, to lead the uprising.

13th May 1958

The Battle of Algiers, commanded by General Massu, lasted from January to October 1957 and was a victory for the French army. However, it used questionable methods to achieve victory, in particular torture, and «the Algerians learnt to hate the name of France» (C-R. Ageron). Although the French people in mainland France were preoccupied by the effect of this war, the supporters of French Algeria within Algeria itself became increasingly active and the army was tempted to agree with them. Successive governments (M. Bourgès-Maunoury, F. Gaillard, P. Pflimlin) appeared fragile, and the idea of calling back General de Gaulle began to gain ground. On 13th May 1958, during the Pflimlin government, a huge demonstration took place in Algiers involving supporters of French Algeria. It led to the setting up of a Committee of Public Safety with Massu as its chairman. The military had seized power. General Salan, who had been granted full powers in Algeria by the government, called on General de Gaulle who had retired from political life in 1953 and was living in Colombey-les-deux-Eglises. On 15th May, De Gaulle announced that he was ready to take over the reins of the Republic. France feared a violent takeover by the army in Algeria. On 29th May, President Coty called on General de Gaulle to form a government. It was sworn in on 1st June.

FRANCE AND THE FIFTH REPUBLIC

Charles de Gaulle had a new constitution drawn up by one of his loyal supporters, Michel Debré. Presented on 4th September 1958, the text was covered by a referendum and massively approved by the French people on 28th September.

New institutions

The role of the President of the Republic was reinforced. Under the terms of Article 16, he could take full power on a temporary basis. The National Assembly retained the power to overthrow the government which was thenceforth managed by a «Prime Minister». Legislative elections gave victory to the party including the Gaullists and supporting De Gaulle's policies, the Union for the New Republic (Union pour la nouvelle République). Left-wing parties were defeated. On 21st December 1958, De Gaulle was elected President of the Republic by a college of 80,000 major voters. From then on, political life was dominated by the General's personality. He was impressive during his trips in France or abroad, in his press conferences at the Elysee Palace and, in serious circumstances, during his television broadcasts, a method he used with great talent. Michel Debré was appointed Prime Minister.

The Evian Accords

De Gaulle, who was initially in favour of French Algeria, offered the FLN an «honourable peace», with economic and social reforms. In vain. He then recognised the Algerians' right to self-determination and international pressure underlined this approach. De Gaulle, however, gave the impression that he was betraying those who had paved the way for his return. The Europeans in Algeria showed their anger in Algeria during the «week of the barricades» in January 1960. Self-determination was approved by a referendum held on 8th January 1961.

Four generals (Salan, Challe, Jouhaud and Zeller) attempted to implement a putsch on 22nd April 1961. De Gaulle denounced the «quartet of retired generals» and the coup d'état failed. The Secret Armed Organisation (OAS, Organisation armée secrete) continued the struggle for French Algeria by organising bomb attacks in Algeria and in mainland France.

Eventually the government negotiated with the FLN and, on 18th March 1962, the Évian Accords were signed. They were then approved by referendum. Algeria became independent (5th July 1962). People of French or European extraction who had lived in Algeria, in many cases for several generations, preferred to leave the country. Certain French people never forgave De Gaulle for abandoning Algeria.

Presidential Changes

Having escaped with his life after an attack by the OAS in Le Petit-Clamart on 22nd August 1962, De Gaulle took advantage of the emotional response throughout the country and suggested that the President of the Republic should be elected by universal suffrage. This was accepted by a referendum on 28th October 1962 and a new link was established between the President and the French people. De Gaulle appointed Georges Pompidou, one of his close colleagues, as Prime Minister in April 1962.

Back in 1958, the government had struggled to fight inflation, balance the budget and defend the value of the franc – symbolically, the «new franc» was created, valued at 100 «old» francs. As the international economic climate was favourable, the efforts made since 1945 bore fruit and France enjoyed the most marked and longest period of growth in its history. The modernisation of the economy continued. The first nuclear power plants were built, the motorway network came into being and industrial or harbour complexes were uelques pages Both of these projects were technical success stories and commercial flops. The changes also brought with them social unrest and the long miners' strike of 1963.

The Politics of Grandeur

In 1960, France acquired the atomic bomb. De Gaulle succeeded in implementing the politics of «grandeur» which he wanted in order to give back to France, despite its defeats and failures, a role as a leading international power. De Gaulle distanced himself from the USA. In 1964, France was the first power to recognise Communist China then, in 1966, it left NATO although it remained in the Atlantic Alliance. In Cambodia in 1966, De Gaulle criticised American intervention in Vietnam where the war was gaining in intensity. He used long world tours to try and develop cooperation between France and developing countries. He was, however, mistrustful of a supranational Europe. While strengthening dialogue with West Germany, De Gaulle vetoed the entry of the United Kingdom into the EEC.

Re-election in 1965

Within the country, the political situation was changing. A strong Gaullist majority supported the government in the National Assembly. Public opinion seemed to be satisfied with General de Gaulle's actions yet he was not re-elected outright in 1965 as he had hoped. The centre right preferred to vote for Jean Lacanuet and the left united to support François Mitterand who described Gaullist practices as a «permanent coup d'état». The second round of voting opposed the left-wing candidate, who obtained 45% of the vote, and the General who won with 55%. De Gaulle's authority was somewhat shaken by this modicum of failure and the 1967 elections marked the revival of the left wing.

The University Crisis of May 1968

The May 1968 crisis was to break like a thunderstorm in a quiet sky. The mounting tension began on the university campus in Nanterre. The number of students had increased two-and-a-half times over in seven years and new universities had been set up in the Paris area early in the 1960's. Although some of the students came from families steeped in the university tradition, others discovered a world of which they knew nothing. An extreme left wing with anarchist, Trotskyist or Maoist tendencies became increasingly influential. By using the works of political theorists or by taking revolutionary examples (e.g. Che Guevara), students cast doubt on the global order of society in which they saw servitude and inequality. The movement of 22nd March was launched by Daniel Cohn-Bendit, named after an administrative building that had been occupied by students on that date. Unrest spread to other universities in Paris. The government reacted with firmness, closing Nanterre. Then, because a meeting was being held in the Sorbonne on 3rd May, the government ordered the police to move in and arrest those attending it. They were taken to Court. Increasing numbers of demonstrations were held in support of their liberation and, on the night of 10th/11th May a veritable street battle broke out, with barricades, cars set alight and police baton charges. On 13th May, demonstrations were held in numerous towns throughout France.

May Surprises

Soon the student crisis turned into a social crisis. Strikes broke out and, within just one week, the entire country was brought to a standstill. The trades unions joined the students. Emphasis was placed on wage increases and on the hierarchy in companies and universities. De Gaulle, who considered these claims as nothing more than the action of the «rabble», made a television broadcast. Calm did not return. On the contrary, it was followed by another night on the barricades. Georges Pompidou decided to negotiate with the employers' organisations and trades unions (25th/27th May).

The Grenelle Accords included a rise in the minimum guaranteed wage and salaries, as well as other social measures. The decisions, however, were rejected by the striking workers despite having been accepted by the trades unions which were, therefore, disavowed. Power seemed to be in a vacuum, ready for the taking. A demonstration was held at the

Charléty Stadium on 27th May, in the presence of Mendès-France; it was followed by other demonstrations on the 29th. F. Mitterand announced that he would stand for President if De Gaulle resigned. On 29th May, it was learnt that De Gaulle had left Paris. It was a mysterious trip. He had travelled to Germany to see general Massu, one of his military companions. On 30th May, De Gaulle dissolved the National Assembly and announced an early election: «… I shall not resign. I hold a mandate from the people. I shall fulfil it». That same day, a huge demonstration was held on the Champs-Elysées to show the scope of support for De Gaulle. Strikes and the occupation of factories gradually ceased and legislative elections brought Gaullist candidates to power.

What was May 1968? A Utopian revolution that failed or the sign of crisis in civilisation itself? A dream of the young at university or a tremor within the consumer society? Although the results were thin compared to the scope of the claims, the movement left deep marks on cultural life, especially at university level, and within society as a whole.

The 1969 Referendum

After these events, De Gaulle removed Pompidou from office and named Couve de Murville as Prime Minister. He had been an immovable Minister of Foreign Affairs. In his efforts to meet the country's aspirations, he proposed a regionalisation policy that would give greater power to the members of the regional councils set up in 1964 and greater corporate profit-sharing among salaried staff. The project was the subject of a referendum but it frightened conservatives and liberals without satisfying the left-wing. Valéry Giscard d'Estaing, acting for the independent Republicans, called upon the electorate to vote no. It was the «No» vote which won the day on 27th April 1969. Charles de Gaulle immediately resigned. He died on 9th November 1970. While a very simple funeral ceremony was being held in Colombey, heads of State from all over the world came to pay homage to him in Notre-Dame in Paris.

Georges Pompidou's Presidency

Georges Pompidou was elected easily to the presidency of the Republic. A graduate from the Ecole Normale, the former teacher and banker had been De Gaulle's private secretary before showing himself to be an energetic, clever politician. He was concerned to modernise the country in economic and cultural terms but, at the same time, he was careful in social affairs. He selected as his Prime Minister Jacques Chaban-Delmas, a «historical» Gaullist. Central government encouraged high-tech industries such as aeronautics, telecommunications, computing and the nuclear industry with European projects such as Airbus and the Ariane rocket. Chaban-Delmas drafted a project for a «new society» and launched an innovative social policy in which employers and salaried staff became «social partners». In 1973, Pompidou was in favour of extending the Common Market to include the UK, Denmark and Ireland. It was on European politics that he wanted to be judged, by a referendum held on 23rd April 1972. The high abstention rate was seen as a partial failure and this led Pompidou to remove Chaban from office, replacing him by Pierre Messmer.

The Common Left-Wing Programme

The government was faced by an opposition that had reorganised itself. The SFIO tried to revive its flagging fortunes in 1969 but, more importantly, F. Mitterand succeeded, in 1971 at the conference in Epinay, in taking over the leadership of the Socialist party. He allied it to the Communist party, signing, in June 1972, a joint programme of government. At the 1973 elections, the Gaullist UDR lost members of parliament but retained an absolute majority. However, political life was shrouded in uncertainty because G. Pompidou was ill. He died on 2nd April 1974.

The Thirty Glorious Years

The death of G. Pompidou marked the end of the «Thirty Glorious Years» as economist J. Fourastié had called the years of growth. The population of France had increased and towns were markedly predominant. This led to the expansion of the suburbs which sometimes posed social problems. By 1975, the primary sector represented only 10% of the working population; the tertiary sector was already exceeding 50%. The overall duration of work decreased. Infantile mortality had almost disappeared. The average lifespan of the people had increased. The standard of living had varied from an index of 100 in 1938 to 87 in 1946 to 320 in 1975.

A Liberal, Advanced Society

It was V. Giscard d'Estaing who was elected to the presidency, defeating F. Mitterrand, the joint left-wing candidate, by a very small majority. The new President appointed Jacques Chirac, who had been close to G. Pompidou and who had called for support for him in preference to the Gaullist candidate Chaban-Delmas. Giscard d'Estaing, who came from the wealthy ranks of society, was a graduate of the Ecole polytechnique and E.N.A. He succeeded in projecting an image of modernity. He wanted to «relax» political life and prepare for an «advanced, liberal society». From the outset, he implemented a programme of reforms, lowering the age of majority to 18, authorising abortion (a measure which was defended before the National Assembly, with some difficulty, by Simone Veil) and dividing up the broadcasting service (ORTF) into three national TV channels. Some of these measures displeased his electorate.

Giscard d'Estaing was a stalwart European who relaunched European politics through elections to the European assembly by means of universal suffrage (1979) and through the setting up of the European monetary system (1979) which limited variations between European currencies.

The Oil Crisis

The 1973 oil crisis (Arab countries used oil as a weapon in economic warfare and suddenly increased its price) accelerated a crisis that had, until then, been latent. Unemployment increased (900,000 unemployed) as did inflation, and growth stagnated. Jacques Chirac implemented a policy aimed at boosting the economy but to no marked effect. His relationship with the President of the Republic became difficult and, in July 1976, he resigned. Jacques Chirac then took control of the Gaullist party, turning it into the Rassemblement pour la République (RPR). He also succeeded in having himself elected Mayor of Paris, against the candidate supported by the President.

Raymond Barre, the new Prime Minister, was an Economics professor. He launched an austerity plan which limited public spending, re-balanced the Social Security budget, and held down salaries and prices. However, the second oil crisis ruined these efforts. In 1979, inflation was running at 13.4% per annum and there were 1.5 million unemployed.

The opposition was weakened by the split in the left-wing coalition in 1977, but it seemed to be in a position to win the 1978 elections. Despite this, it was the parties within the majority which won the day. Giscard d'Estaing, on the other hand, failed to be re-elected in 1981. F. Mitterrand was elected on 10th May 1981 with 51.7% of the vote.

10th May 1981

F. Mitterrand's election led to enthusiastic demonstrations. The new President decided to dissolve the National Assembly and a majority of Socialist parliamentarians was elected. The government, under the Mayor of Lille, Pierre Mauroy, included four Communist ministers. Mitterrand's programme was quickly applied. The death sentence was abolished. New nationalisations strengthened the economic weight of central government. Decentralisation, implemented by the law of 3rd March 1982, increased the responsibility of those elected to «county» and regional councils and the Chairman of the Regional or «County» Council thenceforth held executive power. In order to stimulate consumerism, the Socialists increased the minimum wage and benefits. However, the economic policy was a failure. The increased purchase of foreign goods worsened the balance of payments deficit and the government measures increased the budgetary deficit. Inflation remained high and the number of unemployed increased still further (to 2 million in 1983). Mitterrand also wanted to give potency to his presidency by a number of major building projects (the Grand Louvre, the Opera House on Place de la Bastille etc.), and private local radio stations became legal.

Resistance

The Mauroy government introduced «rigour» by freezing prices and salaries and increasing taxes. Mitterrand's popularity collapsed and the right-wing opposition won seats in municipal elections in 1983 and European elections in 1984. The Communists also criticised government policy. An extreme right-wing party, the National Front under Jean-Marie Le Pen, found new support by exploiting the subjects of insecurity and the dangers of immigration. This rendered the situation more complex on the right.

Alain Savary's project for education, which focussed on a unified, public, non-religious service, was seen as a threat for church schools and anxiety on the part of families resulted in vast demonstrations in 1984. P. Mauroy was replaced by Laurent Fabius, a graduate of the Ecole Normale and ENA, a man of 37 who was close to Mitterrand. Rigour began to bite. Inflation had dropped to 5% and the franc had been stabilised. However, L. Fabius' government was faced with difficulties in New Caledonia and embarrassed by the Greenpeace affair (when a boat belonging to the ecology movement was destroyed in a harbour in New Zealand by France's secret services) and the seizing of hostages in Lebanon. The Socialists lost the March 1986 elections despite the introduction of proportional representation which resulted in the election of 35 extreme right members of parliament.

The First Period of Cohabitation

As leader of the largest party in the opposition, J. Chirac was appointed Prime Minister. This new political situation was referred to as «cohabitation». The new policies were designed to break with the Socialist authoritarianism by restoring economic liberalism, inspired by the lessons learnt from Margaret Thatcher in the UK. National companies were privatised, price restrictions were lifted, direct taxation was decreased, companies could dismiss workers without prior authorisation, and the tax on large fortunes, which had been introduced by the Left, was discontinued. The government ended the wave of bomb attacks linked to problems in the Middle East and dismantled terrorist networks.

Despite low inflation and renewed growth, unemployment did not decrease. Demonstrations by students and high school pupils against a draft law on the University (late 1986) and the Stock Exchange crash of October 1987 weakened the government. François Mitterrand was again seen as a form of recourse and elected against J. Chirac in May 1988 with almost 54% of votes. Jean-Marie Le Pen obtained more than 14% of votes.

François Mitterrand's Second Term of Office

The Prime Minister was Michel Rocard, an Inspector of Finances and former leader of the PSU, the party which had tried to renovate the left-wing at the end of the 1960's. He had been Mitterrand's rival prior to 1981.

After the dissolution of the National Assembly, the Socialists obtained only a relative majority. The Rocard government succeeded in settling the problems in New Caledonia. It also created a minimum «reintegration» benefit (RMI, revenu minimum d'insertion) for the most seriously deprived and re-established the tax on large fortunes which was renamed the Solidarity Tax on Fortunes. He also created the CSG (contribution sociale généraliseé), a new tax on all income, of whatever type.

Government action quickly seemed to have been paralysed for it failed in its attempt to open up to the group of parliamentarians in the centre of the political spectrum. The Socialist party was divided and politicians as a whole were damaged by corruption scandals, right up to those closest to the President of the Republic.

Major Upheavals Worldwide

This was a period of international upheaval. On 9th November 1989, the fall of the Berlin Wall paved the way for the collapse of the Soviet and Communist system and for the reunification of Germany in 1990. After the invasion of Kuwait by Iraq on 2nd August 1990, France took part in the war against the invader in the early months of 1991. The war revealed the weakness of a traditional army in new conflicts in the contemporary world. Shortly afterwards, Michel Rocard was replaced by Edith Cresson, who was close to Mitterrand. She was the first woman to lead the government in France (May 1991) but her time in office was short-lived and she was replaced by Pierre Bérégovoy, another person close to Mitterrand, a self-taught man from a humble background who was appointed Prime Minister in April 1992. He continued to implement a policy aimed at a strong franc, maintaining stable parity with German currency.

The Treaty of Maastricht, signed on 7th February 1992, provided for the introduction of a single European currency in 1999 at the latest, and a central European bank. François Mitterrand decided to submit the ratification of these agreements to a referendum. A political debate arose, with Europe as its subject. On 20th September 1992, the «Yes» vote won by a very short head, after an election with a particularly high abstention rate. Disenchantment with successive Socialist governments led to a crushing victory for the right-wing in the 1993 elections.

Jacques Chirac

Since Jacques Chirac did not wish to repeat his 1988 experience, he left one of his loyal supporters, Edouard Balladur, to become Prime Minister. E. Balladur had once worked with Georges Pompidou and, during his period of government, he did his utmost to lighten the load on F. Mitterrand whose health was declining and who found himself forced to justify his attitude during the Second World War. Having won the trust of part of the electorate, Edouard Balladur was tempted to run for the office of President of the Republic, against Jacques Chirac who was forced to highlight social issues in his pre-election speeches, insisting on the need to «reduce the social fracture» running through French society because of the large number of unemployed. His conviction enabled J. Chirac to bridge the gap separating him from Edouard Balladur and to overtake him during the first round of the 1995 presidential election before going on to win against Socialist Lionel Jospin. François Mitterrand died a few months later, on 8th January 1996.

IMAGES OF FRANCE

The life of the French people began to change in the 1950's and underwent rapid metamorphosis in the 1970's.

Modern France

The movement of the population has been marked by speed. There are large numbers of cars, the train has evolved to become the TGV (high-speed train) and planes are no longer reserved for the elite. Telecommunications have undergone rapid change and computers have completely revolutionised work, from letter-writing to satellite construction. In homes, domestic appliances developed along American lines have provided new levels of comfort and hygiene has made enormous progress. France has, then, been involved in the modernisation that has been a characteristic of developed countries. It has made a contribution to this through innovations and inventions and scientific and technical successes have been achieved in the aeronautics and space industries, especially within a European context but under French impetus. The country has also been very successful in medical research.

Work

Work has changed. Increasing numbers of women now work. In 1988, they represented 42% of the working population. Machinery and computers have transformed industry which has become less labour-intensive. The tertiary sector has expanded, employing 64.2% of the working population in 1990. It required qualified staff and this has forced education to change. Universities have had to take in larger numbers of students. Yet the country continues to suffer from chronic unemployment. Numerous contradictory explanations are given – particularly stiff international competition, the «globalisation» of trade, the modernisation and rationalisation of the economy, the high rates of employers' contributions and corporate taxes etc. Political solutions have been envisaged but the absence of any visible results contributed to numerous changes of government and policy in the period between 1980 and 1990.

The «Cultural State»

Television has transformed leisure time and, to a certain extent, the common culture of the French people by bringing into homes diversified information, images from all over the world and imaginary works, using the new artistic creativity enabled by the cinematography invented by the Lumière brothers and developed, in particular, by the American film industry. The State controlled television, only relaxing its grip gradually. It continued to monitor culture, in line with French tradition, creating museums (Beaubourg, the modern art museum desired by Georges Pompidou, the Musée d'Orsay) or libraries (the new National Library of France desired by François Mitterrand). Through music and drama festivals, especially in the summer months, major exhibitions or historic monuments, the «cultural State», to use an expression created by M. Fumaroli, has attempted to reach new sections of the population and democratise culture.

A New World Vision

The vision of the world has also changed over the past few decades. The Roman Catholic Church has changed and has increasingly emphasised its worldwide and social vocation. Yet its influence on most French people has undoubtedly declined. There is, however, a renewal of religious life among Catholics with new forms of attendance which can also be seen among Jews and Muslims. This need for spirituality sometimes changes course to become an attraction for sects or for all sorts of radicalism. Yet, it can also be seen in great causes such as assistance for the poor, for the persecuted and for victims of war, or the defence of the natural environment.

All this has led to changes in personal lives. Sexuality is more liberated, especially thanks to contraception. This situation changed again with the outbreak of AIDS. Divorce has become frequent. Woman have fought for de jure and de facto equality with men. Same-sex marriage has been legalised. The family, too, has changed but without losing its importance in social life, of which it forms the basis.

The Future

In the 20th century, France has lived through two World Wars that left it materially and spiritually shaken. It has lost most of the colonial empire which it had built up a century earlier. It is not in a position to impose its solutions in international affairs and has to give way in areas where it still has some influence as well as in Africa, a continent that is completely disorganised. By involving itself in the construction of Europe, it gave itself an aim and a timetable, in particular as regards the adoption of the single currency, the Euro, but these choices made the reduction in the public deficit even more necessary. These clear perspectives should not conceal the shadows that hang over Europe, where nationalism is raising its head again after the disappearance of the Soviet empire and where the political map has been totally redrawn in just a few years.

France must work, in particular, to solve the social difficulties resulting from unemployment. It can also find the way to a new French presence in Europe and in the world as a whole. By giving greater depth to the country's leading principles of liberty, equality and fraternity while combining the tenets of the Republic with the demands of democracy, the French people will be able to define more clearly a unique identity which, by seeking support in the past and the diversity of its eventful history, will be the identity of the future.

Thanks

This text owes much to the collective work that produced two history books for junior high schools in 1988-1989 and I should like to thank those who worked on the project at that time – Alain Barbé, Janine Barbé, Jean-Marie Flonneau, Serge Touam and the sorely missed Bernard Grosjean and Jacques Montaville.

A few passages from this book have been, or are due to be, published. I should like to thank the editors who authorised me to use them in this summary of our history.

I should like to express my deep gratitude to Géraud Poumarède, Jacques Briard and Isabelle Richefort who agreed to reread the manuscript.

However, the author assumes full responsibility for this book.

BIBLIOGRAPHY

Barjot (Dominique), Chaline (Jean-Pierre), Encrevé (André) - *La France au XIXe siècle, 1814-1914* - Paris 1995.

Barthélemy (Dominique) - *L'ordre seigneurial, XIe - XIIe siècle* - Paris, 1990.

Bély (Lucien) - *La France moderne 1498-1789* - Paris, 1994, 3e édition 1996.

Bély (Lucien) dir. - *Dictionnaire de l'ancien Régime* - Paris, 1996.

Bourin-Derruau (Monique) - *Temps d'équilibres, temps de ruptures, XIIIe siècle* - Paris 1990.

Briard (Jacques) -*La Préhistoire de l'Europe* - Paris, 1995.

Charmasson (Thérèse), Lelorrain (Anne-Marie), Sonnet (Martine) - *Chronologie de l'histoire de France* - Paris 1994.

Favier (Jean) - *Histoire de France. Le temps des principautés* - Paris, 1984.

Gauvard (Claude), *La France au Moyen Age du Ve au XVe* - Paris 1996.

Jouanna (Arlette) - *La France du XVIe siècle 1493-1598* - Paris, 1996.

Lebecq - *Les origines franques, V^e-IXe siècle* - Paris, 1990.

Romain (Danièle et Yves) - *Histoire de la Gaule* - Paris 1997.

Sirinelli (Jean-François), Vandenbussche (Robert), Vavasseur-Desperriers (Jean) - *La France de 1914 à nos jours* - Paris 1993.

Sirinelli (Jean-François) dir. - *Dictionnaire historique de la vie politique française au XXe siècle* - Paris, 1995.

Theis (Laurent) - *L'héritage des Charles* - Paris, 1990.

ulard (Jean) - *La France de la Révolution et de l'Empire* - Paris, 1995.

Werner (Karl Ferdinand) - *Histoire de France. Les origines* - Paris, 1984.

Table des matières

THE FRENCH ISTHMUS 5
THE BEGINNING...8
ROMAN GAUL..17
CLOVIS AND THE MEROVINGIANS 24
CHARLEMAGNE AND THE CAROLINGIANS....................29
THE FRANCE OF THE FIRST CAPETIANS 35
THE DAYS OF GREAT MONARCHS.....................................45
THE HUNDRED YEARS' WAR 52
NEW HORIZONS 64
THE WARS OF RELIGION..68
FRANCE IN A EUROPEAN WAR DURING
THE DAYS OF LOUIS XIII AND RICHELIEU 77
LOUIS XIV...84
THE END OF PRE-REVOLUTIONARY FRANCE 100
THE REVOLUTION AND THE KING 111
THE FIRST REPUBLIC...117
THE CONSULATE AND EMPIRE 122
THE RESTORATION AND THE JULY MONARCHY.........130
FROM SECOND REPUBLIC TO SECOND EMPIRE 136
THE FIRST WORLD WAR...153
THE INTER-WAR YEARS..156
THE SECOND WORLD WAR 165
LIBERATION AND THE FOURTH REPUBLIC 171
FRANCE AND THE FIFTH REPUBLIC 177
IMAGES OF FRANCE 186
BIBLIOGRAPHY..189